TITOISM and
THE COMINFORM

TITOISM and
THE COMINFORM

Adam B. Ulam

GREENWOOD PRESS, PUBLISHERS
WESTPORT, CONNECTICUT

Preface

I have attempted in this book to describe some of the facts of Communist politics in Eastern Europe. Titoism, both in the sense in which it exists in Yugoslavia and in the much broader sense in which it has reached the Communist Parties of the satellites of the U.S.S.R., forms, of course, the central part of the picture.

It is often assumed that the "real" story of Communist politics can never be learned or studied in the West, that the politics of an authoritarian regime provides suitable material for sensational exposés or queries, but never for a factual study. Fortunately, there has been recently a number of books which have dealt in a scholarly and informative manner with the government of the Soviet Union. I hope that this book, written about a related problem, may make a modest contribution toward the understanding of Communism in power.

My treatment of Titoism and of the Communist Parties of Eastern Europe has of necessity been conditioned by the availability of materials. Some Communist Parties rejoice the heart of a researcher by publicizing their activities and thus providing a mass of data to be sifted and analyzed; other Parties earn his displeasure by being unduly secretive. Hence this book deals in some detail with the

Communist Parties of Yugoslavia, Poland, and Bulgaria, and draws only a general picture of the remaining Communist governments.

Every study dealing with Eastern Europe confronts the same minor but vexing problem: how to render in English names of both persons and places written in the Cyrillic and modified Latin alphabets used by the Slavic nations of the area. Russian and Bulgarian names can be transcribed phonetically without appearing unfamiliar to readers of American and English newspapers, but the same principle of transcription would only lead to confusion in the case of the other Slavic languages. The use of the diacritics is, on the other hand, bothersome both to the printer and to the reader. Here, I have adopted a rule of thumb which I hope will be convenient. The little dots, bars, and hooks are either disregarded or phonetized, and foreign names are otherwise preserved in their original spelling.

This book was written under the auspices of the Russian Research Center of Harvard University. To its director, Professor Clyde Kluckhohn, I owe a great debt not only for his interest in my work but also for his suggestions and encouragement. I can but very inadequately express my gratitude to Professor Merle Fainsod, since for over three years he has watched the progress of this work with constant interest and advice. Professor Philip Mosely of Columbia University was kind enough to read the manuscript and to offer his criticisms and suggestions. Mr. Anton Ciliga generously set his great knowledge of Communism in Yugoslavia at my disposal by allowing me to read some chapters in his manuscript on the history of the Communist Party in Yugoslavia. This work has often called for a bit of specialized information or a linguistic skill which I did not possess but which was kindly provided by my friends and fellow members of the Center. Some of them cannot be named here. But I want to mention with gratitude Professor Robert Wolff, Mr. Alexander Erlich, Mr. Mark Neuweld, and Mr. Marian Dziewanowski. Mrs. Lotte Knieger transformed my untidy manuscript into an orderly typescript. My special thanks go to my friend Dr. Lahut Uzman for his original and witty reflections on politics and related subjects.

A. B. U.

Cambridge
December 1951

CONTENTS

TITOISM and
THE COMINFORM

CHAPTER 1

The Communist Party of Yugoslavia

The history of revolutionary movements has always witnessed the struggle between the spirit and the organization of revolution. The spirit is one of impatience with any authority. It believes that every form of political authority implies oppression. It appeals to anarchism, which is always present in a historical upheaval. Revolution always appears romantic, and the word itself imparts the feeling of something spontaneous and elemental.

The organization of a revolutionary movement means, on the contrary, discipline, planning, and conformity—discipline not only of action, which is perhaps easily endurable, but also of thought and expression. Revolutionary movements in the past have often lacked the organizational hardness which alone keeps a movement together after its first objective has been achieved. For in order to keep the initial impetus, the original ideas and spontaneity which enabled the movement to succeed have had to be sacrificed. Hence a revolution has not infrequently been like an attacking army which, having breached the walls of the existing system, has spent itself, allowing another force to enter and to occupy the real objective of the struggle.

Communism in the twentieth century has been the movement which has most consistently attempted to combine revolutionary organization with the revolutionary spirit. The seeds of Marxism, which contained, originally, the possibilities of both a constitutional and a revolutionary development, took root in a society with a tradition of authoritarianism. The carrier of Marxism, the Social Democratic Party of Russia, transformed itself into the Communist Party (Bolshevik)—eventually the Communist Party of the U.S.S.R.—and by generalizing and applying on a world-wide scale the conspiratorial and authoritarian part of its tradition presented our era with its most pressing challenge.

Communism has grown as a centralistic and totalitarian creed. Its original strategy, developed largely for self-defense and attuned to the weaknesses and vulnerabilities of the Western state system, became eventually transformed into a strategy of attack. It has patiently probed and exploited social discontent, nationalism, racial barriers, and discrimination. Its ability to exploit the weaknesses of its enemy in a series of tactical maneuvers rather than in a frontal attack, which would have been disastrous to the Soviet Union, has compelled the increasing dogmatism of the creed; this in turn has paralleled and contributed to the bureaucratization of the U.S.S.R. and that body of its foreign sympathizers which, owing to the same inexorable necessity, has had to become a projection of the Soviet state —the international Communist movement. Once the expected world revolution failed to materialize following the First World War, the full fervor of the revolutionary spirit could not be released all at once and everywhere and translated into a struggle. It had to be doled out here and there, restrained or temporarily extinguished elsewhere, increasingly in accordance with the interests and wishes of the Communist state. To be a Communist one had to believe more and more and to question less and less, and gradually the distinction between a revolutionary party and a religious sect became obliterated.

But the old dilemma of all revolutionary movements has remained to plague every Communist Party. In order to achieve power or even influence before 1945, each Party had to rely on a broad basis of revolutionary and humanitarian fervor. But in order to remain a part of the international Communist movement, as defined and directed by Moscow, it grew increasingly regimented and incapable of spontaneous expression. This fact explains the heightened influence and seeming stature of the Communist Parties, when, as in the period of the popular front or during the war after June 1941, they could appear—and not only to the world but to themselves as well—to be "natural" revolutionaries sharing in a widely popular and democratic movement. Such periods were infrequent, once the mold of Russian and international Communism was set after 1928, and they were invariably followed by a stern reversal to the usual position and role of the Communist Party. But the dilemma of Communism—its inner contradiction, to use an expression of which the Communists are so fond—remained, and after the war it was to confront Soviet Russia with the greatest challenge to its claim of leadership. The most successful, and the most fanatically revolutionary and Communist, group of followers of the creed found itself compelled to defy the claims of the Kremlin to dominate unconditionally every Communist Party in the world.

The history of the Communist Party of Yugoslavia is not materially different from the histories of many other Communist Parties. It offers no clear clue to the Party's eventual rebellion against Moscow. But it illuminates those possibilities and tendencies which during and after World War II crystallized to present world Communism with the most concrete expression of the inner conflict that has always characterized it.

The Party was born in the era just after World War I as a pure if not very coherent expression of various brands of radicalism pervading the newly created state of the Serbs, Croats, and Slovenes which was later to be renamed Yugoslavia—the state of the Southern Slavs. Communism in 1919 meant, outside Russia, little more than a revolutionary expression of and aspiration for socialism and radicalism. The impetus given by the Russian Revolution found its echo in this predominantly agricultural and, in the main, technologically backward Balkan society. Yugoslav Communism was to follow the pattern of the Communist Parties everywhere. At first, in the early twenties, it was pervaded by a revolutionary romanticism which could express itself naïvely, as in the resolution for the propagation of Esperanto,[1] or in acts of terrorism against the government. The period of spontaneity and romanticism was followed by an era when a "real" Communist Party was being forged, when the definition of Communism was made dependent on obedience and then complete subservience to the Third International. The early Congresses and Conferences of the Party were full of debates and disputes about the road to be taken on questions of ideology, of national and agricultural policy, and so forth. One reads in their accounts expressions quite untypical of organized Communism later on: "There was a great deal of discussion on this point," or "This resolution was passed almost unanimously."

In its early days the Communist Party of Yugoslavia lived and functioned, for all its conspiratorial methods and organizations, as a political party, as a body of people joined together by a community of aims and ideas, but not so tightly knit that the individual members were willing to surrender their right to free thinking and occasional disagreement. It was but gradually that the new pattern set in. In 1928 the Fourth Party Congress held at Dresden heard the representative of the Third International, "Ercoli" (the Party name of Palmiro Togliatti), chide the assembled Yugoslav Communists as if they were children,[2] telling the leaders of the "opposition" within the Party exactly what they were supposed to do in order to expiate their sins. After 1928 any resemblance to a political party ended. The C.P.Y. became but a body of agitators and agents directed from outside Yugoslavia, electing unanimously as its leaders whoever the Balkan section of the Third International decided should be the Yugoslav Central Committee. The fortunes of the Party followed the tortuous path of Soviet Communism. The great purge in Russia was paralleled by a similar process in the ranks of the Yugoslav Communists. The last traces of independence, the last links with the pre-Stalinist phase of Communism, were erased, and by 1937 the Yugoslav Party was in the hands of the people who knew no loyalty but that to Soviet Russia.

In April 1919 the delegates from the various socialist organiza-

---

[1] *Congresses and Conferences of the Communist Party of Yugoslavia, 1919–1937* (in Serbo-Croat), Historical Archive of the Communist Party of Yugoslavia, vol. II (Belgrade, 1950), p. 53. From hereon referred to as *Congresses and Conferences of the C.P.Y.*

[2] *Ibid.*, pp. 460–468.

tions which now found themselves in the new "Kingdom of Serbs, Croats, and Slovenes" convened in Belgrade and formed the "Socialist Workers' Party of Yugoslavia (of the Communists)." The materials of which the new Party was composed, like those of the new state, were heterogeneous. They included the old Social Democratic Party of Serbia and several socialist parties which had functioned in the Yugoslav lands under the Austro-Hungarian Empire. The Russian Revolution had sounded the tocsin, and all over Europe socialists, whether revolutionaries or parliamentarians, were at first ready to make the cause of the revolution their own. The Unification Congress voted an affiliation with the Comintern, but what Communism meant or would mean was not entirely clear to the assembled intellectuals and trade-union officials. Many of them had been brought up in the tradition of the Austrian Social Democratic Party, the tradition of intellectual and legal Marxism. Others had been trade-union officials for whom socialism had meant largely material advance of the working class. Though the Congress attacked the "betrayal" of the international workers' movement by the Second International, its program was but a rephrasing of the old Social-Democratic postulates. It was natural for a Yugoslav Communist who in 1949 was editing the Archive to add, a bit contemptuously, that the Congress did not have a correct policy on certain basic issues. It neglected the national question, and the organizational structure of the Party remained of the social-democratic type.[3]

The Second Party Congress, which took place in June 1920 at Vukovar, gave to the Party a definite Communist mold. The Party now became the Communist Party of Yugoslavia. Its program called openly for a Yugoslav Soviet Republic which would join in a Balkan Soviet federation and then eventually in a universal Communist union.[4] The Congress changed the statute and organization of the Party to conform with the Russian pattern. It was after the Congress that the first purge took place. A body of "centrists" issued a manifesto protesting the compliance of the Party with the twenty-one conditions of the Comintern, which demanded, among other things, submission of every Communist Party to the Comintern. The opposition wanted full autonomy for every constituent

[3] *Ibid.*, p. 10. The editor of the Archive was Mosha Pijade.
[4] *Ibid.*, p. 35.

member of the Third International. It was this claim which found an echo in Tito's revolt against Moscow twenty-eight years later. But in December 1920 the signers of the manifesto were excluded from the Party. The Communists of Yugoslavia took the first and decisive step in their submission to the Comintern—a step which was to mean the subordination of Yugoslav Communism to the interests of the Soviet state. How pervasive this subordination was to be, and how far-reaching the effect of its psychology, can be seen in the comment made upon the Second Congress by the Titoist editors of the Historical Archive. In 1949 one would have expected them to hail the 1920 opponents of Communist centralism as being the first fighters in the struggle which Tito and his group carried to a successful conclusion. But to the Yugoslav Communists of 1949 the purge of 1920—the purge of those who wanted a small degree of freedom from Moscow—appears to have been perfectly logical and justified.

The Party was launched on its revolutionary course. In its proclamations the Communist Party of Yugoslavia was from now on to add under its name: "A Section of the Communist International." In many respects the Communist Party of Yugoslavia was to prove to be an exemplary Communist Party insofar as its allegiance to Moscow was concerned. If its pre-1941 history is a long story of fractionalism and of purges, this was not because the problem of its allegiance to Moscow was still a major issue after 1921. The Party split and often foundered internally on the same issue that has plagued the Yugoslav state ever since its birth—nationalism.

The Yugoslav state, like Communism, is a nineteenth-century dream which has fitted rather uneasily into the realities of twentieth-century politics. The nationalism of the nineteenth century, like socialism at that time, concealed under a violent and revolutionary verbiage an essentially democratic and liberal vision. The Kingdom of the Serbs, Croats, and Slovenes was a response to and a seeming fulfillment of an old idea of the unity of the South Slavs which was to be accomplished under conditions of equality and democracy. Here, as in many other things, the idealists and liberals of the nineteenth century forgot to take into account the essential problem of political power. There was no reason, it seemed, why the fraternal nations of the Balkans—Serbia, Croatia, and Slovenia—could not live together in peace and democracy. The things which united them, their language (Croats and Serbs have a common language which is not dissimilar to the Slovenian) and the logic of their union from the historical and economic point of view, were taken to mean more than the accident of history which caused the Serbs to be Greek Orthodox in their religion while claiming the Croats and Slovenes for Catholicism. History has shaped out of the same material very different national psychologies and viewpoints, but to the liberal spirit of the nineteenth century such differences were quite secondary.

The century ended in 1914, but the postwar settlement was still formulated under the aegis of its beliefs and preconceptions. Nationalism was taken to mean the aspirations and ideals of the intellectuals of the given nation. Thus the more westernized Croats and Slovenes were linked in the same state with the Serbs. In addition, Yugoslavia inherited a large part of the Macedonian problem. Within the new state there was also the former principality of Montenegro, Serbian in its culture and language, but even poorer and more backward than old Serbia. This mélange of cultures and nationalities was expected to live and prosper within the frame of a unitary state which had at first the external paraphernalia of constitutional parliamentarism. From its very beginning, the disruptive forces of the new world were to triumph over the old concepts. The story of Yugoslavia is one long story of a clash of nationalisms. Every new phenomenon in European politics—the accentuation of social radicalism resulting from the economic crises of the interwar years, the emergence of fascism, the weakening of moral and material resources of the Western democracies—served to deepen the basic conflicts within the Yugoslav state. The main one, the Croat-Serb dilemma, exacerbated by the extremists on both sides who sought either to transform Yugoslavia into a Greater Serbia or to destroy the state by erecting an independent Croat nation, proved too great a strain upon the fragile constitutional framework. The struggle was symbolized dramatically by the murder in 1928 of Stjepan Radich, the leader of the Croat Party, by a fanatic. The murder took place during a parliamentary debate, the murderer being a Montenegrin deputy.

But in addition to the main conflict there were several other national grievances. The Macedonians were officially denied the recognition of their separate nationality, though the dialects they speak are quite distinct from both the Serbian and the Bulgarian, and their country was considered as Southern Serbia. Both the Communists and the Macedonian separatists, the two categories sometimes overlapping, were to allege that their country was treated as a colony by the "Serbian bourgeoisie and officialdom."

In 1929 the shell of constitutionalism collapsed, and King Alexander proclaimed a dictatorial regime. Though government control was afterwards relaxed and a modicum of parliamentarism allowed, especially following Alexander's assassination in 1934, Yugoslavia was not again to know genuine parliamentary institutions and political freedom. The regime despite its occasional accommodations with some Croat and Slovene leaders was to remain mainly Serbian in its personnel and attitudes. On the brink of the Second World War this small country, with a population of about sixteen millions, was a welter of conflicting nationalisms and extremisms.

The Communist Party of Yugoslavia could find a fruitful field of activity amidst the discontented nationalities. In the elections of 1920 to the Constituent Assembly, the young Party scored a major triumph. It was the third strongest party in that extremely "Balkanized" legislative body, obtaining 58 seats out of 419. Characteristically, it won its greatest successes in two disaffected and most backward regions: in Montenegro it won 40 per cent and in Macedonia 33 per cent of the seats in the Constituent Assembly.[5] Communism could have meant little for the vast majority of Montenegrins and Macedonians. They simply expressed their chagrin over the new regime by voting for the most radical party that was available. Montenegro was to furnish Tito with a disproportionately large number of his generals and Party leaders. In Croatia and Slovenia, the two most advanced and industrialized provinces where the national problem was also important, the Communists did, paradoxically, very poorly. Slovenia and Croatia are of course Catholic, and in Croatia the nationalist aspiration was well represented by Radich's party.

But Yugoslav Communism was not yet in the position either to sink its roots very deeply in Yugoslav soil or to exploit the na-

[5] I owe the figures to Mr. Anton Ciliga.

tional issue. It was already undergoing the process of ossification and subordination to a foreign power. In commenting upon the Vukovar Congress, the last legal Congress until 1948, the editor of the Archive comments dryly that the Party's "line" on the national issue paralleled the attitude of the "great Serbian bourgeoisie," [6] that is, the Party then still stood on the platform of national unity. But the rapid decline in the popularity of the Party which began in 1921 cannot be explained exclusively by its line or even by the regime's legal suppression of the Party which began by late 1920 and which led in August 1921 to the dissolution of the Communist Party and of all its legal organizations. The C.P.Y. managed to lose within an amazingly short period of time most of its revolutionary and radical spontaneity. It became, in fact as well as in name, a section of the Communist International, and for all its internal squabbles and contradictions, which made it quite different from the Stalinist pattern it was to have after 1928, it stood as an alien force in Yugoslav life. In 1923, when the Party created a legal "front," the Independent Workers' Party of Yugoslavia, it managed to capture only 18,000 votes in that year's elections—a loss of more than 90 per cent of the previous achievement of the Communists at the polls.[7] What revolutionary fervor the Communist Party possessed was expressed in a series of terroristic acts against the regime, including the assassination of the Minister of the Interior in 1921. Clearly the C.P.Y. was on the decline. By 1928 it was to possess only 3,000 members. The Party ceased, between 1922 and 1928, to be a major force in Yugoslav political life.

In 1948 Tito was to review the history of the Party and to place the blame for its eclipse, especially between 1922 and 1928, upon fractionalism and an incorrect stand on the national question. It was a characteristic review, more telling about the personality and attitude of the reviewer than about the history of the Party in the relevant period. For the Communist Party in Yugoslavia, as elsewhere in Europe at that period, suffered already from one great defect, not mentioned by Tito, which made it, even more than its

[6] *Congresses and Conferences of the C.P.Y.*, p. 28.
[7] Tito, *Political Report of the Central Committee of the Communist Party of Yugoslavia*, delivered at the Fifth Congress of the C.P.Y. (Belgrade, 1948), p. 25.

legal suppression, incapable of exercising a strong influence on the discontented masses of its country. It was already a servant of Moscow. Why was it then continually divided and full of fractional strife? The answer is that until 1928 the leadership of Russian Communism was itself full of fractional strife. The Communist Party of Yugoslavia was fast becoming a foreign-directed conspiracy; but it was not to have all the advantages of discipline and unity accruing to a conspiracy until 1937, when, after a series of purges, Josip Broz-Tito took over the leadership of the Party.

The other cause of fractionalism was, as indicated above, the problem of nationalism. The Party had to take a position on the subject of the rights of the non-Serbian nationalities within Yugoslavia. Should the Croats and Slovenes be granted a right to secession, or should the Party, as it did at the Vukovar Congress, maintain its stand on the ground of Yugoslav national unity, while declaiming vaguely against the hegemony of the "great Serbian bourgeoisie"? And should the right of secession be granted to the two "secondary" nationalities in Yugoslavia, not even acknowledged officially by the state—the Macedonians and Montenegrins? The whole problem would have amused a Stalinist after 1930: it is obvious that the given Communist Party should declare for the solution which has the greatest revolutionary possibilities, that is, which promises most speedily to deliver political power into the hands of the Communists. But it is significant that the Yugoslav Communist Party, for all its subordination to the Comintern, could not bring itself until the 1928–1930 period to consider the problem of nationality as a purely tactical rather than an ideological question. The Comintern itself was in that period not sufficiently "Stalinist" to force its Yugoslav subordinates to adopt a hard-boiled position on the national question. The Balkan Communist Federation, a body uniting the Communist Parties of Yugoslavia, Greece, and Bulgaria, during its existence between 1920 and 1930 followed, for instance, a very hesitating and tortuous policy on the question of Macedonia, with the Yugoslav and Greek Communists quarreling with their Bulgarian colleagues on that body.[8] The Comintern was called upon to adjudicate the claims of the three Communist Parties, but again it was unable or unwilling to force a resolute policy which would be

[8] See Elizabeth Barker, *Macedonia* (London, 1950), pp. 48–70.

immediately and without reservation obeyed by all Balkan Communists. It is no wonder that the Yugoslav Communists, for all their attachment and filial obedience to Moscow, could not present a clear-cut strategy on the national issue. The most influential leader of the Party in its early days was "Semich," the name concealing the identity of Sima Markovich, a Serbian intellectual. It is on him that many accounts of the Party's history place the blame for the "incorrect" stand on the national question. Markovich is reputed to have considered the whole problem as a primarily constitutional one, with which a Communist Party should not concern itself too much. He failed to realize the revolutionary potentiality of an appeal to Croat and Slovene nationalism, and he was purportedly unwilling to grant the right of secession to the non-Serb nationalities.

It is difficult now to estimate properly the position of Markovich and his adherents. Since the official historians of the Communist Party of Yugoslavia are bent upon discrediting all of Tito's predecessors in the leadership (with one exception), and since they attribute the Party's decline after 1921 to everything but its real cause, it is impossible to evaluate the charges against Sima Markovich with any degree of accuracy.[9] Markovich was criticized, by Stalin among others, for his "constitutional" attitude on the issue of nationalism. But the real problem went much deeper and is highly characteristic of the Yugoslav Party in this period (1921–1928). The Comintern felt undoubtedly aggrieved because it could not get through what it must have felt were the thick heads of the Yugoslav Communists that the problem of nationality was a tactical one rather than an issue of ideology. Since there was a rich field for the exploitation of national grievances in Croatia, Macedonia, and so forth, within the Yugoslav state, why not advocate the right of secession of those people? Why should the Yugoslav Communist Party fail to explore, for instance, Croat separatism? Why leave this fruitful field to the Croat Republican Peasant Party of Radich? The right to separate does mean the duty of separation on the part of a constituent nationality.[10] The Comintern, speaking in 1924 and 1925 through Manuilski and Stalin, hinted very strongly that once the

---

[9] Markovich's book on the national question was not, unfortunately, available to me.

[10] See Stalin quoted in Barker, *Macedonia*, pp. 65–66.

Yugoslav Communists had achieved power the rights of the Macedonians, Croats, and Slovenes could be satisfied in the same way that the Georgians and Ukrainians had had their right of secession guaranteed in the Soviet state. But in the meantime, the Comintern said in effect, for Heaven's sake, use whatever national slogans you find opportune to gain you the maximum of adherents among the discontented nationalities in Yugoslavia. But the Yugoslav Communists remained obtuse and irresolute. Markovich's hesitations were attributed to the baneful heritage of the Second International and to the idiotic tradition of Continental Socialism, which insisted upon interminable ideological examination of every problem instead of seizing upon a formula with concrete revolutionary possibilities.

The case against Sima Markovich is, even from the Communist point of view, probably exaggerated. An open call for the destruction of the Yugoslav state through its fragmentation among the constituent nationalities might have hurt the Communists' influence in Serbia more than the resulting advantage in Croatia and Macedonia would have justified. In 1949 it was the Cominform which ordered the Greek Communists to declare for an independent Macedonia, and the spectacle of the "Free Greek Government" declaring for a partition of Greece at the bidding of Moscow cost the Greek Communists heavily in terms of popularity with their own people. It may have been a similar reflection, rather than their reputed Serbian chauvinism, which restrained Markovich and his adherents. And they were by no means intransigent. In December 1923 the Third Conference of the C.P.Y. took place. The Party was then illegal, but there was in existence the Independent Workers' Party, its legal front. (The device of the various fronts used by the Communists in the satellite countries during and after the war is not an invention of the 1940's.) The amount of independence possessed by the latter can be judged from the fact that the conference of the C.P.Y. proceeded shamelessly, and without any attempt to conceal it, to formulate the platform of the Independent Workers' Party. The platform flirted openly with the right of secession without committing itself too much to a definite solution.

The Party [the Independent Workers' Party] is obligated to conduct the struggle to secure the right of every nationality to self-determination, with all the consequences of such a right . . . The Party should demon-strate to the proletariat that the national question in Yugoslavia is not a matter of simply revising the Constitution, but that there is a need to change fundamentally the present situation and to create a situation in which the sovereign will of all the peoples in Yugoslavia will be mani-fested and which will show their desire to live in friendship in one federa-tion of the worker-peasant republics.[11]

The declaration went on, not without ambiguities, to elaborate on the right of secession, asserting, however, that it had to be subordi-nated to the "interests of progress and class struggle of the prole-tariat," [12] and that it might be economically unwise. It was equally ambiguous on the subject of Macedonia, whose right to freedom was asserted provided that it got a "worker-peasant" government which would enter freely into the federation of independent Balkan republics.

The somewhat Pythian tone of the declaration was resented by the "right" fraction of Sima Markovich.[18] But the Fifth Congress of the Third International criticized severely the reluctance of the rightists, and underscored heavily the fact that Serbs, Croats, and Slovenes were three separate nations oppressed by Serbian im-perialism. The fight for national self-determination, the Comintern decided, could not be solved by constitutional methods.[14] Stalin him-self, as noted above, chastised "Semich" Markovich for his views. The rightist opposition now capitulated, and the Party could, at its Third Congress, held in Vienna in 1926, present for the first time the spectacle of Stalinist cohesion and of unity on the national question.

The Party, however, was too deeply divided to endure unity of any sort for very long. Soon after the Third Congress sectarian strife again raised its head. Communism was finding that it could not endure that division of opinion which is so normal to any po-litical party. In order to become unified, an ideological movement has to cease being a party and to become an army. Yugoslav Com-munism could not as yet settle down to the latter condition. And the declining conditions of the Party brought with them an irritation

---

[11] *Congresses and Conferences of the C.P.Y.*, p. 65.
[12] *Ibid.*, p. 70.
[18] Tito, *Political Report of the Central Committee*, p. 26.
[14] *Congresses and Conferences of the C.P.Y.*, p. 420.

of those personal conflicts which always lie at least dormant within the high command of an authoritarian movement. It is as if the normal channels of revolutionary activity were denied to those in command, and they put the full vehemence of their temperaments into quarreling among themselves.

Another cause motivated the violence of partisan strife. In Russia between 1926 and 1930 the Communist Party of the U.S.S.R. was being purged of the adherents of those Communists who had, in the past, had most contacts with foreign Communists. First the Trotskyites, and then the followers of Zinoviev and Bukharin, were being eliminated, as yet slowly, from positions of power and influence. It was natural that their foreign contacts and friends would lose favor with the new leaders of Russia and of the Third International, but there were as yet no fully fledged Stalinists to take the place of the veterans.

The official historian of the C.P.Y. turns his spotlight in the years from 1926 to 1928 to Zagreb, in Croatia. There, according to the Historical Archive, a leader arose who was determined to put an end to factionalism within the Yugoslav Party and whose first step in politics was an act of submission to the Third International. The Zagreb branch of the C.P.Y., led by Tito, sent an appeal to the Comintern imploring it to take the C.P.Y. in hand and to end its fractional strife. This act of submission to Moscow was proudly recalled by Tito himself at the Fifth Party Congress, held, it is well to remember, after his breach with Moscow in 1948.[15] It did not occur to Tito when narrating the incident that this initiative of his in 1928—going over the heads of the leaders of the C.P.Y. and appealing against them straight to Moscow—was an act for which a Yugoslav Communist would have been severely punished, as many were, from 1945 to 1948. It is likely that the Zagreb conference of 1928 and its letter created a good impression in Moscow and drew its attention to the promising young Croat Communist, who instead of being "left" or "right" wanted simply to receive marching orders from the Comintern.

In 1928, following the Zagreb letter, the Fourth Congress of the C.P.Y. was held in Dresden. This Congress marked the complete subordination of the C.P.Y. to the Third International. From then

[15] Tito, *Political Report of the Central Committee*, p. 29.

until its rebellion, the Communist Party of Yugoslavia was to be simply an agency of Moscow, reflecting unconditionally, in its program and its strategy, the desires of the Soviet state. Factionalism remained, of course, but only in the sense that some of the old leaders were liquidated for their past opinions and associations, or intrigued against each other, not so much within the Party itself as with the powers of the Third International.

At the Fourth Congress of the C.P.Y. the Third International did, in fact, take its Yugoslav component in hand. The Party was told to end its factional strife. Sima Markovich was again severely reprimanded for his scruples against exploiting the nationalist discontents in Yugoslavia. He had to humiliate himself by writing an open letter, in which he repudiated his former views, to the Party organization in Belgrade. The Third International nominated a new leadership of the C.P.Y. headed by a Croat Communist, Djuro Djakovich, and including Josip Broz-Tito.[16] It was a Party congress of a new kind: the Party delegates assembled in a German town to listen to an Italian Communist announce to them the orders of what was not only the Third International but also the government of Soviet Russia.

The *Congresses and Conferences of the C.P.Y.* contains the full text of the speech of the delegate of the Third International, Comrade "Ercoli," now better known as Palmiro Togliatti, Secretary-General of the Italian Communist Party. There is a good reason for the inclusion of the speech, though it is a part of the paradox which is Yugoslav Communism today. Its leaders accept the Fourth Congress of their Party as being in the historical succession that was eventually to bring the leadership to Tito. They hail its "resolutions," that is, its complete subordination to the dictates of the Third International, as being correct. But they cannot miss the opportunity to display the representative of Moscow at the Congress in his full arrogance and in his too obvious contempt for what he thought were those ignorant and unruly Balkan Communists. And Togliatti's speech is interesting to an outsider, for it shows a certain continuous trend in the thinking of the high command of international Communism about their Balkan comrades. There is a line running from Togliatti's remarks to the letters of the Central Committee of the Communist Party of the U.S.S.R. in 1948. These letters also casti-

---

[16] *Congresses and Conferences of the C.P.Y.*, p. 195.

gated, but this time more violently, the intransigence of the Yugoslav Party. The continuous theme in both is the strong conviction that the Balkan Communist Parties have to be handled with an iron hand and that there should be no nonsense about negotiating with them, appeasing them, or respecting their susceptibilities. For all their Communism, the Yugoslav delegates could not have failed to resent it when an Italian described their activities in the following terms:

> The basic characteristic of the working movement in all Balkan countries is the disunity and disorganization of the working class. This is not incidental. This is the result of so-called "Balkanism." What is "Balkanism"? It is a fragmentation into small groups, the tendency of the smallest component parts toward full independence; it is a continuous fight among those groups by means of intrigues and deceit.[17]

The editor of the Archive comments bitterly that Togliatti's invention of "Balkanism" has nothing to do with Marxism, but is a contemptuous slur against the Balkan peoples.[18] But at the Fourth Congress no one, including the future rebels, dared to throw back the insults of the representative of the Third International.

Togliatti made fun of Sima Markovich's reluctance to use whatever means available to undermine the Yugoslav state. The Marxist, and perhaps the Serb, in Markovich made him reluctant to use, hypocritically, Croat and Macedonian nationalism to create a revolution. Here is what Togliatti had to say, well illustrating the unchanging strategy of Communism:

> I listened when Comrade Gorkich in his speech stressed the great significance of the mistake made by the Party after the imperialist war [World War I], when it accepted and helped . . . the frightened bourgeoisie to disarm the masses. Comrade Number One [Sima Markovich] interrupted at that point with a remark that the masses which were then armed were marching under the banners of nationalism . . . That remark of Comrade Number One shows that even today he does not fully realize the Party's mistakes concerning the national question. In his concept there was missing, as Zinoviev has said, revolution. There are no clean revolutions. The armed working masses, though nationalistically inclined, could have been the starting point for the further development of the revolutionary movement.[19]

Communism, Togliatti told the Balkan "boors," uses anything and everything to achieve its ends. He omitted to explain how the

[17] *Ibid.*, p. 463.   [18] *Ibid.*, p. 486.   [19] *Ibid.*, p. 462.

"armed masses" which in 1918 and 1919 had finished fighting for an independent South Slav state could have been persuaded to turn around and destroy the very same state. His audience may have reflected in silence that the "armed masses" of his native Italy not only failed to be guided by his Communist Party after World War I, but watched Mussolini establish Fascism. To the Third International as represented by Togliatti anything which broke down the legal framework of a state, which introduced chaos and promised civil war, was welcome. He overlooked the fact that the "armed masses" in Germany were, at that moment, beginning to wear brown shirts.

Togliatti's speech is illuminating on many other questions. For the first time a representative of the International called for absolute submission to its will—submission which would require not only agreement on general policy but also a complete renunciation of individual identity and a transformation of all Party workers into mere tools of the Communist International. Thus, the unfortunate Sima Markovich had not only to recant but "the Party has the duty to ask him to capitulate absolutely and unconditionally." [20] No mere declarations, no diplomacy, no hind thoughts—nothing but full submission would do. Markovich had to write to his followers announcing his capitulation (which he did) and ordering them to subordinate themselves to the Party. He was ordered to leave Belgrade and go wherever the Party sent him. Markovich himself, said Togliatti, was unimportant. He had already committed so many anti-Party acts that the Congress could simply throw him out of the Party.[21] Togliatti went on to imply with considerable cynicism that since Markovich still had his followers in Yugoslavia the Third International was willing to use him in the future, though it would never trust him. Have we not here more than a faint promise of Moscow, twenty years later, calling upon the leaders of Yugoslav Communism to humiliate themselves and to acknowledge their mistakes, so that after they had performed their last act of "usefulness" they might be, in time, replaced by more faithful servants and told to go "wherever the Party sends them"? Thus the Communist Party of Yugoslavia got in 1928 its first systematic lesson in Stalinist Communism. It is equally characteristic that Togliatti chose Markovich's case as an example of the unfortunate consequences which

[20] *Ibid.*, p. 465.   [21] *Ibid.*, p. 466.

result from confiding the leadership to an intellectual. "There is no need to cast off the intellectuals, but they must understand what their role is to be." [22] They were to be used, but they were not to lead.

The Party functionaries returned from Dresden more as Soviet agents than as Yugoslav Communists. The Congress, or rather the Third International, had charged them to work most emphatically toward a complete disintegration of Yugoslavia. The ambiguities in the appeal of the Third Congress on the national question now disappeared. The Fourth Congress was compelled to proclaim "self-determination until secession" as its slogan.[23] Not only was Croatia to be independent but also Slovenia and even Montenegro. In its frantic and crude effort to steal the thunder of the most extreme nationalist groups, the Communists were forced to declare for the rights of secession for the Hungarian and Albanian minorities in Yugoslavia. The Internal Macedonia Revolutionary Organization (United), a Communist offshoot of the notorious terrorist organization, was solemnly declared to possess the sympathy of the working class of Yugoslavia, and especially of Serbia, in its struggle for an independent and united Macedonia.[24] There was no limit to the extent to which the Yugoslav Communist Party, while persisting illogically in its name, was willing to go to outbid every nationalism within the state. The Historical Archive unblushingly records all the resolutions of the Fourth Congress, though today it would be a capital offense for a Yugoslav Communist to advocate the cession of a single square foot of Yugoslav territory to a foreign power.

The Party's fortunes were not improved by this reprehensible and at the same time childishly Machiavellian policy. It did not gain any additional popularity. In view of its self-professed aim, one can hardly share the indignation of its official historians at the savage repression which hit the Party in 1928 and 1929. The new leader, Djuro Djakovich, fell in 1929 into the hands of the Yugoslav police and died in jail, purportedly after having been tortured. Today, he is the only pre-Tito leader who is venerated by the Yugoslav Party and the only figure in the history of the C.P.Y. for whom the Soviet commentators have a kind word to say. (They have not alleged as yet that he had been betrayed by Tito.)

[22] *Ibid.*, p. 468.   [23] *Ibid.*, p. 162.   [24] *Ibid.*, p. 163.

In 1928 Josip Broz appeared before a Zagreb court and, after making a defiant speech, was sentenced to five years in jail—years which he spent in the congenial company of his future adviser, Mosha Pijade. The Party's remaining leaders, headed by Djakovich's successor, Jovan Martinovich, a Montenegrin, fled abroad. From their foreign exile they urged an armed rebellion against the regime of King Alexander, who in 1929 had established a dictatorship. The ridiculous attempt almost finished off what had remained of the Communist Party of Yugoslavia. The leaders, still quarreling among themselves, issued chaotic and fantastic instructions from Vienna, with the result that most of the young fanatics in Yugoslavia were killed or imprisoned. In 1932 a new leader was designated, Milan Gorkich, whose real name, Chizhinsky, indicates his probable Czech origin. The change did not succeed in repairing either the inner-Party strife or the Party's declining fortunes in Yugoslavia.

The European situation was changing, however, and so was the Communist International's appraisal of the "objective conditions" in Yugoslavia. The threat of Hitlerism and Fascism was raising some serious doubts in Moscow about the advisability of "armed masses" overturning the governments of Soviet Russia's potential allies. Beginning with the Seventh Congress of the Third International, held in August 1935, Communism in Europe donned its peace-loving and democratic clothes. The Communist Party of Yugoslavia began to beat a frantic retreat from its policy of "self-determination until secession." In 1935 the Politburo of the C.P.Y. explained to the "subjugated nations" of Yugoslavia that secession was at present not practical and that they should not lean on foreign imperialisms.[25] In 1936 the Central Committee of the C.P.Y. was invited en masse to Moscow. It was a bad time to go there, since the foreign even more than the Russian Communists were then being liquidated right and left during the great purge. To be sure, the Central Committee was purged, and the climate of Moscow must have had a definite effect on its deliberations, for the new Central Committee adopted a resolution which among other things repudiated most definitely the old policy of the Party on the question of separation. Frankly avowing that its new policy resulted from the rise and threat of Hitler, "the Communist Party of Yugoslavia comes out against the

[25] *Ibid.*, p. 369.

break-up of the present territory of Yugoslavia, because it wants to achieve the reorganization of the state by peaceful means, on the basis of national equality." [26]

In 1937 Milan Gorkich and the rest of the leaders of the Communist Party of Yugoslavia were made to walk the plank. The one exception was the newly designated Secretary-General of the Communist Party of Yugoslavia—Josip Broz, "Comrade Walter," to become famous during and after the war as Tito.

II

World War II and its aftermath have served to change our perspective on Communism and its leaders. It is difficult now to visualize what kind of people they must have been to endure the existence they led before the war, the existence which was abnormal and illegal in their own country, and which was fraught with even greater danger whenever they reached the seemingly friendly soil of the Soviet Union. In 1937 Josip Broz-Tito, at the age of forty-five, moved into the leading position in Yugoslav Communism. He had literally to step over the bodies of many of his predecessors, in full knowledge that the political life-span of the leader of the Communist Party of Yugoslavia was, as a rule, very short and unpleasant. His predecessors had either been liquidated or had led a wretched existence, abused at every occasion, intermittently thrown out of then readmitted into the Party, and yet in many cases unable to divorce themselves completely from what had been their entire life. Had he not been a Communist fanatic in 1937, Tito could not have helped knowing that any major shift in the policy of the Comintern or the liquidation of one of his Russian protectors was likely to mean for him the fate of Milan Gorkich or Sima Markovich.

The circumstances of his selection for the position remain somewhat obscure. Twelve years afterward when "Comrade Walter," the exemplary servant of Stalinism, had become Tito, the greatest object of hatred for good Communists everywhere, an attempt was made to present his original selection in 1937 as a devilish plot on the part of the Trotskyites. At the trial of an alleged Bulgarian "Titoist," Traicho Kostov, it was claimed that as far back as 1934

[26] *Ibid.*, p. 399.

Tito had been favored by two notorious Trotskyites, the Pole Maximilian Walecki and the Hungarian Béla Kun, then ensconced in the Balkan section of the Third International.[27] The charge was, of course, completely nonsensical. Tito's predecessor, Milan Gorkich, was removed precisely because he was supposed to be a Trotskyite. By 1937 the only people being appointed to foreign Communist posts were those with unblemished Stalinist records. Tito seemed to fill the bill. He had entered Communism not from a Social Democratic background but on the basis of his stay and indoctrination in Russia, where, as a captured Austro-Hungarian soldier (he had been brought up a Croat in the old Austro-Hungarian Empire), he had witnessed and then joined the Bolshevik Revolution. He was not an intellectual, but of peasant and working-class origins and background. In 1928 he demonstrated his Communist loyalty as one of the leaders (though possibly not the leader the Historical Archive makes him) of the anti-fractional Zagreb Communist group which appealed to the Comintern to take the Communist Party of Yugoslavia firmly in hand. He must have appeared in 1937 as an ideal example of the new Communist leader: a man who was not likely to bother with problems of ideology, who was enamored of action and organization, and blindly loyal to his superiors in Moscow. Here was not a brooding and ascetic Communist, personally attached to the fallen great of Communism and perhaps susceptible to ideological scruples, but an essentially uncomplicated and childishly loyal follower of Stalinism. So it seemed, and so it was in 1937 and for a long time afterward.

The change of command coincided with a new period in the history of the C.P.Y. The leadership of the Party was told to get back to Yugoslavia. According to Tito's not unbiased account, Gorkich's "contacts" with the situation in the country where he was leading the revolutionary masses consisted of sitting in a café in Vienna and listening to the most recent arrival from Belgrade,[28] and then sending a report to Moscow. Tito and his high command went back to Yugoslavia and there worked clandestinely with an amazing degree of success. The Party rebuilt its shattered organiza-

[27] *Rabotnichesko Delo* (an organ of the Communist Party of Bulgaria), November 30, 1949.
[28] Tito, *Political Report of the Central Committee*, p. 35.

tional structure. In 1937 the Croatian and the Slovenian Communist Parties were established for the first time as parts of the C.P.Y.[29] Thus, though the decision to form them had been taken in 1934, it was only in 1937 that the attempt was made to develop a more systematic Communist appeal in Croatia and Slovenia as well as elsewhere in Yugoslavia. Tito and his colleagues managed to do what their predecessors had failed to accomplish since 1922: they had an actual Communist organization operating illegally within Yugoslavia, and they had escaped a wholesale liquidation of the Communist command by the police—a common and recurrent event before 1937.

Numerically, the Communist Party remained insignificant. Had the Communists been allowed to compete for power legally and freely, it is unlikely that they could have obtained more than a handful of seats in their country's parliament. But Tito and his lieutenants acquired in the years from 1937 to 1941 an asset more valuable to Communists than popular support: they acquired the "cadres," a body of experienced and well-trained followers who, for once, were not split into innumerable factions and groups. At every level of Yugoslav society and in every nationality the Party had a group of supporters which, in a crisis, could be counted upon to provide the elite of a revolutionary movement.

The achievement cannot be credited exclusively to the new leader. As in other countries of Southeastern and Eastern Europe, the atmosphere in Yugoslavia during the thirties was one of increasing apprehension of a national catastrophe. The rise and accomplishments of Nazism and its then overestimated ally, Fascism, were being resisted but feebly by the democracies of the West. King Alexander was killed in 1934 as the direct result of the activity of the Croat and Macedonian terrorists supported and abetted by Mussolini's Italy and its satellite Hungary. After his death, Yugoslavia moved more and more from its alliance with France toward the position of benevolent neutrality toward the Axis Powers. The semi-dictatorial regime of Milan Stojadinovich (1935–1939), and that of Dragisha Cvetkovich, which followed, openly flirted with the Axis, despite the fact that Italy, at least, never renounced her territorial ambitions in the Balkans. It was relatively easy for the Communists

[29] See *Congresses and Conferences of the C.P.Y.*, pp. 404–414.

to capitalize on the resentment against the policy of the regimes and to pose as defenders of democracy and of the anti-Axis sentiment in Yugoslavia. Until August 1939 they could play the role of inveterate enemies of Germanism and Fascism and friends of Russia's ally, France.

The Party's influence spread to the intellectuals and the students. By 1939 the C.P.Y. had been purged of most of the old-line Communists, whose quarrels and recantations had comprised so much of its history in the twenties and thirties. In 1939 it was announced, for instance, that a whole group of the old guard had been excluded from the Party, including its former leaders Gorkich, Sima Markovich, Antun Mavrak, Jovan Martinovich, and Djuro Cvijich.[30] Many of those excluded had been thrown out and readmitted several times since 1928, and how many of them were still in Yugoslavia or even alive must remain a subject of conjecture. The Party was becoming one of young men. It remained small numerically, but it was getting to be strong and militant. By 1939 some veterans of the International Brigades of the Spanish Civil War were trickling back to Yugoslavia to provide the Yugoslav Communists with experienced fighters and commanders. Tito was building a new Party free from sectarianism and constructed on the basis of Stalinist precepts and tactics. Alexander Rankovich in his 1948 report mentions casually that the Communists organized regular courses which were held in jail for the benefit of imprisoned comrades.[31] The University of Belgrade became a beehive of Communist activity.

The Archive of the Communist Party of Yugoslavia stops the account of its Congresses and Conferences in 1937, the year of Tito's accession to power. To some extent this is quite understandable. An account of the Party's activity between 1937 and 1941 would underline a fact which was already becoming painful to recollect for Tito and his group at the time of publication of the Archive in 1948–49: the fact that the Party in those years was, even more than before 1937, fully subservient to the Soviet Union. Thus there is no authenticated report of the Fifth National Conference of the C.P.Y.,

---

[30] Alexander Rankovich, *Report of the Central Committee of the Communist Party of Yugoslavia on the Organizational Work of the C.P.Y.*, presented at the Fifth Congress of the C.P.Y. (Belgrade, 1948), p. 5.

[31] *Ibid.*, p. 10.

held in October 1940. War had in the meantime engulfed Europe, and Soviet Russia was now an open accomplice of Nazi Germany. The Cvetkovich-Machek government of Yugoslavia had now become subservient to the Axis. The Fifth Party Conference confined itself to a studiedly vague analysis of the international situation. It stressed the need for organizing Party cells in the army, the railway service, and so forth. The Communist Party of Yugoslavia—that is, the Soviet Union—expected a period of troubles and opportunity in the Balkans.

Organizationally, the Fifth Conference elected a new Central Committee of 29 members, composed largely of Tito's nominees, and a Politburo of 7 members. Tito was now officially designated as Secretary-General.[32] The fact that the Conference could be held in Zagreb with 105 delegates participating is a tribute to the skill in clandestine work displayed by the new leadership. It was held "in agreement" with, that is, at the orders of, the Third International. Rankovich prudently does not mention who were the delegates of the Comintern at the meeting. If the archives of the Comintern are ever opened and revealed to the world, it is very likely that one will find in them a high praise for the loyalty and ability of the leaders of the Communist Party of Yugoslavia between 1937 and 1941. Nowhere else in Eastern Europe did a clandestine Communist Party in that period function so well and so usefully for the U.S.S.R.

The war was to test the Yugoslav Communists from a different point of view. This study is not the place to review the military history of the war in Yugoslavia, but certain things have to be noticed, since they are most revealing about the Communist Party of Yugoslavia both before and after 1941.

In February 1941 the Yugoslav government of Prince-Regent Paul, as represented by its Prime Minister Cvetkovich and Foreign Minister Cincar-Markovich, entered into negotiation with the Axis, concluding a long period of diplomatic approaches. France had been defeated and Germans were masters of the Continent. The Nazis needed the permission of Yugoslavia to send their troops through the country to invade Greece, which was then trouncing Hitler's Italian allies. On March 25 the Yugoslav government acceded to the Axis. Two days afterward, a group of Serbian officers

[32] *Ibid.*, p. 14.

led by General Dushan Simovich executed a *coup d'état.* The pro-Axis government of Cvetkovich was overthrown. Prince Paul was compelled to flee the country, and King Peter was declared to have come of age and to have assumed the rule. It was a brave and even foolhardy act. The Serbian officers who executed the coup could not be accused of being overly democratic or of having enlightened views on the national problem of Yugoslavia. But like the Greek government before them, their political shortcomings did not make them tremble before the dictators and did not make them give up their country's honor and independence without a fight, as did so many "democratic" politicians in France, Belgium, and Holland.

The Yugoslav coup was a direct defiance of Hitler. The master of Europe had to postpone his plans for the invasion of Russia in order to dispose of the insolent little Balkan country. By their courageous act the small group of Serbian "reactionaries" may well have saved the U.S.S.R. from an even greater disaster than befell it in the first months of the war.[33] The blitzkrieg hit Yugoslavia within a few days; Germany struck on April 6, and after an unequal fight old Yugoslavia ceased to exist. The country was distributed among Germany and its satellites, Italy, Hungary, and Bulgaria. Croatia finally had an "independent" state—with the assassin Ante Pavelich as its fuehrer, and a member of the Italian royal house as its king. The latter, rechristened Tomislav II, hid with a girl friend in Milan before receiving the news of his royal fortune, and thereafter had the good sense never to visit his kingdom.[34] Italy's wartime exploits in the Balkans provide the only relief in an otherwise bloody and depressing story. Dalmatia and a part of Slovenia, like Croatia, were allocated to Italy. Montenegro was to be set up as a puppet state. Bulgarians occupied Yugoslav Macedonia. Serbia and most of Slovenia were to be within the German sphere of occupation. Hungary also was to receive some crumbs

[33] The executors of the coup must have anticipated, at least to some extent, Hitler's reaction to it. Though they did not repudiate their predecessors' formal accession to the Axis, they chased out Hitler's favorite Yugoslav government. See a discussion of their attitude in Hugh Seton-Watson, *The East European Revolution* (London, 1950), p. 66.

[34] Galeazzo Ciano, *The Ciano Diaries,* ed. by Hugh Gibson (New York, 1946), p. 348.

off the German table. Everywhere, of course, real control and supervision belonged to the Germans, and in many places there were puppets, traitors, and "reasonable men" to serve the Nazis' purposes,
though none of them approached Pavelich and his clique in the
bloodiness of their regimes.

What was the attitude of the Yugoslav Communists toward the
destruction and partition of their state? On June 22, the confusion
between patriotism and Communism disappeared. When Soviet
Russia was attacked, they could fight as Communists and also as
Yugoslav patriots. But how about the period from April 6 to June
22? The Communists were to boast long after the events that they
took up arms in defense of their country *before* the German attack
on Russia.[35] They were to resent, especially after their break with
Moscow in 1948, any insinuation that their fight had been for Soviet
Russia and not for Yugoslavia. According to Stephen Clissold, in his
book, *Whirlwind* (the best account of the war, but unfortunately
not documented), the Party's reaction to the coup of March 27
was a further effort to destroy the Yugoslav state and to split it
into its national components during the German onslaught.[36] Where
is the truth?

In order to clarify the situation, let us juxtapose two statements
from the published diary of Vladimir Dedijer, a young Communist
and Partisan leader, who in 1941 was in contact with all the leading
lights of the Communist Party of Yugoslavia. The first entry is
dated April 27, 1941—that is, after the occupation by the Germans:
"We have received our directives to organize attacking groups of
ten and to investigate conditions for sabotage." [37] Then, on September 15, Dedijer notes: "I heard from Comrade 'Crni' that the first
shot fired in Serbia *after June 22* was on the highway Valjevo-
Uzhice . . . *This happened in the beginning of July.*" [38] By the first
shot Dedijer means, of course, one fired by the Communist Partisans, for there were many fired by others before June 22. But the
juxtaposition is characteristic. Before the "Fatherland of Socialism"

[35] See Kardelj's statement at the meeting of the Cominform quoted in the
next chapter.
[36] Stephen Clissold, *Whirlwind* (London, 1949), p. 27.
[37] Vladimir Dedijer, *Dnevnik* (*Diary*), in Serbo-Croat, 3 vols. (Belgrade,
1945, 1948, 1950), I, 18.
[38] *Ibid.*, p. 28. My italics.

was attacked, the Communists went on in their old way. The destruction of the old regime and the substitution of the successor puppet states represented simply a change from one bourgeois regime to another, but it was a change which provided the Party an enhanced opportunity to fish in troubled waters and to prepare for its own Communist action. The fact that on April 5, one day before the German attack, Soviet Russia had signed a treaty of non-aggression and friendship with Yugoslavia may have given the Communists a pause in their hostility to the Yugoslav state. But then the destruction of the state, its division and occupation, seemed, from the Communists' point of view, a new and wonderful opportunity to carry on and intensify their work. They did not collaborate with the Germans; on the contrary, they sabotaged their puppets and began to prepare for armed action; but they were ready to throw everything into the fight and to give their all only *after* Soviet Russia had been attacked. And we don't need much testimony on this point. For all their protestations to the contrary, the Yugoslav Communist leaders themselves betrayed more than once, even after their break with Moscow, that their real fight against the invader began only after Russia had been invaded on June 22.[39] Until then they were ready to sabotage and obstruct and infiltrate the puppet regimes in Yugoslavia, just as they had done with every government in Yugoslavia since the country's inception, but after that they were ready to risk all and to give all in their unmeasured loyalty to Soviet Russia.

The war against the invader in Yugoslavia was complicated and at times overshadowed by several civil wars raging at the same time in the unfortunate country. Pitted against the Communists, who took the name of Partisans for their fighting units, were the Chetniks of General Mihailovich. The Chetniks perpetuated both a name famous in Serbia's history and a para-military organization which had existed in peacetime Yugoslavia. The organization placed its members at the disposal of the Serbian puppet, Milan Nedich, but a great many among them followed the appeal of Drazha Mihailovich and joined him in a resistance movement against the invader.[40] The "illegal Chetniks" under Mihailovich soon became associated

[39] See, for example, the quotation from Kidrich's speech in Chapter 4, below.
[40] Seton-Watson, *The East European Revolution*, p. 126.

with the royal Yugoslav government-in-exile, and Mihailovich became its war minister while leading armed guerrillas in Yugoslavia. The case of General Mihailovich is the most notable *cause célèbre* of the war. In February 1944 Winston Churchill was to condemn Mihailovich's Chetniks and to assert that from then on Great Britain intended to support the only effective anti-German force in Yugoslavia—the Partisans of Tito. The man who in the earliest days of Yugoslavia's occupation had been hailed as the embodiment of his country's indomitable will for freedom found himself, after 1943, steadily denounced in London and in Washington. The Allied missions were withdrawn from the Chetniks. It was asserted that Mihailovich was collaborating with the enemy. The flow of materials from the West was directed to Tito's forces. The Communist Partisans were said to be the only true defenders of Yugoslavia. And at the end of the war the Western Allies forced the exiled government of Yugoslavia and its king to repudiate Mihailovich and to enter into a suicidal "compromise" with Tito. Were the Allies taken in by Communist propaganda and did they betray the only true Yugoslav leader, or did they rightly denounce a collaborator and near traitor?

To give a full answer one must go into the incredibly complex situation in Yugoslavia, with its civil wars, its fight against the invaders, and its puppet regimes with their differing shades of treason and collaboration. (At least one of these regimes, that of General Nedich in Serbia, claimed that it owed its allegiance to King Peter and that it was collaborating only to spare the lives of the Serbian people.) In a work devoted to the problem of Titoism, the case of Drazha Mihailovich cannot be fully appraised. It should be pointed out, however, that it is extremely naïve, to say the least, to attribute the Allies' conversion to Tito to a group of British and American Communists and Communist sympathizers who had wormed their way into the Allies' information and strategic services connected with Yugoslavia.[41] The strongest adherents of Mihailovich feel constrained to admit that some of his commanders collaborated with the enemy, especially with the Italians.[42] It is well documented that

[41] This is the case made by Leigh White in his *Balkan Caesar* (New York, 1951), especially pp. 45–54.

[42] See David Martin, *Ally Betrayed* (New York, 1946), for example, pp. 131–149.

Drazha Mihailovich had the foolish habit of issuing blank command slips containing his signature to his commanders, who sometimes made treasonous use of them, thus apparently implicating their leader. His own position appears to have been that of a Serbian patriot who at times, regretfully, had to sanction somewhat questionable dealings of his subordinates. It is true that the military effort of Mihailovich's forces, largely but not completely because of reasons beyond his control, could not compare with that of the Partisans. On military grounds, the Allies' decision to supply Tito and the Partisans was well founded. What was inexcusable, and in some quarters intentionally misleading, was the effort to present the Partisans as anything but a Communist-led and a Communist-controlled movement. But that was, of course, a part of a much vaster and more tragic story of illusion and self-deception.

More relevant to our study is the problem of how the Yugoslav Communists, in 1941 but a handful of workers, intellectuals, and professional agents, could by 1944 emerge as undoubted masters of Yugoslavia, enjoying considerable popular following and ready to take over and run their country with but slight assistance from the Russian army. Was it the Allies' support of Tito and betrayal of Mihailovich that determined the issue? [43] To some extent, yes. The Russians during the war gave Tito practically nothing in terms of supplies. He received supplies, encouragement, and at one time shelter away from the mainland of Yugoslavia, from the Allies. But the Allies' help does not begin to explain fully his success.

There were three major reasons for the Communist victory in Yugoslavia. First, there was the tremendous psychological advantage enjoyed by the Communist forces over their opponents in the civil wars, not to mention the invaders. The war was an opportunity the Communists had expected and prayed for, for years. For them it was a period of relative freedom. To be able to stage guerrilla marches and attacks from hide-outs in the mountains, to endure enemy offensives, represented a decided advance over their previous position of hiding from the police and leading a clandestine activity with the certitude of sooner or later falling into the hands of the regime. It was a period of revolutionary enthusiasm, when the interminable ideological discussions and the incessant search

[43] As it is asserted in White, *Balkan Caesar*, p. 51.

for Trotskyites and deviationists were pushed into the background. For the first time the Yugoslav Communists could live and breathe as fighters and revolutionaries. And they were peculiarly suited for the type of fighting they engaged in. The café type of revolutionaries had been previously eliminated. It is characteristic that the one occasion when a Partisan operation was entrusted to a Communist of the pre-1937 school—the Montenegro uprising of July 1941, conducted by Mosha Pijade—ended in a failure not unrelated to the attempt to combine a doctrinaire social revolution with a national uprising.[44] The leadership was by and large young and resilient.

The second advantage enjoyed by Tito was a peculiarity of the Yugoslav situation. His rival, General Mihailovich, was a Serb, and he led a purely Serbian movement. While the Yugoslav government-in-exile contained Slovene and Croat ministers, it proved impossible to create within the country a correspondingly broad Yugoslav movement under Mihailovich. The news of the massacre of Serbs by the Croat puppets of Pavelich, one of the most hideous occurrences of the war, accentuated the deep split between the two kindred nations. The Communists, while strongly resentful, were hard-boiled enough to disregard such "sentimental" considerations. Their organization included cells in every subdivision of Yugoslavia, and within every nationality they had a small group of adherents. The Partisans began, as did Mihailovich's Chetniks, as a mostly Serbian movement. But their leader was a Croat, and the core of the movement—the Communists—did not care for nationality for its own sake. By 1943 they were gaining followers all over the territory of Yugoslavia; and everywhere, whether in Slovenia, Macedonia, or among the Moslems of Bosnia, there was a small Communist group to lead and to indoctrinate the nonpolitical adherents who wanted no more than to fight the Germans and their own traitors. The Communists did not look down upon any useful human material. When former Ustashis (armed followers of Pavelich), some of them not innocent of the slaughter of the Serb minority in Croatia, came over to Partisan units, they were cheerfully accepted, though watched and reindoctrinated. A former collaborator or a Chetnik was always welcome in the Partisan camp, provided he could be useful. The Communists were for once flexible and

44 Clissold, *Whirlwind*, pp. 78–85.

maneuvered with ease in the morass of national and ideological problems. The problem of losing their own men or of inviting savage German reprisals for an isolated act of terrorism did not bother them greatly. A village razed to the ground by the Germans meant an influx of men into the Partisan ranks. Their own losses could be endured since they were fanatics fighting with no regard for life. Their country had been attacked. Whether by their country the Communist leaders of the Partisans meant Yugoslavia, or the U.S.S.R., or the two somehow joined together, became less and less clear as the war progressed. Dedijer's diary offers many examples of this confusion. The patriotic songs the Partisans sang were often songs about Stalin, the Red Army, and Comrade Tito. Among the pictures reproduced by Dedijer, some of which purport to show the ghastly details of the Ustashi massacres, appears more than once the cheerful figure of Tito's boss painted by the Partisans on the walls of some reconquered town. Partisans falling before a German firing squad would often die with praise of the Soviet Union or even of the Third International on their lips.[45]

The third major factor in the Communists' success was the quality of leadership displayed by Tito and his group. Alone of the Communists of Eastern Europe, the Yugoslav Party was prepared when the war came, both organizationally and psychologically, to engage in armed operations. That the credit for their preparedness should be attributed to their patriotism is more than doubtful. They were simply, as far back as 1938, laying the foundations for armed struggle for power at a favorable moment, and it so happened that their opportunity coincided with a patriotic and civil war. There was no duality of command among the Partisans. Tito, alone of the Communist leaders of the future satellite states, was both the boss of the Party and the commander in chief. The Party had previously succeeded in recruiting several career officers of the Yugoslav army. The most outstanding of them was Tito's chief of staff, General Arso Jovanovich. In addition, many veterans of the International Brigade of the Spanish Civil War added their experience to the fight against their old enemy. All the channels of command and influence within the Partisan movement were safely in Tito's hands. While he was undoubtedly in contact with Moscow,

[45] Dedijer, *Diary*, I, 39.

the Russians were too busy, until the battle of Stalingrad, to pay much attention to the Yugoslavs. By then, things were going so well for their side in Yugoslavia that there was no reason for them to interfere more directly with Tito's conduct of the war and to stir up suspicions among the Western Allies.[46] What more could the Soviets demand in Yugoslavia? What was happening there was a Communist dream come true. There was no incident during the war which could even vaguely suggest that in his national struggle Tito ever forgot that he was a Communist. For all their preoccupations, the Yugoslav Communists did not forget their fraternal Communist Parties. They helped the Albanian Communists to organize their partisan activities. They established contact with the Greek and Bulgarian Communists. If these actions indicated a certain unhealthy tendency of Tito's to spread his influence too far, then, Moscow probably thought, that could be handled after the war.

The only troublesome thing about Tito was the excess of his Communist zeal—a zeal which made him overly impatient to get everything into the Communists' hands as soon as possible. The National Liberation Committees were being created by the Partisans as early as 1941 to provide the new political structure.[47] The short period of uneasy alliance with Drazha Mihailovich came to an end in November 1941, and it is obvious it could never have worked in view of the objectives of both sides. The Communists were not looking for allies among the non-Communists; they were looking for dupes and puppets. The "front" they wanted to establish in Yugoslavia was to be more on the order of the old Independent Workers' Party than a genuine coalition of radical and progressive forces. To accuse Tito of duplicity is beside the point. No one who could read the orders of the National Liberation Army and Partisan Detachments could be left in any honest doubt regarding the character of the movement. In his report in 1948 Tito was to use the characteristic phrase, "the Central Committee of the C.P.Y., that is, the Supreme Headquarters." [48] The core of the Partisan army, the Proletarian Shock Brigades, wore the five-pointed star with hammer and sickle on their caps.[49] Moscow may have believed that

---

[46] This subject is treated more fully in Chapter 3 below.
[47] Tito, *Political Report of the Central Committee*, p. 67.
[48] *Ibid.*   [49] *Ibid.*, p. 82.

such openness went too far, but no one can accuse the Yugoslav Communists of hypocrisy. "Our Party did not carry out its role of leader in the Liberation War obtrusively, illegally, in disguise," said Tito afterwards, and to some extent he was speaking the truth.[50] In their public activity, however, the Communists felt constrained to create a "broad, national" body which would serve as the rallying point for the non-Communist adherents of the Partisans and, eventually, as counterfoil to the Yugoslav government-in-exile. In Bihach, in November 1942, the Anti-Fascist Council for the National Liberation of Yugoslavia was created as the front for the Partisan movement. The delegates included a variety of politicians from such legal parties of old Yugoslavia as the Croat Peasant Party, the Democratic Party, and the Agrarian Party. The A.V.N.O.J., as the new body was called in brief, issued a six-point declaration "guaranteeing," among other things, "the inviolability of private property" in agriculture, industry, and trade.[51] More truthful was the pledge to recognize national rights of all the peoples of Yugoslavia. The pledge, however, should have been interpreted to mean that in Tito's Yugoslavia, Croats, Slovenes, Macedonians, and Moslems, as well as Serbs, would enjoy the right to serve the Party and the state.

Even before Bihach the Communists had entered into negotiations with various political parties which could not stomach Mihailovich or the Yugoslav government-in-exile. People like Milan Grol and Dragoljub Jovanovich, genuine democrats and social radicals, were enticed into a hopeless alliance with Tito, an alliance which could have only one end: their ejection and imprisonment, once their usefulness to the Communists had passed.

One year afterward, at Jajce, the A.V.N.O.J. became the acting government of the territory held by the Partisans. The king and the government-in-exile were warned not to return to Yugoslavia without the consent of the people. A federal Yugoslavia was sketched out, composed of six federal republics and some autonomous districts —a faithful replica of the federal structure of the U.S.S.R. Dr. Ivan Ribar, a distinguished prewar politician, became the figurehead of the projected state. Ribar, a future president of Tito's Yugoslavia, was

[50] *Ibid.*, p. 105.
[51] Clissold, *Whirlwind*, p. 113.

attached to the Communists by the strongest personal ties. His two sons, Ivan Lola and Jurica, though only in their twenties, were among the leading Yugoslav Communists, and both gave their lives during the war. The presidium of the new government was a strange hodgepodge of Communists, a few bona fide representatives of democratic movements, and even some Macedonian and Bulgarian professional revolutionaries.[52] There was no question where the real power belonged. Tito became acting Prime Minister and Minister of Defense. The current Communist fashion was recognized when the Secretary-General of the Communist Party of Yugoslavia was also designated a marshal. The framework of new Communist Yugoslavia was set. Germany's collapse in the Balkans, and the Western Allies' inability or unwillingness to stem the tide of Communism in Eastern Europe, completed the picture. By the end of 1944, Soviet troops were on Yugoslav soil and Belgrade was occupied by the Partisans. For a few months Tito had to go through the comedy of a "compromise" with the government-in-exile. In March 1945 he accepted a few members of the royal government into his "unity" government. They did not stay there long, but the transition from the monarchy to the republic could thus be accomplished legally. "We had to consent to this agreement because the Western Allies stubbornly insisted on it," [53] said Tito, but it did not cost him very much to do so. By the end of 1945 Yugoslavia was safely in the hands of the Communists. Behind the cover of the Peoples' Front, they monopolized all political power and were busy introducing Communist social and economic measures with a speed unmatched in the countries under direct Soviet control.

It is relevant to compare the Partisans' wartime accomplishments with those of the Communists in the other East European countries. Here, of course, the true achievements of Tito and his group are fully illuminated. True, the Partisans were helped by the nature of the terrain, the fact that for the Germans the Balkans were after all a sideshow, and the reluctance of the British to land their troops in Yugoslavia (as they had in Greece in 1944). Yet the Communists in Yugoslavia, unlike those in other satellite nations, won their country by their own exertions during the war, with scant help from

---

[52] See Barker, *Macedonia*, pp. 95–96.
[53] Tito, *Political Report of the Central Committee*, p. 119.

the Russians and with relatively little terrorist activity. There was terror in Yugoslavia during and after the war and legal chicanery which eliminated people like Ivan Shubashich, Milan Grol, and Dragoljub Jovanovich from the government and influence. But the main conquest of power took place during the war. In Poland, Hungary, and Rumania, the Communists needed the help of the Soviet Union first to keep their foot in the door and then to achieve and hold political power. Even in Bulgaria, traditionally the most pro-Russian of all Balkan states, with a strong Communist Party of its own, it was the postwar period of terror, possible only because of the shadow of the Soviet Union, which enabled the Communists to grasp the government. The Czechoslovak Communists, despite a considerable popular following, managed to carry off the coup of February 1948, which really gave them the monopoly of power, because of the fear of a direct Soviet intervention. Compared with the Yugoslavs, the Communists elsewhere were like clumsy pupils always running to the teacher to tell them what to do next and to extricate them from a difficult situation.

In Greece, the Communists, who were masking behind the People's Liberation Army (the E.L.A.S.), came very close to duplicating the feat of the Yugoslav Communists; but for the British intervention in October 1944, the E.L.A.S. and its political counterpart, the E.A.M., would have held most of Greece at the time of the Germans' withdrawal and defeat. The understanding between Stalin and Churchill that Greece would remain within the "British sphere" was largely responsible for the splits and indecision which affected the Greek Communists at the crucial period of late 1944 and early 1945. But the fact still remains that, compared with the Partisans, the E.L.A.S. was weak numerically, and the Greek Communists themselves during the war never achieved the degree of cohesion and direction which Tito's forces possessed. The Yugoslav Communists, the scorned "Balkanized" Party of Togliatti's speech of several years before, now showed themselves masters of their revolutionary craft. It is no wonder that between 1944 and 1947 Tito was widely considered, and considered himself, as the future deputy of Stalin for all the Balkans and as already the overlord of Communist Albania, protector of the Greek Communists fighting against their government, and even an acknowledged superior of the Bulgarian Communists, who had previously been the favorites of the Comintern in the Balkans. And what sentiments must have stirred the Yugoslav Communists when in 1947, at the founding meeting of the Cominform, the Italian and French Communists were blasted for their mistakes at the end of the war! It was the Italian Communist Party, led by the Yugoslavs' old persecutor, "Ercoli," which in 1947 was criticized and humbly acknowledged its sins for allowing the "armed masses" of Italy to be disarmed when the Allies took over. The Yugoslav Communists could strut and boast of their achievements, convinced of the lasting obligation their Russian colleagues felt toward them.

The success of Tito was due to an unusually fortuitous arrangement of events and personalities. Old Yugoslavia was divided and seemingly incapable of regeneration. Whatever else the Partisans were, they exemplified energy and purpose. During the war they acted, talked, and sometimes even thought as free revolutionaries rather than as servants of an alien government. It was no accident that they attracted so many of the young among the former ruling class of their country. Tito's versatile secretary, Olga Ninchich, was the daughter of a minister of the Yugoslav government-in-exile. Drazha Mihailovich's tragedy is underlined when it is reflected that his own children left him during the war to join the Partisans.[54] In contrast to the continuous wrangling which went on among the Chetniks, excellent morale pervaded Tito's headquarters. His high command, including even his two future enemies, Generals Sreten Zhujovich and Arso Jovanovich, preserved a picture of harmony and discipline. The "old man," as Tito is called in Dedijer's diary, appears to have been the undoubted master of both the military and the political structures. If there were quarrels and debates about military and political problems, they do not seem to have affected the unity of the Partisans. On the death of Rankovich's wife, Milovan Djilas wrote Rankovich a touching letter, testifying to an unusual phenomenon—a strong personal friendship between two people who would usually be close competitors for power.[55] Even Andrija Hebrang, Tito's greatest enemy in the Party in the crisis of 1948, appears in Dedijer's diary (printed in 1945) as a brave

[54] Monty Radulovic, *Tito's Republic* (London, 1948), p. 197.
[55] Dedijer, *Diary*, I, 178–179.

Communist leader in Croatia, with not the slightest hint of the horrible sabotage and treason attributed to him by Tito once he cast his lot in with Moscow and against the Party.[56] Hebrang's prison interview with the Croat "fuehrer" Pavelich is mentioned casually, as something the Party knew all about, rather than as an act of treason.[57]

The life of the Party was obscured but not submerged by the struggle of the Partisans. The schizophrenic quality of Communism in action is well illustrated by the fact that Dedijer could become honestly indignant at the "rumors" spread in London that the Partisans were Communists, while expounding, at the same time, Marxism-Leninism to the Partisan recruits. Logic is a great handicap to would-be revolutionaries. The Communist leaders were fortunate in their capacity to see themselves, and sincerely, as both Soviet and Yugoslav patriots.

It has been the fashion recently to trace the beginnings of the Russo-Yugoslav conflict to the period of the war. This point of view is true, but only if it is qualified immediately by the assertion that neither the Russian nor the Yugoslav Communists, and especially the latter, were at any time during the war conscious of anything but complete harmony of their aims and interests. There were minor irritations.[58] But to the Russians Tito's unexpected rise as a Balkan Stalin was something that could be taken care of after the war, and to the Partisans the lack of concrete help from the Soviet and the hints that Tito should be more prudent in his professions of Communism were explained by Russia's embattled situation and temporary obligation to the Western Allies. When the first British officers joined the Partisans, Dedijer's elation was tempered by a twinge of conscience that a proletarian movement should beg for and receive help from the representatives of an

---

[56] *Ibid.*, pp. 300–301.

[57] Like the lenient treatment of Traicho Kostov by the Bulgarian authorities during the war, so does that of Andrija Hebrang by the Ustashi remain something of a mystery. Kostov was the known leader of the Bulgarian Communists; Hebrang was obviously known as one of the leading Communists in Croatia. Yet he was exchanged with thirty-one other Communists for two Ustashi officials held by the Partisans. In both instances their Communist colleagues did not see anything "fishy" in their cases, until they were liquidated for other things.

[58] The subject is examined below in Chapter 3.

arch-capitalist power. He reconciled himself by observing that the British needed the Partisans as much as the Partisans needed the British. "We must be realists too," he said, and the decisive consideration was that *"strengthening and broadening of the Anglo-Soviet-American alliance is the basic task of all freedom-loving nations of the world."* [59] Could a man like that conceive of any conflict between Communist Yugoslavia and the U.S.S.R.? And Dedijer was probably typical of the younger generation of Communist leaders.

Among the few older leaders the question was more complicated. When the war ended another struggle was to begin. Yugoslavia was to be made into a Communist state, and the democratic phraseology of the A.V.N.O.J. during the war was simply to be tossed aside. Organization, planning, and the security police were to take precedence over the spirit of revolution. But new Yugoslavia was still to be run by the same people who had conquered it for Communism. The story of Sima Markovich and Milan Gorkich, ignored by the youngsters as merely a tale of treason from the distant past, could not have been entirely absent from the minds of Tito and his older colleagues as they exchanged their wartime occupations for ministerial offices.

[59] Dedijer, *Diary*, II, 272. My italics.

CHAPTER 2

The Establishment of the Cominform

The existence of an international social or religious movement which is led and represented by a great secular power is not a new phenomenon in European and world history. It is the fact that Communism has grown and developed within the fully matured modern state system that has made it a disturbing element in international society. The challenge represented by Communism has counted not only in the call for a violent transformation of existing political and economic institutions but also in a straightforward advocacy of the viewpoint and, sometimes, the political interests of a great power—Soviet Russia. A historian comparing the history of the Third International with that of the Second will be struck by the disunity of the Socialist movement when contrasted with the seemingly monolithic cohesion of Communism. The incidence of purges and deviations cannot erase the fact that in almost every civilized country Communism under the Third International managed to preserve a nucleus of well-organized followers. The official ideology moved along the most tortuous road; at times nothing seemed to remain as an article of faith save a firm belief in the infallibility of the leaders of the Soviet Union. A man brought up in the liberal tradition in politics could rub his eyes and still not believe that the followers of a "scientific" philosophy of life could be pushed, through faith or discipline, into the most unreasonable sequence of beliefs and actions. There were people of liberal persuasion who, in the interwar period, could and did admire much of the achievement—supposed or real—of the Soviet Union, and yet who found it impossible to join in the absolute devotion to the U.S.S.R. that was required by organized Communism. The Communist Party of the U.S.S.R. had succeeded by 1930 in alienating the great mass of organized labor outside of Russia. By its rigidity, its purges, and its departure both from the democratic principle and, seemingly, from orthodox Marxism, it aroused the hostility of the Socialist Parties. Communism by its tactics, if indeed not by its very existence, may have facilitated the rise of fascism in Europe. The persistence of the Communist International must have appeared to many as the triumph of faith over reason, or simply as the result of Soviet Russia's determination to perpetuate an instrument of its foreign policy under the guise of an international Communist movement.

Those reflections are only natural from the point of view of an outsider or even of a person who feels some sympathy with the aim of Communism, who is impressed by the economic and social achievements of Soviet Russia, but who nevertheless still questions the validity of the methods employed by Communism both in Russia and abroad. Conversely, to a person steeped in Communist ideology and familiar with the official version of the history of the Party since 1903, those methods have preserved the nucleus of world Communism, first in Russia and then in the well-disciplined and active Parties all over the world. The Third International in its activity, if not in its theory, was built upon the premise that the Soviet Union had to be defended at all costs, and the choice of the enemy and of the means to defeat him had to be left to those holding the ramparts of victorious socialism. Even the elimination or defection of the most brilliant leaders of Communism, whether in Russia or abroad, did not matter. Could international Communism afford to become a loose confederation of debating societies when Russia, still in the process of transition to socialism, was surrounded by hostile capitalist states? History taught that socialism had often failed because of its lack of cohesion and discipline, and even the annals of the Bolshevik movement bore testimony to the evil of "factionalism." A variety of interpretations, ranging from philosophical idealism to syndicalism, had in the past been superimposed upon the original doctrine and had threatened to destroy the revolutionary mission of Russian socialism.

Communism in the years between the two wars was increasingly conditioned by this protective sentiment toward the Soviet Union, which, in the minds of its devotees, finally displaced their original Marxist dogma. Certainly, it is striking to contemplate the contrast between the early days of Communism both in Russia and elsewhere, when the essence of the movement appeared to consist in continuous discussion, in the urge to survey and remake all the existing social and political institutions, and the thirties, when its discussions turned into recitations and its revolutionary dynamism became tamed and harnessed to the tactics of the Soviet Union. Toward the end of its existence the Third International became almost superfluous. It had fulfilled the educational function of training Communist leaders, and their mental processes were now synchronized with the policies of the Communist state. By 1943, when the Comintern was dissolved in a gesture widely interpreted as one of courtesy toward Russia's allies, it was already obvious that the postwar world would require a different type of Communist organization or collaboration. Communism had achieved both maturity and respectability. It was almost certain that the end of the war would witness the emergence of new Communist states and that even in the West, particularly in France and Italy, Communist ministers would appear. The existence of the Third International, and the fact that its seat was in Moscow, had proved in the past one of the main reasons for the distrust with which even the most radical French and English Socialists looked upon the Communists in their own countries. In addition to being an incubus upon the future development of Communism, the Comintern had too much of the flavor of the conspiratorial past to befit a movement now firmly established as a leading social tendency of the age. When at the end of the war the government of the U.S.S.R. abolished the title of "commissar" and reverted to the commonly used designation of "ministries" for its administrative agencies, it illustrated once again the tendency prevalent since the early thirties of discouraging the outward trappings of the revolutionary tradition. The dissolution of the Comintern was in the same vein, and yet the move was not without great symbolic significance: it was the fullest expression yet of the belief that the Soviet Union *as a state* will always enjoy the allegiance of Communist leaders all over the world, and that the allegiance no longer required the fiction of an international organization. The demise of the Comintern has often been cited as a typical example of Soviet hypocrisy. It was, on the contrary, a very clear and unambiguous statement of the nature of the relationship between the Soviet Union and world Communism.

The Second World War exerted a profound influence on the character of organized Communism both in Eastern and in Western Europe. In the East the Red Army occupied Poland, Hungary, Rumania, Bulgaria, and parts of Yugoslavia and Czechoslovakia toward the end of the war.

With Soviet armies came the veterans of the movement who had spent the war years in Moscow. The roster of the distinguished Communists who then for the first time in many years were traveling to their native lands under their real names and without the fear of arrest reads now like a "Who's Who" in politics in Eastern Europe. It is possible that upon his arrival home many a veteran Communist had to rub his eyes not only to convince himself of the reality of his own good fortune but also in order to believe that the Party which he had abandoned as a small group of conspirators working clandestinely was now a tremendous organization, a partner in the government of his country, and soon without doubt to become its master. Before 1939 the Communist Parties in the future satellite states were numerically weak to the point of insignificance. Except in pre-Munich Czechoslovakia, they could not operate legally, and their illegal existence was hampered by innumerable disputes ranging from Trotskyism to the national question, which was particularly acute among the Communists of Yugoslavia and Czechoslovakia. The great purge of the thirties was especially hard on the Communist Parties of Eastern Europe. The Polish Communist Party was officially dissolved in 1938, since its entire leadership in Moscow had been liquidated some years before and the Party organization in Poland was shot through with Trotskyites and police agents. In Yugoslavia about the same time a "Moscow man" by the name of Josip Broz-Tito, then "Comrade Walter," reorganized and purged the C.P.Y. Now after only seven or eight years those shadowy figures of obscure Communist leaders, completely unknown to the average citizen of their countries, emerged from their obscurity to become ministers, generals, and masters of the lands where a few years before they had been hunted men. Those arriving from Moscow after the war were to find in many cases a new class of Communist leaders in their countries. In Yugoslavia the Party hierarchy was composed exclusively of those who had stayed in the country during the war and had added to their Party titles an equally imposing array of military ranks and decorations. The same situation prevailed, though to a much smaller degree, elsewhere in Eastern Europe. The returning dignitaries had to share Party and government offices with the people who had risen from obscurity during the war and who could not be simply pushed aside by their former superiors. The men who had fought the invader and faced danger during every moment of their underground existence could not, on their part, look with excessive joy on the arrival and immediate prominence of their fellow Communists who had spent the war years in the U.S.S.R. A considerable mental gulf separated the two groups of Communist leaders. Those who had held the most exposed position had, under the exigencies of the war, learned to make their own decisions; in the process, they had become somewhat alienated, both literally and metaphorically, from the realities of Soviet politics. Their nationalism, urged and applauded by Moscow during the war, and their ability to get along with their non-Communist partners in the resistance movement (which had been the case in many countries but not in Poland or Yugoslavia) now seemed to agree with them almost too well from the point of view of their newly arrived colleagues. The latter brought with them no military exploits or acts of personal heroism, but they did have the more important assets of contacts in Moscow and knowledge of the ways of thinking of the official circles in Russia. A Communist Party, from what we can gather, does not require personal intimacy or the same pattern of thinking among its leaders. It goes without saying, however, that the men who day after day have to make crucial decisions, and in a way which suggests their complete agreement with each other and with the decisions as well, must possess a certain similarity of background and temperament. The situation which prevailed in the People's Democracies between 1945 and 1948 was bound to increase dissension and clashes between the two groups of leaders. It is erroneous to assume that all the conflicts and purges which the satellite states have undergone within the past few years have been due to Soviet orders or to the issue of nationalism versus the Soviet brand of internationalism. On the contrary, there is a great deal of evidence to suggest that diversity of background and temperament led to personal conflicts which became invested with a political significance. What has happened in Poland, Hungary, or Bulgaria within the past five years is in a sense similar to the developments in the Communist Party of the U.S.S.R. in the twenties, when the original group of leaders had to crystallize their divergent views and personalities into a seemingly uniform mold. Only then could the country become truly totalitarian.

The struggle for power in a totalitarian system often has its roots not only in the desire to achieve eminence, patronage, and the ability to dictate policies, but also in the companion urge to destroy what there is of the unfamiliar and the unpliable, first within the society, then within the Party itself. The situation in the satellite states between 1944 and 1947 was complicated by the fact that their Communist leaders were not entirely free agents and that the most important decisions could not be settled by an inner party struggle but had to be resolved by, or at least with the permission of, Moscow.

A parallel phenomenon had taken place among the rank and file of the Communist Parties of Eastern Europe: by 1946 they were no longer the small conspiratorial groups that had been recruited by clandestine propaganda and intensive study of Marxist literature. The Parties had become mass movements, with people joining them often for purely opportunistic reasons. They were thus far from being reliable instruments of power during a period of social and economic transformation, and the transformation itself had for this and other reasons to be gradual and calm. Hence popular fronts and blocs spread profusely in postwar Eastern Europe from Czechoslovakia to Bulgaria. In addition, the qualitative weakness of the material within the Communist ranks compelled the Party to look almost with tolerance upon its former bitter enemies, the Socialist and Peasant Parties of the satellite states, once they had been purified of their anti-Russian and generally more intransigent elements. These parties contained a great number of experienced organizers and politicians, many of them increasingly favorable to the ascendant philosophy; those leaders could, after a period of careful training and selection, become valuable members of the ruling group.

The task of transforming Eastern Europe into a group of satellite states must have appeared from the perspective of 1945 as a long and laborious process. Any attempt to hasten it unduly would have led to considerable trouble and would have delayed the economic reconstruction of the most devastated area in Europe. Hence the Communists could not afford violent upheavals and social transformation. The name of the ruling party in many cases (for example, in Poland and Bulgaria) purposely did not contain the word "communist" in order to facilitate the process of recruitment of those radically minded but still not ready to swallow the full connotation of the term. The more extreme elements among veteran Communists had to be reminded repeatedly that violence and ultra-left measures would not be tolerated and that the newly won "converts" to the cause of socialism should not be treated with undue suspicion. As a matter of fact, from the point of view of Communism, the idea of political toleration seemed at times to be pushed to the extreme: in Poland some members of prewar Fascist organizations were allowed to publish newspapers and to engage in a mild variety of political activity; certain politicians of prewar vintage, like Kimon Georgiev in Bulgaria and Tatarescu in Rumania, found themselves for a while members of the Communist-dominated governments of their countries. It was only against their main competitors for power, or against decidedly anti-Russian organizations, that the Communists ran true to form. There was no compromise with Dragoljub Jovanovich in Yugoslavia, Petkov in Bulgaria, Maniu in Rumania, and Mikolajczyk in Poland, for there could be no question about the real seat of political power. When the issue was posed sharply in February 1948 in Czechoslovakia, the response of the Communists illustrated the nature of political life in a Communist-dominated country: there can be relative political freedom in such a country, but only on the sufferance of the Communist Party; it can never be the result of a free interplay of political forces.[1] In only one Eastern European country did the process of liquidation of non-Communist political groups and social forces proceed at a pace reminiscent of Russia after the Revolution. Trotsky's "law of multiple development," which proclaims that a backward country might "skip" some stages in its revolution, found a new and ironic application in Yugoslavia, for by 1947 what might be called the Stalinist pattern of political life prevailed in that country.

It is easy to visualize from the preceding the variety of political problems which Communism confronted in Eastern Europe. The transitional period from 1944 to 1947 evidenced tendencies which, unchecked, might have gone far in dividing and weakening the Communist Parties in the area. The air of independence and the habit of making their own political decisions may have slightly intoxicated the new Communist rulers. Aside from the ever-present dangers of complacency and neglect in applying the more disturbing elements of the Communist program, their political reflexes appeared at times to lag behind Soviet policies of the moment. It is well known that the Czech and Polish governments had been eager at first to participate in the talks leading to the drafting of the Marshall Plan for Europe and that they abandoned the idea only after a remonstrance by Moscow. The incident of Georgi Dimitrov's untimely talkativeness about the Balkan federation followed rather than preceded the creation of the Cominform, but it was a mode of behavior which could not be duplicated in Soviet Russia and which was typical of the "uncoördinated" period of European Communism which the Cominform was supposed to end.

The creation of the Cominform was probably one kind of answer to the multitude of problems sketched above. The puzzled inability of many observers in the West to understand the creation

---

[1] The attempt made here to generalize about the whole satellite area has its obvious limitations. To get a complete picture and explanation of the variation of the Communist tactics it would be necessary to go much deeper into such factors as the strength of the anti-Russian feeling in Poland, the hold of the Smallholders Party on the Hungarian electorate, the varying degrees of influence possessed by the Catholic Church in Eastern Europe, and so forth.

of a new Communist international organization four years after the Comintern had been dissolved was a consequence of the failure to understand ways of political thinking and operation which are quite alien to the liberal tradition of the West. This tradition understands the concept of an international political movement and it understands conspiracy. But Communism, owing to its domination by Moscow, is not a bona fide international movement; and if it is an international conspiracy, why has it been necessary to publicize its character by a formal association of several Communist Parties? What possible difference can it make to have Malenkov or Suslov meet the leaders of the Communist Parties abroad as fellow members of the Cominform rather than as fellow Communists? Is the Russian viewpoint any more prevalent in the Communist Party of Belgium, which is outside the Cominform, than in the Communist Party of France, which is a charter member? A similar question is also asked about Soviet Russia proper: Why do the rulers of the U.S.S.R. bother to have a constitution with an elaborate bill of rights when such a document is largely irrelevant in regard to the actual situation in the Soviet Union? The queries spring from an understandable effort of people in the West to comprehend the "Soviet mind" by visualizing themselves in the situation of the Soviet leaders (but still with their Western beliefs and ideas), and on this basis trying to reconstruct the motivations and aims of Communist policy. They are thus likely to reconstruct problems inherent in Soviet policies without taking into account the ingrained habits of thought and action which motivate the people facing these problems. A more promising approach must seek a clue to Soviet policies in the character and tradition of the people who initiate and conduct the policies.

It has been a cardinal belief of Communism, and especially of Communism in power, that the nature of politics requires a vast educational and agitational effort. The rulers of the Soviet Union have not achieved their present position, or their country's status as a great world power, by practicing the naïve brand of Machiavellism which is sometimes ascribed to them. They have not attempted to run their own country or the other Communist Parties by purely manipulative devices, but they have always supplemented the technique of command and suppression by devising institutions which, by their very existence and functioning, indoctrinate their members along a desirable line. The Cominform was to temper by its operation the nascent nationalist and independent spirit of the leaders of the most important Communist Parties in Europe. The Comintern had become, as Zhdanov himself later admitted, a purely administrative agency, associated in the minds of the new generation of Communist leaders with complete domination of world Communism by Soviet Russia. The new agency was to be more exclusive, situated outside the U.S.S.R., and endowed with an air of the complete equality of the nine participating parties. At the same time, the Cominform would be a convenient place in which policies, slogans, and attitudes could be manufactured without their "made in Moscow" mark showing too much. The attention of Communists everywhere would be riveted upon the Cominform and its decisions. If its official theory of the equality of the participants could not be taken too seriously by people inside the organization, it could still assuage the feelings of the rank-and-file Communists in the People's Democracies.

In September 1947 the representatives of the Communist Parties of Russia, Yugoslavia, Poland, Hungary, Rumania, Bulgaria, Czechoslovakia, Italy, and France met "at the invitation of the Polish Workers' (Communist) Party." [2] The meeting took place near Warsaw. The stage was thus set most carefully to anticipate and refute the charge of undue Soviet influence in the new organization. Even during the existence of the Comintern [3] it had been suggested that the geographical association with the U.S.S.R. had been a burden on the organization. In the days of the popular fronts there had been some toying with the idea that the Comintern be shifted to Prague. Now the Cominform was born on Polish soil, and it was to have its first "permanent" seat, ironically enough, in Belgrade.

Why only nine Parties? The original principle of selection is very hard to justify on any systematic basis. Unrepresented were

[2] Wladyslaw Gomulka, during his subsequent expulsion as the Secretary-General of the Polish Workers' Party, admitted that he had been opposed to the creation of the Cominform and, by implication, that the initiative had come from another quarter.

[3] For example, in the twenties. See Ruth Fischer's *Stalin and German Communism* (Cambridge: Harvard University Press, 1948), p. 390.

Parties numerically weak, not in power in their countries or conceivably close to power, and the non-European Communist Parties. Even so, it is hard to explain the absence of the Albanian Communists unless on the theory that they were at that time protégés of the Yugoslav Communist Party. The presence of the French and Italian Communists must have been due to the fact that they represented two powerful Parties which, though not in power in their countries, were still conceivably within reach of power. For the reasons stated above, a Communist Party out of power is likely to be much more docile toward the Soviet Union than are those whose leaders are not only Communists but also leaders of their state and nation. The first meeting of the Cominform was to witness an exemplary lesson in self-criticism performed by the French Communists for the benefit, no doubt, of their Polish or Yugoslav colleagues who may have had the notion that they had outgrown such things.

The Cominform, as its full name—the Communist Information Bureau—indicates, was established by the nine Communist Parties as an organization for the exchange of information rather than as a policy-making body. In accordance with its "information" character, the Cominform was to publish a biweekly organ (now a weekly), whose title reflects the current slogan of Soviet policies: *For a Lasting Peace, For a People's Democracy.*

The initial meeting of the Cominform deserves some attention, for it abounded in moments of ideological and political drama. Among those present—an illustrious aggregation of names in international Communism—were three men whose names soon became anathemas to their Communist colleagues: Edward Kardelj and Milovan Djilas from Yugoslavia, and Wladyslaw Gomulka from Poland. Andrei Zhdanov made the keynote address for the Soviet Union. Barely a year was to separate Zhdanov's taking the limelight at this meeting of Communist chieftains and his sudden death. Accompanying Zhdanov, but still playing a secondary role, was Malenkov, for whom another year and the death of his colleague were to signify an ascent to near the very top of the Soviet hierarchy. Veterans of the movement, like France's Jacques Duclos and Luigi Longo from Italy, encountered the formerly lesser known Communist leaders such as Rudolf Slansky from Czechoslovakia and Vulko Chervenkov from Bulgaria, who, however, unlike their Western colleagues, could boast that they represented not only the Communist Parties of their respective countries but also the dominant element within their governments. Some of the non-Russian delegates were probably reminded of the days when, their names unknown to the world, they had attended the meetings of the Comintern as the representatives of small and often clandestine Communist parties. Now their good fortune and the help of Russia had enabled them to reach the pinnacle of power. But their power was not merely to be enjoyed; it was a means through which their countries would enter the road to socialism, the length of the road and the speed with which they were to traverse it depending largely on the wish of their Russian colleagues. The new organization which they were founding stood as the symbol of their dependence upon the U.S.S.R. For all the phrases about the equality of socialist states that they were to hear, they were not allowed to forget that the Soviet Union did not choose to abandon its task of guiding and instructing foreign Communists, whether they were obscure agitators or ministers and generals of their nations.

The speeches as reported in the official organ of the Cominform bear witness to the awkwardness of the ambivalent nature of the new organization: it is an organ echoing the official Soviet policy, yet it is dedicated to the principle of equality. Andrei Zhdanov, fresh from his victorious encounters with the supposed new "Westernizers" in Russian arts and philosophy, proclaimed the principle: "The Soviet Union unswervingly holds the position that political and economic relations between states must be built exclusively on the basis of equality of the Parties and mutual respect for their sovereign rights." [4] He was at pains to stress the distinction between the new organization and the Comintern:

> The dissolution of the Comintern, which conformed to the demands of the labor movement . . . played a positive role . . . [It] once and for all disposed of the slanderous allegation that Moscow was interfering in the internal affairs of other states and that the Communist Parties in the various states were acting not in the interests of their nations but on orders from outside. [5]

[4] *For a Lasting Peace,* November 10, 1947.
[5] *Ibid.*

Frankness about the past often serves to conceal something very far from frankness about the future. Yet it is startling to see Zhdanov admitting what, a few years before, he would have classified as slanders against the Third International. The soothing words and the disarming admission that the Communists fear political contacts implying the "hand of Moscow" reveal, probably without undue hypocrisy, one of the dilemmas which the Communist movement has always had to face and which in 1947 was focused with particular gravity on the relations between the U.S.S.R. and the satellite states.

Zhdanov's other points—his review of the international situation and his indictment of the United States for entering the imperialist path formerly followed by Hitler's Germany—clash in a sense with his main point about the need for absolute equality among the members of the Cominform. His was not an address by a participant in an international conference, nor was it a chairman's report at a meeting of free and equal parties. Zhdanov's speech was a complete and authoritative statement about what the policy and general orientation of the Cominform had to be. Parliamentarism and the technique of negotiation consist largely of asking questions and of leaving wide areas open to discussion. They consist in a real or pretended uncertainty, and the willingness and ability to discuss. But discussion before the Cominform has nothing to do with parliamentarism.

Malenkov's talk at the same meeting was more in the nature of a "report" than that of Zhdanov. Rather than stressing the general line and "explaining" the facts of the international situation, Malenkov dwelt on the recovery of the Russian economy and on problems involved in the numerical expansion of the Communist Party of the U.S.S.R. during the war. Yet even his speech took on the character of a directive when he reviewed the measures undertaken by the Central Committee of the Communist Party of the U.S.S.R. to fight "cosmopolitanism" among the Soviet intelligentsia.[6] It is no accident that shortly afterward the fight against "cosmopolitanism" was to be prominently featured in the press of the satellite countries. Yet the rationale, or, rather, the "mystique," of the struggle against "cosmopolitanism" has never been quite understood by the

[6] *For a Lasting Peace,* December 1, 1947.

satellite critics, whose efforts to explain the phenomenon reveal an understandable uncertainty about what "cosmopolitanism" is. It is only the more specific aspects of the fight which can be successfully transplanted from the U.S.S.R. to the People's Democracies, such as, for instance, the encomium bestowed upon Lysenko and his theories and the parallel excommunications of the reputed followers of Weismann and Mendel. Malenkov's speech on the subject of "cosmopolitanism" offers a classic example of the type and technique of the "exchange of information" for which the Cominform was created.[7]

The delegates from outside the U.S.S.R. took the floor to discuss their own Parties and their organizational and economic problems. There is an air of slight tension in their speeches. They were called upon to recite a standard piece, but to some of them the task did not seem to come naturally. It was not easy to discard the role of responsible statesmen whose word was decisive in their own lands and to adopt that of docile pupils delivering a recitation full of praises of the Red Army and Comrade Stalin.

The tribute to Soviet Russia must have come naturally to most of the assembled, for it was the U.S.S.R. which after many years had finally led them into the promised land of power. But the set form of the addresses and the constant reminders that each of the countries represented owed its liberation to the Red Army—except for Italy and France, whose representatives practically bemoaned their liberation by the West—must have been a galling performance to the assembled leaders. Here and there a most "proper"

[7] Totalitarian, or would-be totalitarian, regimes exhibit a strange ambivalence in their attitude toward the intellectual. They realize the importance of the intellectual not only as a specialist but also as an agent of social change in society. They reward their chosen artists and scientists with emoluments of all kinds. The Soviet regime, especially, because of its worship of technology and because of its own history, is particularly attentive to the state of mind of its own intellectuals and to the potentialities of gaining converts in similar circles abroad. Yet the intellectual by virtue of his position and training represents a sector of society which cannot be completely propagandized or regimented or protected from outside influence. Hence the continuous effort, of which the campaign against "cosmopolitanism" is but one chapter, to break down the spirit of political objectivity or political indifference whenever it reappears in various fields of scientific or artistic activity in totalitarian countries.

speech revealed a sign of tension or portended a future conflict. Speaking for the Polish Workers' Party, its Secretary-General, Gomulka, mentioned, perhaps not too tactfully, the great work being done by his Party in eradicating the anti-Soviet sentiment in Poland; then he added significantly: "The principal lever in this question is the problem of our Western territories and the knowledge that the Soviet Union helped Poland settle its frontiers on the Oder and Neisse." [8] Gomulka's colleague from Czechoslovakia, Slansky, dwelt on the expulsion of Germans from Sudentenland, the task made possible only "thanks to the Soviet Union and especially Comrade Stalin." [9] There was an unmistakable warning, or at least a warning mixed with a plea, in the two statements. The German question has remained, even in 1951, an imponderable yet vital factor, limiting the free maneuverability of Soviet policies in Eastern Europe.

It may have been a nice sense of etiquette which prompted the editors of *For a Lasting Peace* to print a résumé of the speech by Yugoslavia's foreign minister, Kardelj, after that of Zhdanov. After all, Belgrade was to be the seat of the Cominform, and Yugoslavia's leaders had already shown themselves unduly sensitive on questions of prestige and national pride. Kardelj's speech must have struck a discordant note among the assembled Communist dignitaries. The former Slovenian schoolteacher, now a close collaborator of Tito, did not mention once, at least in the report as printed, that his country owed its liberation to the Soviet Union or the Red Army. With a certain violence to facts, and in startling distinction to the speeches delivered by the Yugoslav leaders during the war, Kardelj attacked with bitterness "those who slandered our Party . . . to the effect that the national liberation uprising developed fully only after Hitler's attack on the Soviet Union and not before." [10] Kardelj went on, rather pedantically, to remind his hearers that his Party as far back as April 1941 had begun to form military committees. The remainder of Kardelj's speech also contrasted vividly with the tone of the other representatives of the People's Democra-

[8] *For a Lasting Peace*, November 10, 1947.
[9] *Ibid.*, December 1, 1947.
[10] *Ibid.*, November 10, 1947.

cies. Neither Kardelj nor Djilas in his coreport for the Yugoslavs chose to be unduly thankful to the Soviet Union for its help in liberating the Balkans.

With our accumulated hindsight it is easy to see in Kardelj's departure from the etiquette required at a Communist meeting a sure portent of the crisis which one year later was to rock the Cominform and cause the great break between Moscow and Belgrade. Yet such an explanation would be far-fetched. The Yugoslavs were probably indulging in a typical exhibition of their bad temper, occasioned by Moscow's attempt to set them at the same level as, say, the Hungarian or Bulgarian Communists, who had received their freedom from the Red Army instead of working for it themselves. They were not as yet rebelling; they were sulking. The meeting, which to a casual observer would have appeared as a conference between equals with the Soviet Union playing merely the role of *primus inter pares,* must have been recognized by the initiated as the setting for a new stage in the development of the Communist-dominated governments of Eastern Europe— a stage which would be characterized more and more by a stress on uniformity and subordination and less and less on the right of each government to follow its own route to socialism with only general guidance by Soviet policy and directives. The Yugoslav leaders had come to the conference with a profound irritation over certain aspects of Soviet policies. But their irritation was as yet not equivalent to defiance. It is necessary to draw this rather subtle distinction if the whole course of the Russo-Yugoslav dispute is to be understood.

Yet, if the idea of future conflicts, purges, and changes in their status worried the assembled Communist chieftains, there was little on the surface to indicate gloom or apprehension about the future. The leaders could contemplate their lifelong dream come true: almost all of Eastern Europe consolidated under the banner of Communism. And at their side sat the leaders of the Communist Parties of France and Italy, representing at the moment the largest political movements in their respective countries and the promise of not too distant Communist power in those two great Western nations. Still, in the speeches there is very little of exaltation or of revolutionary dynamism. Zhdanov's speech is a careful review of the situation, a temperate attack on the protagonist (the United States), and a laborious search for bureaucratic formulas and definitions. Thus, he specifically rejected the claim that democracy consists in a multiplicity of political parties. The speech has the didactic quality characteristic of Communist speech-making since Lenin's time, but in the earlier days it was often combined with the real spirit of revolutionary fervor, which is now missing. Indeed, the meeting was one of Party bureaucrats, though most of those present had a conspiratorial or military background. Revolution in order to continue and succeed must become a system and an administrative technique. It will then lose the major part of its original emotional appeal, with the factor of force and propaganda being invoked to take its place.

II

It was in Eastern Europe that the two world wars found their most immediate and direct beginning. After the end of World War II it was again the extension of Russian influence in the East (which led Mr. Churchill to coin his phrase about the "iron curtain") that became a dramatic symbol of the conflict between the West and the U.S.S.R. The spread of Russian influence over so many formerly independent countries which the Allies had solemnly pledged to restore to independence after their liberation from the Germans, has been to many the most impressive proof that the U.S.S.R. is bent upon world domination. It is impossible to determine, at least at this time, whether it was the course of the war or the ineptness of the Western Allies' diplomacy which practically delivered the whole region to the U.S.S.R. People are apt to judge unfamiliar situations by the nearest equivalent they are able to find within their own experience. There is much to suggest that many Englishmen during the war viewed the possibility of territorial expansion by the U.S.S.R. in the light of their recollections of Tsarist Russia, and that to some American leaders the ruling circles in the Soviet Union appeared strikingly similar to the city boss and his entourage in their own country. It was thus easy to minimize the problem or to postpone its serious consideration.

It is probably fallacious to assume that the Russians have always had a clear but cleverly concealed design for Eastern Europe. On the contrary, Soviet foreign policies have exhibited a variety of improvisations and sudden shifts, and nowhere has it been more evident than in Eastern Europe. After Stalingrad the Russians concentrated more and more on the political aspect of the war, but the seeming resolution and inflexibility of Russia's foreign policy is an optical illusion created by the secrecy surrounding the decision-making process in the U.S.S.R.

Such considerations are in order if the internal policies and problems of the Cominform countries are to be evaluated. It is ridiculously absurd to imagine that every aspect of every policy elaborated, say in Poland or Hungary, between 1945 and 1948 was decided upon orders from Moscow. The administrative problem involved in any attempted regulation of a vast area filled with so many nationalities, each with a peculiar cultural and political tradition, obviously could not be handled by the Soviet Union alone. It was probably wise on the part of the U.S.S.R., which could and did dominate the satellite countries by its mere proximity, to allow a period of transition and trial before embarking on a more decisive attempt at political and economic integration of the area. Yet in certain respects this postponement of direct intervention by the U.S.S.R. did not enable the satellites to enjoy the privileges of real independence. In their foreign policies the People's Democracies had, of course, to follow Soviet Russia's wishes and even to anticipate them. They likewise could not resist Russian pressures in the economic sphere. Through the use of "mixed companies" and through their quite obvious advantages in commercial negotiations, the Russians were able to exact a heavy price from their reputed friends and protégés.[11] Politically, the Russians long before 1947

---

[11] "Russia, however, apparently was frequently able to secure terms of trade which were more favorable to it than seemed justified on the basis of price developments in world trade. Thus, Russia is supposed to have secured a price per ton of Polish cement which was almost equal to the price per ton of Polish coal in 'non-political' exports of coal to Russia, while normally the price of cement tends to be more than twice that of coal . . . It is primarily in the case of Hungary that over-all terms of trade vis-à-vis Russia can be compared with those vis-à-vis other countries. The comparison . . . indicates considerable Russian advantages" (Alexander Gerschenkron, "Russia's Trade in the Post-War Years," *Annals of the American Academy of Political and Social Science,* May 1949, p. 95).

started the process of infiltration of the military and administrative apparatus of the People's Democracies with their own men, some of whom happened to be of Russian ethnic origin. The presence of the Red Army in many of those countries was, to be sure, of great initial advantage to the Russians, and the advantage persisted beyond the withdrawal of the Soviet troops. But the greatest argument in favor of whatever claims the U.S.S.R. might be making was the frightening phenomenon of Russia's power and its evident ability to arrange Eastern Europe to its liking with barely a perceptible murmur from the Western Allies.

The period between 1945 and 1947 appears now as the time of consolidation of Soviet influence in Eastern Europe: the period during which the Communist Parties in the various satellite states were allowed and even encouraged to follow their own lights in dealing with the double problem of reconstructing their countries after the ravages of the war and grasping more firmly the instruments of political power. These twin objectives could be accomplished only with the collaboration, or at least the acquiescence, of some other political parties in these countries; for, as has already been explained, aside from the political expediency of collaboration, the purely technical task of ruling Eastern Europe, of handling the vast multitude of administrative and economic problems, could not be managed by the mere handful of experienced Communists then at the head of their numerically swollen, but unwieldy and unindoctrinated, Parties. Hence the device of the "united front" (a coalition of several Parties, run, in fact, by the Communists) was used as the most convenient holding arrangement until the groundwork could be prepared for the edifice of the Communist state.

The period of the united front (under whichever of the various names used to designate it in Eastern Europe [12]) is not to be considered as a purely tactical maneuver, however. It was undoubtedly a tactical ruse in its conception. It was like an injection of a sedative which allows the patient to recuperate free from his most acute anxieties until the time comes again for violent exertion. The seeming quiet; the concentration on the task of economic reconstruction; the political tolerance, not excessive from our point of view

[12] See C. E. Black, "Soviet Policy in Eastern Europe," *Annals of the American Academy of Political and Social Science*, May 1949, p. 157.

but amazing in a Communist-dominated land—these surprising phenomena which a casual observer from the West could notice in countries like Poland and Czechoslovakia between the end of the war and early in 1948 all testified to the great effectiveness of the medicine. The most violent apprehensions of an outright annexation by the U.S.S.R. or of a Saint Bartholomew's night for all the anti-Russian or non-Communist elements in the satellite countries in Eastern Europe, were almost dispelled by those years of caution and moderation. Again, the picture has many local variations. In Bulgaria, and especially in Yugoslavia, the extent and method of the liquidation of non-Communist political organizations had none of the gradualness or moderation of the corresponding process in Poland or Czechoslovakia. But there is much to suggest that the initiative for a rougher way of dealing with the problem came from the local Communist Party bosses and not from the Russians.

While the concept of the united front was primarily tactical, the way it had worked out in practice confronted Communism in Eastern Europe in 1947 with most serious problems. For some of the Communist leaders the collaboration with certain non-Communist parties and forces came almost too easily. For others the mere fact of collaboration whether tactical or not represented a betrayal of their principles.[13] From a purely tactical device the united front had become, by the time the Cominform was organized, a major issue causing a variety of disputes within the Communist Parties themselves.

There was no real issue insofar as the question of power was concerned. No Communist was ready to concede that political power should be shared between the Communists and some other political party or parties. Hence the direct competitors of Communism in Eastern Europe had to be eliminated whenever they disputed the overwhelmingly dominant role of the Communists: Maniu in Rumania early in 1945; Mikolajczyk in Poland in January 1947; and, finally, the illusion of peaceful collaboration between the Communists and the democratic parties burst open and empty in

---

[13] Thus we find criticisms, such as that by J. Revai, that some members of the Hungarian Communist Party imbued with "Left-wing sectarianism" are in favor of violent measures against their non-Communist colleagues in the National Independence Front in Hungary (*For a Lasting Peace*, December 15, 1947).

Czechoslovakia in February 1948 after a feeble attempt on the part of the non-Communists to reassert themselves. Whatever remained of non-Communist political forces in Eastern Europe had, by early 1948, become emasculated and impotent. The Peasant Party in Poland and the Smallholders in Hungary had been deprived of their leaders and had in fact become auxiliary organizations of the Communist Parties of their countries. The Socialist Parties, long the vanguard of the progressive movement in countries like Poland and Czechoslovakia, were now being readied for absorption into their Communist counterparts.

But for some Communist leaders the period of the united front was the period of accommodation with the "nationalist" and "moderate" forces in their own countries.[14] For over two years the Communist leaders in Eastern Europe had to preach moderation and national unity. Some of them, especially those in Poland and Czechoslovakia, had to assuage the fears of the peasants and to reassure them that any approach to collectivization would be gradual and based on the voluntary principle. As late as February 1948 Clement Gottwald was to remind the Czechoslovak peasants and small tradesmen that the new constitution would guarantee their status for a long time to come and that the process of nationalization and land distribution would not go beyond certain clearly defined and legally guaranteed limits.[15] Similar assurances were heard in Poland, Rumania, and Hungary. The Catholic Church, which has never concealed its opposition to Communism, was not attacked between 1945 and 1948, as an institution, in any of the three Catholic countries of the area: Poland, Hungary, and Czechoslovakia. The extent of toleration for various religious orders and institutions displayed by the Communist-dominated governments during the period would undoubtedly have dismayed a forthright socialist of the old school. In anything not touching the instruments of power—the army, the police, and the administrative machinery—the Communists were expected to, and by and large did, display a rather frightening toleration and willingness to compromise. Even their attack against the

---

[14] Both adjectives are in quotation marks, for the forces in question were moderate and nationalist only by comparison with the extreme pro-Russian viewpoint within the Communist Party.
[15] *For a Lasting Peace*, March 1, 1948.

"Western imperialists" contained a measure of moderation which was allowed to decrease only gradually.

Is it then surprising that some of the Communist leaders were carried away by their own tactics and that the goals of Communism and its avowed object of destroying all unreliable elements in society and of assimilating the social structure of the satellite countries as closely as possible to the conditions in Soviet Russia became in their minds the ends to be achieved some time in the future but not now? There were undoubtedly those who entertained thoughts of bolstering their own position in the government of their country with the help of the new element which, having been "processed" through the united fronts, was ready to be amalgamated into the Communist Parties. It is unlikely that even the people who, like Gomulka in Poland or Patrascanu in Rumania, in the two years after the formation of the Cominform were to be singled out as the most extreme "nationalist deviationists" were deviationists in any real sense of the word. Their fault lay in the fact that, in the years preceding the creation of the Cominform, they pursued the official and Moscow-approved policies of their Parties with too much enthusiasm. When the time came for an abrupt shift following the Yugoslav crisis within the Cominform, they found themselves lagging behind their colleagues, and they were never allowed to catch up. The road was barred to them, and instead of being allowed to accommodate themselves to the new situation just as they had accommodated themselves to the united front period of the People's Democracies, they were pictured as spies and "Titoists." Why were they singled out for purge along with the two prominent Communists who had never been known as exponents of softness in dealing with class enemies—Kostov in Bulgaria and Rajk in Hungary? The answer must again take into account the character of the period before the creation of the Cominform. Today this period appears in retrospect as a time of trial, during which the Communist leaders of the satellite area were given relative autonomy by Moscow. Some of them failed the test, and if in addition they made powerful enemies within their own Parties, enemies who were ready to magnify and emphasize any incident or utterance that could be interpreted as representing an anti-Russian bias, their political and even physical life was to be threatened during the new period signaled by the establishment of the Cominform. It has already been mentioned that the new organization aroused an instinctive distrust in the top layer of the Communist hierarchy in Eastern Europe. The most immediate fear was that of enforced uniformity in the process of the social transformation of the People's Democracies. Up to 1947 the issues of the collectivization of agriculture and the rights and privileges of the Catholic Church were handled by each of the Communist-dominated governments of Eastern Europe according to its own discretion. The success in economic reconstruction achieved in those years, for instance in Poland, would not have been possible without a policy of moderation on these two most explosive issues. Again, there is no doubt that in the long run both collectivization and a drastic attack at the position of the Roman Catholic Church figured on the agenda of the People's Democracies. In the short run, however, the peasants of Poland, Hungary, and Czechoslovakia were to be reassured, and the attack upon private property in agriculture was to be prepared only gradually; violence was to be avoided, and subtle methods, such as governmental lending and price policies, were to be employed.

The Catholic Church was a more immediate problem for Communism, especially in Poland, Hungary, and Czechoslovakia. The Church, entrenched in education and dominating so much of the countries' intellectual and even political life, stood as a formidable barrier to any real conquest of the people's minds by Communism. But even this problem, many Communist rulers thought, could be handled individually by each country. Little need was felt for a uniform anti-Church policy. The Cominform from its inception stood as the symbol of the tendency toward uniformity, and though in fact it did not exert its power until the summer of 1948, its potential function must have preyed on the minds of the Communist leaders in the short interval between its formation and the outbreak of the Yugoslav crisis.

Some of the leaders must have felt that they were doing well without any prompting by the Cominform or Moscow. The two Balkan satellites fell into the hands of fanatical Communists who proceeded to "communize" their countries at a much faster pace than would have been dared or wished by their Polish, Hungarian, or Czech comrades. In the more sober days after 1948, Marshal

Tito and his economic advisers were to complain of the undue haste with which radical reforms had been introduced in Yugoslavia following the Partisans' victory. In Bulgaria the extent of enforced collectivization and of the peasants' opposition to it was to be disclosed only during the liquidation of Kostov. The two least industrially advanced countries among the People's Democracies were the most precipitous in their approach to the Soviet pattern. The dream of complete industrialization led the Yugoslav leaders into overambitious plans which caused serious hardships for their people.

But, whether one sees moderation or undue haste in the process of transforming the satellites into the Communist pattern, it remains almost axiomatic that the tempo of the transformation between 1945 and 1947 was largely dictated by the Communist rulers of the given countries and not by Moscow. The Soviet Union's main interest in these years was to vest reliable Communists with the instruments of power within the People's Democracies. During the period in question there was no attempt to correlate fidelity to the Soviet Union with the character and speed of social and economic reforms undertaken by the satellite countries. When the great crisis of 1948 and 1949 broke within the Cominform ranks, among those destroyed or denounced were not only the advocates of radical reforms like Kostov and the leadership of the Yugoslav Communist Party but also those who believed in a slow and cautious approach to collectivization and other economic and social goals of Communism like Gomulka. It was only then that the "ideological" issue was allowed to become a test of the pro-Russian reliability of the Communist hierarchy in Eastern Europe, and the test followed very much the same pattern that had been established in the determination of loyalty to the Stalin group in Russia between 1927 and 1930. Here, in Eastern Europe, the yardstick of ideology was to be used even more unreservedly as a tool of political consolidation and purge.

The establishment of the Cominform did portend the coming era of consolidation. It is very hard to decide at this time whether the initial concept of the organization envisaged the creation of the atmosphere of political and economic uniformity which has, in effect, prevailed in the satellite countries since 1948, or whether this tendency, to some degree implicit in the original scheme, became greatly intensified under the impact of the Tito affair. The latter is the more probable hypothesis. Since its first meeting the Cominform has addressed itself to a variety of organizational and ideological problems. Its resolutions have set the tone of the official propaganda in all of the Cominform countries. The main themes of *For a Lasting Peace, For a People's Democracy* have been repeated by the press of the satellite countries. Almost imperceptibly a kind of political and cultural *Gleichschaltung* has crept over the official press and public pronouncements of the governments of the whole region. The impression of variety and real differences which a Western observer experienced between 1945 and 1947 in comparing the political scene in several Eastern European countries under Soviet domination has faded throughout the past few years to the point where its very memory seems distant and unreal.

It is important, however, not to overlook the earlier period. To a considerable extent the seeming ease with which Communism achieved hold over so many countries, possessed of so many divergent cultures and social traditions, was due to the period of moderation, the interval of the seemingly "separate ways" toward socialism which it loudly espoused and propagated. To the war-weary countries of Eastern Europe, the first years of the "united" and "popular" front governments appeared, not as an interlude between the war and the subsequent period of their increasing integration into the Soviet system, but as a possible *modus vivendi* for the small powers, which, having recognized the predominance of their powerful neighbor, would be left to enjoy a modicum of political and economic independence.

Soviet Russia had previously exacted a heavy price in territory from Rumania and especially from Poland. Even the ever friendly Czechoslovakia had had to part with her most backward and economically least important province—the Carpathian Ukraine. Soviet insistence on confiscating this territory, an area insignificant from every point of view, but settled by Ukrainians, can be taken as yet another proof of the extreme nervousness with which the Kremlin government regards the slightest possibility of irredentism or of raising the question of the non-Russian nationalities within the U.S.S.R. Anyway, the price had been exacted and all the possible apprehensions of the U.S.S.R., strategic, political, and economic, were considered to have been appeased. The presence of Communists in the governments of the area, though often enforced by the Russians, could be regarded as a legitimate reward to the movement that had contributed much toward the final victory. The dynamics of economic reconstruction, the enthusiasm engendered in rebuilding the normal national existence which had been shattered in Poland and Czechoslovakia and heavily damaged elsewhere by the German invader, obscured for a while the subtle growth of a new type of authoritarianism, which in its first stages betrayed but little of its foreign origin and connection.

It is well to introduce yet another consideration into the picture. Prior to World War II, the future satellites had by and large not enjoyed what are sometimes described as the blessings of democracy. Except in pre-Munich Czechoslovakia, genuine parliamentary democracy existed in Eastern Europe only intermittently and sporadically. On the other hand, it is possible to exaggerate, and this is indeed often done by writers on the subject, the nondemocratic character of Eastern Europe between the two world wars. Certainly nothing approaching the absolute one-party dictatorship of Mussolini or Hitler ever existed even in the Poland of Pilsudski or the Hungary of Horthy. Insofar as the basic civil liberties are concerned, even the period of moderation from 1945 to 1947 represented a retrogression over the prewar situation in this unfortunate part of Europe. But there is no denying that the contrast between the prewar and postwar regimes could not, at first, appear to be too great nor the transition to the Communist model dictatorship too abrupt. During its first stage a Communist regime often shows its most positive characteristics. In contrast to an East European semidictatorship of the interwar years, characterized by social lethargy and directed by a complacent bureaucracy, its Communist-dominated successor displayed, at the beginning, great and straightforward energy in dealing with the most urgent social and economic problems. Moreover, as pointed out before, its approach to those problems was not as yet encumbered by the dictates of Communist ideology. The early postwar days saw the regime display its typical solicitude for the worker, respect and financial assistance for the intellectual and the artist, and more land for the poor and the "medium" peasant. It would have required considerable sophistication or cynicism to see beneath these favors the promise of the future exploitation of the worker, with its appurtenances of "labor discipline" and "socialist competition"; the attempt at wholesale collectivization of land; and the inevitable regimentation of the intellectual and the artist, which was to be accomplished according to the Russian pattern by the fight against "cosmopolitanism" and the "Westernizers." During the period in question Communism chose to turn its more benign and humane face toward the satellites. It exhibited all the characteristics which its apologists present as being not the initial and tactical phase of the movement but the essence of Communism.

Even so, the relative ease with which the twin powers of Soviet Russia and Communism settled over the lands of Eastern Europe cannot be explained completely by the exhaustion brought in the wake of the war, the sheer physical power of the U.S.S.R., or the air of reasonability and moderation with which the local Communists set about to accomplish their initial aims. A large part of the story lies in the decline of the prestige both of the Western Powers and of democracy, which in this part of Europe has been traditionally associated with the power and political institutions of France and England. France, especially, between the two world wars represented to the small powers of Eastern and Southeastern Europe the model of democratic institutions; and France, until Hitler's Germany demonstrated the fragility of the Versailles system, had stood as the seemingly powerful protector of their independence and frontiers. An educated citizen of an Eastern European country tended to look westward and beyond Germany for his political and social ideas. Even in Bulgaria and Serbia, which had seen the beginning of their statehood and national existence under the auspices of Russia and whose links with the great Slavic power have always been closer than those of the other nations in the area, the Bolshevik Revolution marked a decisive interruption of Russia's cultural and political predominance. It was the decline of the West, symbolized by its passive acceptance of Hitler's rise to power and by Munich, which weakened fatally what was left of democratic movements in the Balkans and inflicted almost the same amount of damage in Poland and Czechoslovakia. The war superimposed its havoc upon the spirit of disillusionment. Yet it brought at the same time the spirit of national reassertion, of collaboration among various parties in the resistance movements, and even proposals looking beyond the victory and toward a solution of some of the most basic national conflicts of the area—proposals such as the projected federation or close alliance between Poland and Czechoslovakia, and similar ideas among the South Slavs. The entrance of the United States into the war seemed to strengthen the hope that the postwar settlement would be accomplished under democratic auspices. Even Soviet Russia, while still in mortal danger, appeared to exhibit a change of heart and a spirit of accommodation toward the national aspirations of the occupied territories. But following the victory of Stalingrad it became obvious that Russia's policy in Eastern Europe was designed to assure her domination, and every Russian victory and every pronouncement from the West appeared to reinforce the impression that the Western Allies were not going to argue too strenuously against a free hand for their ally in the East. The pitiful protests of the governments-in-exile against Russian acts and proclamations concerning their future were treated in the West—with a measure of truth but also with a great deal of blindness and ignorance—as the last gasps of reaction in Eastern Europe. It became quite clear toward the end of the war that the friends of the Western Powers "had nothing to expect" and their enemies "nothing to fear," and that the same proposition could not be advanced about Soviet Russia's friends and enemies.

It is therefore not surprising that there were many non-Communists who during the first two or three years of the postwar world were quite resigned to Russia's domination of their countries and to the new pattern of "people's democracy" which was being impressed on the countries within the Russian sphere. Democracy seemed to have failed. Its foremost proponents in the world left the Eastern European countries to their own devices and, beyond a series of diplomatic notes, showed themselves unwilling or unable to oppose Russia's encroachments or the slow extinction of the limited sphere of free institutions which could still be found in countries like Poland and Czechoslovakia. The battle against the twin powers of Soviet imperialism and Communist dictatorship had been and could be fought only by hopeless idealists and hopeless reactionaries.

The middle-of-the-road politician found himself pushed more and more deeply into collaboration and into external and often internal agreement with the "reasonable" and "positive" postulates of his Communist colleagues. The latter, as observed before, found it not too difficult to collaborate with the non-Communists as long as there was no dispute about where the real seat of power was situated. It is only reasonable to assume that aside from ruthless destruction of "class enemies" and real competitors for power, the local Communists found some things in common with their more complacent colleagues from the Socialist or Peasant Parties. With them they shared a similar social outlook, the task of economic reconstruction, and a measure of nationalism which, not unlikely, found one of its manifestations in common but very private grumbling at the Russian exactions and domineering ways. The last point, however, could not but be overwhelmed by a strong conviction that Soviet Russia's power was bound to be the dominating and lasting influence on the Continent, at least in its eastern part; that the West was committed to a course of reaction if not imperialism; and by the further conviction, which was perhaps the decisive point for an East European politician whether he be Communist or non-Communist, that British and American statesmen, unlike their French colleagues in their ignorance of the Slavic world, appeared blind to the still existing danger of Germany and were not above playing with the forces of German nationalism.[16]

Thus it was that many forces and factors conspired to make the first stage of the Communist conquest of Eastern Europe a relatively easy task. It has been seen that Soviet Russia stood much to gain and very little to lose by continuing the policy of moderation, of subtle and not too visible pressure, which, prior to the Yugoslav crisis, was its ostensible method of dealing with the satellites. Where

[16] The same thing could be said, of course, about certain Russian moves in Germany, and, as will be seen later on, they did not fail to alarm Polish and Czech Communists. Here it is only attempted to point out the effect, strengthened and multiplied by Communist propaganda on Eastern Europeans and especially on the Slavs behind the "Iron Curtain," of the Allies' pronouncements on the subject of Germany, and particularly of the too often expressed horror at the fate of the Sudeten Germans and of Germany's eastern provinces allotted at Potsdam to Poland. If the whole question was a strong card in Russia's hand insofar as Eastern Europe was concerned from 1945 to 1947, it is doubly so today (December 1951).

the ascent toward a more uncompromising Communist dictatorship was steeper, as in Yugoslavia and Bulgaria, the initiative before the creation of the Cominform belonged to the local Communists rather than to their Russian protectors. But in surveying
the situation in the satellite states in 1947 and 1948, the makers of
Russian policies must have felt that neither radical social policies
nor a firm attachment to the Soviet Union and Communism offered,
by themselves, fair guarantees of the complete reliability of the satellites. It must have appeared to them that opportunism and toleration,
the tendency to enjoy power and to relax, and the inclination to
ease into ways of thinking appropriate to leaders of independent nations rather than to faithful servants of international Communism
had been stealing into the leadership of the Communist Parties of
the satellites. Hence the visible, undisputed direction of international Communism had to be resumed by Moscow. The new phase
was begun with caution and with every pretense of respect for the
national feelings of the leaders of the People's Democracies. Yet the
real import of the Cominform, though perhaps misunderstood by
outsiders and by the rank-and-file Communists in the satellite countries, was only too well realized by those who were concerned in
the summer of 1947 with "deciding" to establish an innocently appearing bureau for the exchange of information between the most
important Communist Parties of Europe. And before one year had
elapsed the new organization was to exhibit its real function and
illuminate the true aims and methods of Soviet policies in Eastern
Europe.

CHAPTER 3

The Background of the Soviet-Yugoslav Dispute

The conflict between Stalin's Russia and Tito's Yugoslavia is reminiscent of a quarrel between two old friends whose long intimacy serves only to make their dispute all the more violent and ultimately irreconcilable. Certainly the reaction of the Yugoslavs has followed a familiar pattern: at first, complete incredulity that their old friends and protectors should take a minor dispute centered around a few personalities and a few administrative problems as the opening of a great campaign to proclaim Tito and his colleagues traitors and to call for the destruction of their regime. Then, as the hope of reconciliation vanished (this hope was evident, at least on the Yugoslav side, during the first few months of the dispute), both sides began to recall those moments of strain which at the time of mutual admiration had appeared as only minor dissonances, but which upon reflection were seen as the first clear signs of the other side's brutality or treachery.

The Partisans fought during the war for their own country, but they also fought with a fanatical devotion to the Soviet Union.

NOTE: This chapter appeared originally with some changes in *The Review of Politics* for January 1951, and is used with the permission of the editors of that publication.

Apart from the Communist persuasion of their leaders, the fact that
the Soviet Union was meeting the main fury of German attacks and
that it stood as the main defender of the Slavic nations against Germany's aggression created an atmosphere in which the slightest
criticism of Yugoslavia's great ally would have been inconceivable.
Even a few months after July 1948, Tito in his speech to the Fifth
Congress of the C.P.Y. recalled those Partisans who had died before German execution squads with the praise of Soviet Russia and
Stalin on their lips.[1]

Wartime *Borba* exuded unbelievable exhilaration at the news of
Soviet victories, while similar exploits of the West were met with
scant and perfunctory praise. It was only natural that implicit in
this admiration was the conviction that the Partisans' contribution
to the victory was equally admired in Moscow and that the new
Yugoslavia would be an honored and privileged ally of the U.S.S.R.
The exploits of Tito's armies were exalted throughout Russia. Various Yugoslav visitors to Moscow were encouraged by the respect
of the Soviet leaders for Tito and his Party and by their attitude
of comradely equality. When Vladimir Dedijer asked Stalin in
1944 whether the "line" pursued by the C.P.Y. was correct, the
great man was supposed to have replied: "You alone are in the
position to know, and you alone should judge it." [2]

The same atmosphere of good feeling persisted beyond the defeat of the invaders and the first contacts between Yugoslavia's
population and their Russian brothers-in-arms, though the latter,
represented by Marshal Tolbukhin's army, behaved in somewhat
less than exemplary fashion, as is illustrated by the Djilas episode.[3]
The rulers of Communist Yugoslavia saw their country in 1945
as the leader of the People's Democracies and the center of the
projected Balkan federation. As late as 1947, during the creation
of the Cominform, the C.P.Y. was treated as the first among the
Communist Parties outside the Soviet Union, despite the facts that
from the point of view of population Yugoslavia is far behind Poland and that her economic importance is hardly equal to that of

---

[1] Tito, *Political Report of the Central Committee,* p. 77.
[2] Excerpts from Dedijer's diary in *Tridecet Dana* (*Thirty Days*) for February–March 1950.
[3] See below, pp. 123–124.

Czechoslovakia, Poland, or even Rumania. The primacy of Yugoslavia was undoubtedly seen by her rulers as a fitting reward for their Communist fervor and for their achievements during the war; they well knew that Russia's other allies had had to be liberated by the Red Army and that other Communist leaders, for the most part freshly imported from Moscow, could hardly claim they *unaided* defeated the Germans and set their countries on the road to socialism.

But this wise regard for the sensitivities of a small nation (and what in Moscow was probably interpreted as Tito's "swollen head") was to give way at the beginning of the Russo-Yugoslav crisis to the contemptuous tone in which the official voice of the U.S.S.R. spoke about the Partisans' record during the war and about their pretentions to military glory. No greater psychological error could have been made on the Russian side than the scornful and pedantic way in which the Yugoslavs were informed by the Central Committee of the C.P.S.U. that their wartime achievements had really been not too different from those of the Hungarians or the Rumanians and that they had also been liberated by the Red Army. This insult was completely gratuitous and completely unnecessary. But it is very likely that this reprimand, delivered in the tone of a caustic teacher ridiculing an overambitious pupil, has proved to be one of the most valuable arguments for Tito and his regime in rallying the rank and file of his Party and his army in a resolute defiance of the U.S.S.R.

The background of the dispute as it unfolds itself in the angry replies of Yugoslav Communists has three main elements. There is, first, the story of the Soviet attitude toward the fight of the Partisans during the war, the attitude which, now that the veil has fallen from the eyes of the Yugoslavs, is seen to have been motivated by purely selfish considerations of Russian policy rather than by paternal regard for the cause of fellow Communists. There is also the story of Soviet duplicity concerning the Balkan federation and Yugoslavia's role in it. The third and most important part of the background of the dispute—the Soviet attempt to destroy the leadership of the C.P.Y. and to fill Yugoslavia's army, Communist Party, and the whole machinery of government with Soviet agents—is told by the Yugoslavs with most reserve and with least detail. The men who in 1937 destroyed, at the command of the Comintern, the leadership of the C.P.Y. and reorganized the Party according to the precepts of Moscow stand today as the defenders of their country's sovereignty, but they are unwilling or unable as yet to reveal too much of the inner workings of the conspiratorial machinery which, having brought them to power, has of late turned against them.

The story of Soviet help to Tito's forces during the war is, of course, only a fragment of the over-all Soviet policy during the years 1939 to 1945. The full report about Soviet instructions, or the lack of them, to various Communist Parties in Eastern Europe during those fateful years would be of tremendous value. Had the Yugoslavs chosen to tell fully their own part of the story, our knowledge of the motives and methods of Moscow's policy would be enormously enriched. But even in the face of the incredible abuse daily heaped upon them by Soviet Russia, the ruling circles in Yugoslavia refuse to divulge many of the most important questions concerning their relationships with the Soviet Union just before and during World War II. Some parts of the story might, of course, reflect rather unfavorably upon the official thesis of the unremitting fervor of the C.P.Y. and of its readiness, ever since 1937, to put Yugoslavia's national interest above the dictates of Moscow. Other incidents when fully elaborated might throw grim light on the methods of settling political disputes once employed by the people who are now respectable leaders of their state. It is not that the Party shirks self-criticism. In his review of the war, Tito did not spare harsh words in describing the poor handling of the Partisans' activities in an early uprising in Montenegro, notwithstanding the fact that the leader of the Montenegro uprising had been none other than one of Tito's closest collaborators, Mosha Pijade.[4] The unwillingness to go beyond certain limits in discussing purely political problems connected, first, with the struggle for liberation and now with the stand against the Cominform must be due to the necessity of protecting the legend which has currently been built around the C.P.Y.: its solicitude ever since 1937 for Yugoslavia's interests; its willingness to follow Soviet advice, but not commands; and its unwillingness to sacrifice the slightest bit of the national interest for

[4] Tito, *Political Report of the Central Committee*, p. 107.

the sake of Communist discipline. The present frame of mind of the leadership of the C.P.Y. is thus read into its whole history since 1937, and there is no reason to consider this historical "reconstruction" as being entirely contrived or insincere. The unceasing verbal battle between Belgrade and Moscow touches largely on the insinuation of the Soviet and satellite press that Yugoslavia's liberation, and indeed her very fight against aggression, was made possible only because of Soviet help. For purely psychological reasons, if for nothing else, this is a charge which the C.P.Y. finds most useful to emphasize and discuss before the Yugoslav people. It is also not without its lesson for the historian or for anyone else who wants to reconstruct Soviet policies during the war and draw a moral from them.

The fullest account of the Yugoslav position on the subject is found in a pamphlet published in Serbian by Mosha Pijade, a member of the Politburo of the C.P.Y. and its acknowledged "literary" spokesman.[5] Pijade's booklet takes up the story almost from the beginning of Tito's organized campaign and brings it down to 1944, when Russian help finally did materialize after two years of compliments and unfulfilled promises. The pamphlet is based upon the records of the headquarters of the (Yugoslav) People's Liberation Army, and although some editing must have been done on the original documents, the main points of the story ring true.

Pijade is emphatic on the point that from the beginning of the struggle down to late 1944, when actual contact was established between the two armies, Soviet Russia provided no material or military help to Tito's Partisans. He is willing to concede that there was some English help during the war, but the burden of his argument is that until late 1944 the Yugoslavs fought by themselves with what little they had in the way of armament, and that they fought not only against the Germans and the Italians but also against the traitors, among whom he lists, in addition to the Ustashis and Nedich's forces, the Chetniks of General Mihailovich. The whole argument is, of course, more than debatable, but it is not proposed here to examine it beyond pointing out that it is designed for home con-

[5] Mosha Pijade, *Pricha o Sovietskoy Pomochy Za Dyzanie Ustanka u Jugoslaviji* (*The Story of Soviet Help in the Yugoslav Uprising*), in Serbo-Croat (Belgrade, 1950).

sumption and that it is the argument of a propagandist using certain selected data of history for political purposes, without being interested in the broader aspects of the whole problem.

What is of transcendent interest is the light Pijade's argument throws upon the Soviet official mentality during the early part of the war as contrasted with that of the Yugoslav Communists. On March 5, 1942, Tito's headquarters received the following cable from Moscow:

> Reviewing all your information one gets the impression that with some justification the followers of England and the Yugoslav government believe that the Partisan movement is assuming communist character and that it intends to sovietize Yugoslavia. Why, for instance, was it necessary to organize a special proletarian brigade when *the basic and immediate task consists now in the unification of all anti-Hitler elements in order to crush the occupier and achieve national liberation?* . . . Is it really so that, besides the Communists and their followers, there are no other Yugoslav patriots with whom you could fight against the enemy? It is difficult [for us] to agree that London and the Yugoslav government are collaborating with the invader—there must be some misunderstanding. We beg you to review seriously your tactics and actions, to check whether you did all you could to create a united and real national front of all enemies of Hitler and Mussolini in order to defeat the conqueror and invader, and if not, to take quickly the necessary steps and to inform us about them.[6]

To Soviet Russia, fighting for its life at that pre-Stalingrad stage of the war, the ideological aspect of the struggle was at most secondary. For Tito and his closest associates the armed struggle was but a new form of the fight for Communism in which most of them had spent their adult lives. Tito's own reactions reflect his incredulity at the Russian position. On March 11, 1942, he wrote a letter to Pijade in which he reiterated his annoyance at the insistence of the "Grandpa" [7] that the fight in Yugoslavia be given a wide national basis and that reference to Communism be soft-pedaled. Characteristically enough, the Soviet Union was trying to dampen Tito's public enthusiasm for the "Fatherland of Socialism" and to make him issue official proclamations stressing the alliance between England, the United States, and the U.S.S.R. The Yugoslav zealots had to be cautioned against too frequent references to and

---

[6] *Ibid.*, pp. 11–12. My italics.
[7] Code name for the U.S.S.R.

slogans about Stalin, the Soviet Union, and the Red Army. Tito's own attitude toward all these urgings of political realism was one of amazement and slight exasperation. He concluded wearily in his letter to Pijade that the followers of Mihailovich should now more than ever before be publicized not only as royalists and reactionaries but also as direct servants of the invaders.[8]

The contrast presented by Pijade's story is very revealing. The author, who, incidentally, emerges as Tito's top adviser on matters of foreign policy during the war, seems himself unaware of the fact that his narrative pictures Tito and his wartime high command not as genuine nationalists who left no stone unturned to create national unity against the invader, but as fanatical Communists for whom the struggle for independence was but a phase in the realization of their political aim. The objections of the Soviet government, and its fears of endangering its relations with the Western Allies, were entirely incomprehensible to Tito and his entourage. How could the Soviet government put a higher premium on its relations with the capitalists and its legal obligations to the royal Yugoslav government than on its sacred duty to support its fellow-Communists in Yugoslavia? Such reasoning appears incredibly naïve and incompatible with the *curriculum vitae* of those hard professional revolutionaries. Yet there is probably very little of artifice or invention in Pijade's story. The Yugoslav Communists were receiving their first lessons in international politics. Previously, they had had only to follow directives; now, for the first time, they had to make decisions. It is one of the ironies of the situation that the Russians, probably filled with annoyance, expended great efforts in 1942 and 1943 to have Tito present himself as a progressive nationalist and to make him less voluble in his public protestations of love for the U.S.S.R. and Comrade Stalin.[9]

"We forced ourselves to believe that technical difficulties were the cause [of Soviet hesitations and the lack of help]," says Pijade. But the lesson of wounded pride and disillusioned idealism was not to be lost.

[8] Pijade, *The Story of Soviet Help*, p. 12.

[9] Soviet diplomatic efforts on behalf of the Partisans began actually but cautiously in the middle of 1942. See Wayne S. Vucinich's chapter in *Yugoslavia*, ed. by Robert J. Kerner (Berkeley: University of California Press, 1949), especially pp. 373–374.

The story of the Soviet attitude during the early days of the war is, of course, extremely interesting from the broader point of view. Not until February 1944 did the Russians send a mission to Tito's headquarters, though delegates from Allied headquarters in Cairo had been with the Partisans since May 1942. On the other hand, the Russians attempted on more than one occasion to establish liaison with the forces of General Mihailovich. There is nothing unusual about their attempts, since it is reasonable to assume that the Russians preferred not to arouse the suspicion of their allies and also preferred not to commit themselves in the civil wars raging in Yugoslavia simultaneously with the fight against the invader. Their own military situation was precarious in 1942, and they may have had, at that time, an exaggerated opinion of the political intelligence and motivation of the West. Yugoslavia was simply a small fragment of the larger picture, and it was conceivable that a political bargain, postwar Yugoslavia being one of the items in it, would have to be struck with the Western Allies. It was preferable to have secret communications with Tito and to extol the Partisans in the Soviet press without making any public commitments, but it is perhaps natural that Pijade, viewing those wartime developments from the perspective of 1950, saw in the attitude of the U.S.S.R. the promise of cynicism and selfishness that later was fully developed in the Soviet attempt to oust Tito.

Jarring incidents of the nature described above continued throughout the war period. Dedijer in his diary mentions that as late as 1944 the Yugoslav Brigade, formed and equipped in Russia, was provided with a royal emblem similar to that worn by the Chetniks, and only the most vigorous representations by Tito's emissaries moved the Russians to change the emblem.[10] Prior to the conference between Eden, Hull, and Molotov, held in Moscow in October 1943, Tito had emphatically notified the Russians that his regime would never recognize the London Yugoslav government, or the king, and would never allow them on the soil of Yugoslavia. That, and the formation by the Partisans of their own republican regime in Yugoslavia, was, supposedly, received in Moscow as a stab in the back of the Soviet Union and as an attempted sabotage of Russia's alliance with the West. It was only the lack of a vigorous

[10] *Tridecet Dana (Thirty Days)*, February–March 1950.

reaction from Great Britain and the United States that convinced the Russians that their fears were exaggerated and persuaded them to send an official mission to Tito.[11]

Pijade's account raises several interesting questions. The most important one is now of only historical interest and cannot be answered within the framework of this study: was Soviet domination of Eastern Europe at the end of the war something predestined by the course of events during the war, or was it the result of a policy, beginning in 1944, improvised by the U.S.S.R. when confronted with the unexpected submissiveness of the Western Allies on this issue? Pijade's story, if we accept its reliability, establishes only that the Russians were unwilling to commit themselves publicly for Tito and against Mihailovich at a time when some circles in the West were already denouncing loudly the official Yugoslav government and demanding that all Allied help be denied to Mihailovich on the ground of his collaboration with the invader (something the Russians could not or did not choose to believe completely until late in 1943). But it is also clear that in their worldly and political wisdom the Russians managed to outguess themselves in Yugoslavia. When the Russian mission finally got to Tito's headquarters, and later on when Tolbukhin's armies joined with the Partisans, the leaders of Communist Yugoslavia still constituted as devoted a group of worshippers of the Soviet Union as could be found outside the U.S.S.R. But in addition to this worship, they also had a deep feeling of cohesion and national pride in their liberation, which they felt they had achieved by themselves.

II

The Soviet attempt to subvert Tito's regime, which began while the Marshal was being hailed throughout the world as a Communist hero, is at first glance incredible and incomprehensible. Why was it believed necessary in Moscow to destroy the men who at the end of the war were the most faithful allies of the U.S.S.R., who stood ready to support Soviet Russia in any and all measures against the West, and whose main aim insofar as their own country was con-

[11] Pijade, *The Story of Soviet Help*, p. 27.

cerned was to copy as closely as possible the Soviet pattern? Could there be something to the Russian charges that Tito and his group were plotting against the U.S.S.R. and seeking an overthrow of Soviet supremacy in Eastern Europe?

The Soviet case is presented first in the interchange of letters between the Central Committees of the Communist Parties of Yugoslavia and of the Soviet Union, and then in greater detail in the evidence at the trials of Kostov and Rajk.[12] In the letters exchanged in 1948, there was no hint that Yugoslavia was being charged with overtly hostile acts against the U.S.S.R. The burden of the accusations fell upon the "incorrect" internal policies of the Yugoslav Communists. The trials of Rajk in Hungary and Kostov in Bulgaria pictured Tito and his associates as leaders in a wide conspiracy against the U.S.S.R. and Communism. It is useless to spend any time reviewing the "evidence" offered at the trials. It can be convincing only to a man capable of believing that, all during the war, Tito, instead of being the leader of a Communist Partisan movement, was an agent of the Gestapo and that he worked at the same time, curiously enough, as an agent of the British and American intelligence. The patent impossibility of some of the charges has been discussed elsewhere. Whatever truth there was in the accusations against Rajk and Kostov, the attempt to present Tito as an archtraitor and conspirator collapses of its own absurdity.[13]

[12] The trials are discussed below in Chapter 5.

[13] A French newspaperman asked the Marshal in the course of an interview: "In the light of the trials of Rajk and Kostov, do you consider the [purge] trials in the Soviet Union in 1936 and 1937 as having been 'produced' in the same way?" Tito, whose accession to the leadership of the Yugoslav Communist Party in 1937 was largely a by-product of the purge period, refused to answer the question (*Borba*, December 28, 1949). One example will perhaps be sufficient to illustrate the nature and reliability of the evidence presented in the trials. According to the Hungarian prosecutor and Rajk's own "confession," Rajk and several Yugoslav Communists currently important figures in Tito's regime worked for the Gestapo while in a Vichy concentration camp in the fall of 1940. There have been several testimonies to the effect that the Yugoslavs mentioned in the trial, men like Alesh Bebler and "Tempo" Vukmanovich, were at that time in Yugoslavia. Mr. Stephen W. Pollak, in a letter to *The New Statesman and Nation* of April 8, 1950, writes: "Bebler, an old friend of mine from the days of the Spanish [Civil] War, was released from prison in Ljubljana in September 1940, after serving a one-year sentence . . . and after his release, until my departure from Yugoslavia in March 1941, I was a frequent guest in Bebler's house."

The story of a vast anti-Russian plot presided over by Tito and his clique is nothing but a clumsily constructed propaganda device. But how reasonable is it to reject a less extravagant explanation of the Russo-Yugoslav crisis which would see in Tito, not a spy and foreign agent of long standing, but a bona fide Communist who once in power was ready to construct a bloc of the "people's democracies which would checkmate Soviet domination of Eastern Europe? That explanation has been advanced more than once by non-Communist observers, and it is at least a reasonable effort to determine the rationale of a conflict which otherwise seems inexplicable. But the theory, for all its plausibility, errs essentially because it reads the potentialities of the Balkan situation in 1951 into the realities of 1945–1948. It should be evident both logically and from all the data we possess that the Yugoslav Communists were at that period in no position, either politically or psychologically, to plan an anti-Soviet bloc or even a bloc which would aspire to a position of neutrality in the East-West controversy. No other country in Europe, following the end of the war, went as rapidly down the road to Communism and one-party government as did Tito's Yugoslavia. No other country within the Russian sphere was as ready to challenge both the governments and the public opinion of the West. The trial and execution of Mihailovich; the proclamation of the republic, based from the beginning on the Soviet pattern; the speedy suppression of the remaining non-Communist elements in Yugoslavia, represented by people like Shubashich and Grol; the defiant attitude of Yugoslavia on the subject of Trieste—all these facts testify to the deep and unfeigned hostility of Yugoslavia's rulers once the war ended to anything connected with the internal and external politics of the Western Powers. The official pronouncements of Yugoslav officials equaled and exceeded those of their Russian colleagues in their incessant abuse of the United States and Great Britain. How realistic is it, then, to assume that while thus ready to provoke the West almost to the point of war, the government of Yugoslavia at the same time was attempting to build a combination of states which would challenge and weaken the position of the only Great Power standing behind Yugoslavia? Even if we disregard the fanatical Communism of Tito and his followers, the realities of postwar politics make the thesis that Tito attempted to build a bloc of socialist states apart from and against the Soviet Union completely untenable and fantastic.

It is not improbable that the Yugoslav Communists may at times have encouraged their colleagues in Poland or Bulgaria to take a more independent position vis-à-vis the Soviet Union, or may have urged either by example or by specific advice that the People's Democracies resist Soviet pressures concerning some of their domestic policies. But such actions were undoubtedly conceived as being in the nature of political relations even among the most closely associated states, and the idea of an outright challenge to Soviet supremacy could not enter the minds of the Yugoslav leaders prior to 1948.

Surveying all the available evidence, one must reach the conclusion that the stage for the Russo-Yugoslav conflict had been set by continuous Russian attempts to subvert the position of Tito and his group and that, even in the face of these attempts, the ruling circles of the Communist Party of Yugoslavia did not wish or dare to turn against Moscow until the summer of 1948 when the Russians chose to make the conflict public, in the hope, no doubt, that once their displeasure was announced, the Yugoslav Communists would turn against their own Politburo. The reasons behind the Soviet policies, which ever since 1945 had been intended to find and exploit any weak spot in Tito's personal dictatorship, are hard to ascertain. One can surmise only that the Russians did not like the idea of a Communist Party and a Communist government controlled by a group of non-Moscow Communists, in which the Russians were, so to speak, on the outside, no matter how much their directives were followed by the Yugoslav leaders and how much the latter had shown themselves devoted to Soviet Russia and Communism. It is likely that in their commercial and political dealings with Yugoslavia, the representatives of the Soviet Union found themselves handicapped by the solidarity of the C.P.Y. and by the intransigence of the Yugoslavs on any issue where the interests of their state had to be subordinated without *any ideological excuse* to the interests of the U.S.S.R. There seems to be very little doubt that had the Russians employed diplomacy instead of attempts at compulsion and subversion, Tito's Yugoslavia would still be the most faithful ally of the Soviet Union. But for one reason or another, and in accordance with the character of its development since 1928, the Politburo of the Communist Party of the U.S.S.R. did not choose to plead or to negotiate with its fellow Communists. The latter had to be freed from the romantic nonsense of nationalism which had captivated them during the war, and their conceited leaders were to be chastised and removed in favor of more reliable subordinates of the Soviet Union.

The effort to subvert Tito's regime logically had to start with the two main instruments of his power, the Yugoslav army and the C.P.Y.

The army has been the bulwark of the regime, not only because of its record during the war but also because of its essentially political nature, which has made it, along with the Party, the main foundation of the new Yugoslavia. It is incredible to realize now that during the darkest days of the occupation, when the present rulers of Yugoslavia were organizing their military forces, their first thoughts went to the problem of the political organization and education of their troops. Those who still believe that the Partisan movement had at any point of its development a broad national, or apolitical, character would do well to reread Marshal Tito's report to the Fifth Congress of the C.P.Y., where with characteristic candor he revealed the details of the political organization of the Partisan army. As early as March 1942, an elaborate network of political commissars and agents was prescribed for every unit of the Partisan army, reaching down to at least one political delegate in every platoon (a platoon being a unit of from thirty to fifty soldiers). "The political commissars are the soul of the units. They are the representatives of the people and the guardians of the people's interests in the units. They are the initiators and the leaders in the elevation of the political, military, and ideological level of the units," said an official order of the Supreme Headquarters of the Partisans early in 1942.[14] That expense of energy and manpower for political purposes was being authorized at the moment of extreme peril to the very survival of the Partisan forces. The notion of an apolitical army has never even entered the minds of the Communist leaders of Yugoslavia. The high command of the army and that of the Party have always overlapped. In addition to Tito, several

[14] Quoted in Tito, *Political Report of the Central Committee*, pp. 81 and ff.

other members of the Politburo, Ivan Goshnjak and Alexander Rankovich, for example, emerged from the war as high-ranking officers. Under the new regime the army has remained a thoroughly political organization, and, indeed, it is doubtful whether the Red Army itself has been equally propagandized and organized from the political point of view. The head of the army political administration has stated recently that every officer in the higher ranks has been subjected to several ideological examinations in the Party schools.[15]

It is not surprising that the unity and political cohesion of the Yugoslav army has from the beginning been the paramount objective of the C.P.Y. and its leaders. Soviet attempts to penetrate the army, to infiltrate the officer corps, and to win its highest leaders from their allegiance to Tito were among the most important factors in convincing the Yugoslav regime that for its sheer survival it should stand up to Soviet Russia. As early as 1943 and 1944, the Soviet authorities recruited into their secret service a number of soldiers in the First Yugoslav Brigade, then being formed in Russia from those Yugoslavs who had been captured on the Eastern Front while fighting alongside the German army.[16] After the war Yugoslav officers studying in the U.S.S.R. were frequently approached and urged to join the Russian intelligence service. General Kreachich in his report gives the names of several Russian officers, attached to the army of their ally, who were engaged in Yugoslavia in this process of recruiting spies among the fighting services of a fellow-socialist nation. Since the Russians had good reason to know the efficiency of the Yugoslav secret police, it is obvious that they expected the Yugoslav authorities to look with complacency on the process of subversion of their own army.

Nor were the Russians content to recruit by blackmail or political persuasion a few informants who might give them information of military or political character. In the trial of two Yugoslav officers charged with treason, one of the accused testified that the Soviet attaché, General Sidorovich, had been inquiring of him about the attitudes of such important Yugoslav leaders as General

[15] Lieutenant General Otmar Kreachich, quoted in *Politika* (Zagreb newspaper), December 22, 1949.
[16] *Ibid.*

Goshnjak (member of the Politburo of the C.P.Y.) and General Kocha Popovich (chief of staff of the Yugoslav army).[17] A Yugoslav state trial is usually no more reliable as a source of historical information than a corresponding ceremony in the Soviet Union. In this case, however, there is little reason to doubt the correctness of the information. In the years 1945 to 1948, while Tito was being feasted in the capitals of the People's Democracies and while Yugoslavia was celebrated by the Soviet press as a faithful ally of the Soviet Union, the Politburo of the Communist Party of Yugoslavia must have been receiving constant reports of Soviet agents infiltrating the ranks of the Yugoslav army.

It is impossible to estimate how much success was secured by those activities within the Yugoslav army. Soviet agents did succeed in recruiting one of the highest officers of the army, but his usefulness to his Soviet masters was to be very brief. Among the British officers serving with the Partisans, Tito's chief-of-staff, Arso Jovanovich, had the reputation of being a capable strategist but also of being an extremely vain man. It must have been the latter characteristic, and his lack of political prominence after the war, which urged him to turn traitor. After the conflict with Moscow had erupted with full intensity, Jovanovich was told to flee Yugoslavia. He may have been slated to head a "Free" Yugoslav government on satellite territory; and it is reasonably clear, though not so stated in the trial of his companions, that his activities had not been unsuspected. In any case, his decision to flee in the summer of 1948 could have only indicated that the Yugoslav army was not ready for a rebellion. On the night of August 12, 1948, Arso Jovanovich was shot while trying to cross into Rumanian territory, and his companions in treason and flight, Major General Branko Petrichevich and Colonel Vladimir Dapchevich,[18] were shortly afterward apprehended. Almost two years later they were to confess their treason and the details of their dealings with Soviet agents in a public trial.[19]

The whole course of events in connection with the Soviet attempt to seize control of the Yugoslav army is still largely unre-

[17] An account of the trial is found in the issues of *Borba* for June 3, 4, and 5, 1950.
[18] Brother of Peko Dapchevich, a famous Partisan leader and one of the highest officials of Tito's army.
[19] See *Borba*, June 5, 1950.

ported. The Yugoslavs have released just enough to present their own case, and the Russians have kept silent. Arso Jovanovich has been elevated in the Soviet and satellite press to the dignity of a martyr of the proletarian cause, sharing the distinction with Zhujovich and Hebrang, the two Communist leaders who were discharged from the Central Committee of the Yugoslav Party and imprisoned upon the outbreak of the crisis.[20] Caution is required in interpreting the attitude of outraged innocence which the Yugoslav government has chosen to assume in connection with Soviet espionage activities. The leaders of the C.P.Y had been trained in the school of conspiratorial communism, and many of them had seen service in the Spanish Civil War before they became generals and leaders in their own armies. It was not the existence of Soviet espionage and Soviet agents in their army which gradually crystallized their determination to stand up against the Soviet Union, but the conviction finally established in their minds, probably sometime between 1947 and 1948, that the Russian aim was nothing other than the destruction of the Politburo of the C.P.Y. and the establishment of a new regime dependent upon the U.S.S.R. in a way that those "self-made" Communists could never be. But after the break the story of Soviet subversion in free Yugoslavia, at first not entirely unexpected and grudgingly tolerated, was put on record as an undeserved and unheard-of outrage upon a sovereign and friendly state.

III

Today's Yugoslavia is a curious example of a country where the existence of a highly emotional and self-conscious nationalism is unaccompanied by militant expansionist tendencies. The Communist rulers of Yugoslavia have, of late, been fond of emphasizing that theirs is a small country and that their fight against Soviet imperialism represents the struggle of small countries everywhere to preserve their independence of the two great camps waging an incessant political struggle. There are few governments so desperately devoted to the position of absolute neutrality in time of

[20] Zhujovich lost this distinction upon his release and recantation in November 1950.

peace as is the Communist government of Yugoslavia. Repelled almost equally by the capitalism of the West and by Soviet aggressive designs upon them, the Yugoslavs are determined to follow their own way and to eschew the merest semblance of an imperialist venture.

It is all the more striking to recall the militant and aggressive frame of mind in which the ruling circles of the C.P.Y. greeted the liberation of their country and, later, the full defeat of Germany and Italy. The territorial claims pressed by Tito's government against Austria and Italy would have been advanced by any other Yugoslav government, but the violent and provocative manner which the Communist government adopted, especially on the subject of Trieste, attests the Yugoslav conception of their own rule as that of the advance guard of Communism. Trieste remained between 1945 and 1948 one of the most sensitive spots in Europe; and there is much to suggest that the Yugoslav government was not unwilling at times to risk a major military adventure in support of its claims against Italy and Austria. It is not clear whether the Russians exercised a restraining role in the dispute or whether they incited their allies toward a more uncompromising position.[21] Soviet support and Allied acquiescence enabled the new Yugoslavia··to gain Fiume and other Adriatic territories from Italy; Soviet help was also thrown behind Yugoslavia's claims for Trieste. But the Yugoslav Communists emerged from the war in a state of excitement: their nationalism blended with a fanatical conviction of the inevitability of Communist expansion and the omnipotence of Communist arms. As happens not infrequently, their fantastic success, which they themselves would have deemed improbable a few years before, now only served to increase their irritation with the postwar world for failing to conform *completely* with their interests and desires. It is unlikely that they had more comprehension of the complexities of international politics, which made it impossible for the Soviet Union to force the issue of Trieste in the interest of Yugoslavia, than they had of Russia's reluctance during the war to grant a premature recognition to the Tito regime. Obviously, Soviet Russia, as witnessed by her own territorial expansion, could win any international dispute. Her unwillingness to press the Yugo-

[21] The Russians, as seen below, insist on the former version.

slav case for Trieste with greater firmness could only be due to Russia's ingratitude toward her most faithful ally or conceivably to some previous clandestine arrangements with the West. If this whole train of reasoning appears incredible, it should be kept in mind that militant nationalism has often produced the type of national egocentrism and fanaticism described above, and that, in this case, nationalism was allied with an equally fervent religious conviction of the invincibility of Communism. The accusation by the Soviet authorities that the Yugoslavs were not unwilling to have the U.S.S.R. risk a major war over Trieste is one of the few items in the Soviet indictment of Tito which may come close to the truth.[22]

More important than the unsatisfactory position of the U.S.S.R. on Trieste was what the leaders of Yugoslavia must have viewed as sabotage by Russia of Yugoslavia's plans for the Balkan federation. The concept of the federation was, following the war, the most immediate aim of the foreign policy of Communist Yugoslavia. The year 1945 saw the emergence of three Communist states on the Balkan Peninsula. Albania was clearly within the Yugoslav "sphere of interest," and the Albanian Communist leaders were the protégés of the C.P.Y. Bulgaria was a fellow Slavic nation whose cultural tradition and history made its separation from other South Slav nations illogical at the time when scientific Marxism was removing obsolete political and social forms and foreign imperialisms (so it seemed in 1944 and 1945), which alone had been responsible in the past for the disunity of the South Slavs. The idea of a union between Yugoslavia and Bulgaria, which aside from any doctrinal postulates and Communist tactics would be a progressive and reasonable solution of one of the most difficult dilemmas of the Balkans, must have made a particular appeal to Tito. His own role within the Communist Party of Yugoslavia has been that of the exponent of the "federal" outlook; he has chastised both the "Great Serbian" chauvinism and the separatist tendencies of the Croats and the

---

[22] "Since all other means were exhausted the Soviet Union had only one other method left for gaining Trieste—to start war with Anglo-Americans over Trieste and take it by force. The Yugoslav comrades could not fail to realize that after such a hard war the U.S.S.R. could not enter another. However, this fact caused dissatisfaction among the Yugoslav leaders" (letter of the C.P.S.U. to the C.P.Y. quoted in *The Soviet-Yugoslav Dispute: Text of the Published Correspondence* [London: Royal Institute of International Affairs, 1948], p. 36).

Macedonians. Postwar Yugoslavia has been the visible expression of the same idea, its federal structure proclaiming, at least in theory, friendly association of several nations whose cultural, religious, and political traditions have in the past been further apart than those of the Serbs and the Bulgarians. A union of the two states, which too often have found themselves in armed conflict because of dynastic and Great Power interests, would create a real "Yugoslavia"—a true federation of the South Slavs. Then, the prospective federation would undoubtedly take place under the leadership of Tito and his group and would be a fitting reward for the leading part undertaken by the C.P.Y. in the political and military liberation of the Balkan peoples.

It appears probable that as early as 1944 and 1945, the idea of the federation had the enthusiastic approval of Moscow, if indeed the very initiative for it did not come from that quarter. It is not difficult to see the reasons behind Russia's acceptance and sponsorship of the federation. By late 1944 it was almost certain that both Bulgaria and Yugoslavia would emerge from the war as Communist states. The solution of the agelong conflict between the two states would have proved once more the magic efficacy of Communism in removing the evils of nationalism. The new federated state would have been an effective counterbalance to the American-British influence still lingering in the Balkans and of great moral and material assistance to the Greek Communists just then facing the struggle for power in their own country. It is conceivable that the Russians were not unmindful of the possibility that the union of Bulgaria and Yugoslavia would by its very mechanics produce some counterbalancing to Tito's personal dictatorship and increase the leverage of Moscow both within the Communist Party of Yugoslavia and that of Bulgaria. But the dominant factor must have been the vision of the Balkans united under the aegis of Communism, a testimony to the irresistible march of the socialist idea, and a promise, perhaps, in the more distant future, of a still greater union of Communist states.

The working out of a union was bound to present serious if not insurmountable difficulties. In the first place, the leaders of the Bulgarian Communist Party were not likely to agree to a simple absorption of their country. There was the troublesome problem of what was to be the role of the Bulgarian Communist Party leadership, which included such well-known veterans of the international Communist movement as Dimitrov, Kolarov, and Kostov, in the new federation to be headed by Tito and dominated by his clique of Yugoslav Communists. But the most important initial task in clearing the way for a federation was some initial resolution of the Macedonian problem.

Just as the Macedonian problem has always reflected the national antagonisms of the Balkan states, and as the country itself, its geographical or linguistic limits never clearly defined, has been the historical battleground between Serbia, Greece, and Bulgaria, so has the official Communist line on the Macedonian problems changed and fluctuated through the years in accordance with the Comintern's and, later, the Cominform's appraisal of the international situation. Moscow, it seems, has considered Macedonia the prize to be awarded to its most promising and useful pupil among the Communist Parties of the Balkans. The notion of the "Greater Macedonia" (that is, the area comprising the ill-defined territory now found in Yugoslavia, Greece, and Bulgaria) has never been advocated by itself, but always in conjunction with some larger political scheme sponsored by Moscow: at one time as a part of the Balkan federation to be presided over by Tito, more recently as an anti-Tito move designed to stir up the irredentist movement in Yugoslav Macedonia.

The occupation of Yugoslavia during the Second World War coincided with a curious incident in the Communist organization of Yugoslav Macedonia. That part of Yugoslavia had been awarded by the German and Italian invaders to their Bulgarian allies. The representative of the C.P.Y. in Yugoslav Macedonia, Metody Shatorov-Sharlo, whether impressed by the administrative convenience of the shift or so ordered by Moscow, "transferred" his Party organization with the connivance of the Bulgarian Communist leaders from the Communist Party of Yugoslavia to that of Bulgaria. The Central Committee of the C.P.Y., unmindful of the administrative principle involved, removed Sharlo and "returned" its Macedonian component to the C.P.Y. Sharlo's eventual successor, Lazar Kolishevski, is still the Party boss in the (Yugoslav) Federal People's Republic of Macedonia. The Comintern approved of

Tito's actions.[23] From that time on, until the crisis of 1948, the Yugoslav viewpoint on Macedonia appears to have had the backing of Moscow. The first step in the projected federation was to be the incorporation of Bulgarian Macedonia in the (Yugoslav) People's Federal Republic of Macedonia; and it seems very likely that, implicit in the help extended by Tito to the Communist Partisans in Greece, was an assurance that the latter, once in power, would not stand in the way of still further territorial expansion of the Macedonian republic and the Balkan federation. In the spring of 1949, when their own fight against the Greek government was collapsing, the Greek Communists were to make a public declaration of their willingness to see a part of their country incorporated in the Macedonian Republic—a member of the still nonexistent Balkan federation. By that time Macedonian nationalism was being fanned by the Cominform and Moscow in an as yet vain hope of creating trouble in Yugoslavia.

The Macedonian question has always been one of the stumbling blocks in the way of friendly relations among the various Balkan states. It is natural that its solution was thought to be a preliminary step in the creation of the South Slav federation. But negotiations to work out a formula for the union of Bulgaria and Yugoslavia were started as early as November 1944, when war still lingered in the Balkans. Again, it is striking to contemplate the political sense and dynamism of Communism: with the war still raging, with the internal situation in their own countries still far from settled, the Communists of Bulgaria and Yugoslavia began, with Moscow's authorization, their talks designed to transform Southeastern Europe. They were not as yet, at least officially, masters in their own houses, and Bulgaria was still a defeated country not empowered to conduct its foreign relations without an authorization of the Allies. But the Central Committees of the two Parties knew that they needed only the permission of the Soviet Union and that the non-Communists in their governments—the Shubashiches and Georgievs—would soon be eliminated.

Actually, the official Yugoslav version of the early negotiations

---

[23] See Barker, *Macedonia*, pp. 84–89. For the current Bulgarian Communist view and some unkind things about Kolishevski, see Georgi Madolev's article in *Rabotnichesko Delo*, March 24, 1950.

with Bulgaria on the subject of the South Slav federation fits in very well with what might be called the Cominform version of these negotiations as presented in the indictments of Traicho Kostov, the Bulgarian Communist leader who was purged in 1949. The latter version differs only insofar as it considers the negotiations as part of a plot engineered by Tito and Kostov in order to destroy Bulgaria's independence and to betray the Balkans to the Anglo-American imperialists. There are some other minor differences between the two versions, but the fact remains that the negotiations were started in November 1944, and in December of the same year Tito's right-hand man, Kardelj, was in Sofia consulting with Kostov and his treacherous accomplices, according to Moscow and the Cominform, with the Central Committee of the Bulgarian Communist Party and the Bulgarian government, according to the Yugoslavs. If the Russian version (and it should be so called, despite the fact that it was prepared and presented by a Bulgarian court) is to be considered, then we are asked to believe that Kostov and Kardelj were having their leisurely and treasonable conference under the very eyes of the Russian army, the occupation authorities, and the secret police then ensconced in Bulgaria, and that the blueprint for the Yugoslav-Bulgarian federation had been developed some time before by a representative of the American intelligence service assisted by a special emissary of Hitler! It seems somewhat simpler to assume that the conversations were held with the full knowledge and agreement of the Soviet Union, and it is not unreasonable to accept, with certain reservations, the present Yugoslav thesis that the South Slav federation, and more specifically the Yugoslav concept of it, had in 1944 and 1945 the backing of the highest authorities in Soviet Russia.

Ambiguity arises if one analyzes the story of the Yugoslavs about Dimitrov's position on the federation. If we accept Kostov's indictment and his written confession (which he later repudiated in court), Dimitrov in 1944, when he was still in Moscow, intervened against the Kardelj-Kostov plot and his telegram to the Central Committee of the Bulgarian Communist Party opened their eyes to Kostov's treachery. Conversely, in the Yugoslav version related by Pijade,[24]

[24] In his speech before the eighth session of the National Assembly of Yugoslavia, *Borba*, December 29, 1949.

Dimitrov emerges as the staunchest friend of the idea of the federation and of Yugoslavia, while Kostov, in fact, wanted a federation which would give a privileged position to the Bulgarian Communists. It is understandable that both sides want to exploit the great prestige of Dimitrov in the Communist movement, and, therefore, none of the versions of Dimitrov's position on the Yugoslav-Bulgarian federation in the years 1944 and 1945 can be trusted.[25]

The undeniable fact remains that in November and December of 1944 there were negotiations between the leaders of the two countries on the subject of federation. It is also clear, since it is admitted very good-naturedly by Pijade, that the Yugoslav project envisaged first the union of Yugoslav Macedonia with Pirin (Bulgarian) Macedonia and following that the accession of Bulgaria as the seventh federal republic of Yugoslavia. It is characteristic of the nationalist fervor of the Yugoslavs that they were surprised at the unwillingness of the Bulgarians to submerge their state in the Yugoslav federation and to receive a status equivalent to that of Montenegro or Macedonia. The Bulgarians, for their part, proposed a union based on the principle of parity (between all of Yugoslavia and Bulgaria), or simply, in the beginning, a very close alliance. The negotiations dragged on, and Kardelj in his letters to Belgrade hinted, according to Pijade, the need for an appeal to Stalin, who supposedly had committed himself in favor of the Yugoslav scheme.[26]

It is useful to repeat, since Pijade emphasizes it throughout his speech, that the negotiations were conducted not only with Kostov, then the secretary of the Bulgarian Communist Party, but also with many other Bulgarian notables. Among the latter was a certain "Vladimirov," who, according to the Yugoslavs, was none other than Vulko Chervenkov—and Chervenkov today, having survived

---

[25] The story of Dimitrov's friendship toward Yugoslavia and Tito's regime, a friendship which survived the break between Moscow and Belgrade and the Cominform revolution of 1948, has been consistently pursued by the Yugoslav press. On the other hand, there are those public appearances and utterances of Dimitrov in which, following the Cominform declaration of June 28, 1948, he attacks Tito and the Yugoslav regime. At the Fifth Party Congress of the Bulgarian Workers' (Communist) Party held December 18–25, 1948, Dimitrov lashed out against Tito, accusing him of being a "nationalist" and "Serbian chauvinist" and of having designs on Bulgarian Macedonia! (*For a Lasting Peace*, January 1, 1949.)

[26] Pijade's speech, *Borba*, December 29, 1949.

Dimitrov and Kolarov and having purged Kostov, is the undoubted dictator of Bulgaria. That Kardelj's negotiations were conducted in a veritable glare of publicity, insofar as such matters are usually transacted, is attested by the fact that the Bulgarian Communists even bothered to impart them to the nominal Prime Minister of Bulgaria, Kimon Georgiev, whose official interest in the matter (since he was a non-Communist) was likely to be short-lived.

Reading between the lines of the Yugoslav accounts of the Sofia conversations, one receives the impression that the Yugoslav Communists were exerting heavy pressure upon their Bulgarian colleagues to establish their own postulates in regard to Macedonia and the eventual plan of the federation. The Yugoslavs were after all the representatives of victorious Communism, whereas their Bulgarian confreres owed their liberation and their power to the Soviet army. It is natural that the C.P.Y. expected, and their expectations were not at first disappointed, to have the U.S.S.R. on their side. Were they not the most successful and useful pupils of the Soviet Union, the key to Soviet domination of the Balkans? The Bulgarians had been unable to shake off their weak monarchical regime without Soviet intervention, and their most distinguished Communists, in glaring contrast to the leaders of the C.P.Y., had spent the war years in Moscow. The Russians had to arbitrate between their two satellites, and it was their decision to continue the Sofia negotiations, not in Belgrade as urged by the C.P.Y., but in Moscow. The Yugoslav delegation to Moscow was led by Pijade, the Bulgarian by Anton Yugov, the Minister of Interior and a member of the Politburo of the Bulgarian Party, with Kimon Georgiev tagging along.[27]

Pijade insists that the conversations in Moscow resulted in a full victory for the Yugoslav point of view. Dimitrov's opposition to a federation in which Bulgaria would be merely one of the seven federal units was supposedly overcome when Stalin mentioned that the Yugoslav plan was a good one. It is clear at the same time that Pijade's account is inconsistent with what he himself had to say about the original Yugoslav plan. Prior to the Moscow meeting, which took place in January 1945, the Yugoslavs had insisted that a treaty stipulating the federation should be signed and published immediately. They were, however, to leave Moscow with only a draft of

[27] *Ibid.*

a treaty of alliance with Bulgaria and with a promise, or at most a secret agreement, regarding the eventual and gradual accomplishment of the federation. It is clear why the Russians could never have agreed to a consummation and announcement of a Yugoslav-Bulgarian federation in 1945, though Pijade is either oblivious of the fact or does not choose to mention it. Bulgaria was a defeated country theoretically under the control of the three Allied Powers. For that matter, Yugoslavia, though *de facto* under Tito's regime, was still legally a monarchy, and its postwar constitution (including the federal structure of which Bulgaria was to become a part in 1945) was not to be installed until 1946! With the war still going on, the Russians could not, even if they chose to disregard the sensitiveness of their Bulgarian protégés, ignore the Western Allies and put a public seal of approval upon a Communist federation in the Balkans. But to the Yugoslav Communists, flushed with their triumph, the world in 1945 consisted of their own country, the U.S.S.R., and the Communist Parties elsewhere. It appears almost certain that the Moscow session must have involved a rather stern lecture by the Soviet authorities to the Yugoslav delegation about the facts of international politics. The Yugoslav source merely admits that the treaty of alliance between Bulgaria and Yugoslavia, which was not to become public for some time, was actually drafted by Mr. Vyshinsky.[28]

The attempt to bring about the federation continued from 1945 to January 1948. The Bled agreement of August 1947 between Bulgaria and Yugoslavia (which publicly was merely a treaty of alliance not much different from the whole series of treaties signed at that time between various states within the Russian sphere, and between them and the Soviet Union) is declared by the Yugoslav press to have been the first formal step toward the federation. The treaty almost certainly contained unpublished clauses, and the Yugoslavs are insistent that, at the same time, the Bulgarian Communists, on the initiative of Dimitrov, were ready to cede Pirin Macedonia to the (Yugoslav) Federal Republic of Macedonia.[29] But the Yugoslav press

[28] *Ibid.*
[29] Article in *Borba*, December 11, 1949: "The Trial in Sofia and the South Slav Federation." The Yugoslavs at the same time were to make minor territorial concessions in return to Bulgaria. Yugoslav teachers were sent into Pirin Macedonia to prepare the ground for Pirin's incorporation.

is unable to explain why, despite the supposed willingness of every-body—of the Russians, of Tito, of Dimitrov—the federation could not have been realized in the more than three years that elapsed from its first mention in November 1944 to January 1948, when the whole situation abruptly changed. No explanation is offered by the Yugo-slavs for the failure to realize the union so eagerly awaited by all the interested parties, unless it was the objection of Bulgarian Com-munists, like Kostov, who opposed the "Dimitrov line" and who wanted a federation which would put the Bulgarians in a "privileged position," that is, make the new state a dual union instead of ab-sorbing Bulgaria as the seventh unit of the Yugoslav federation. But it is indeed more than doubtful whether the majority of the Bul-garian Communist notables were eager for a federation in which their traditional rivals—the leaders of the C.P.Y.—would have clearly retained the upper hand. It is to be noted that while Dimitrov spoke often and enthusiastically about the need for closer ties between Bulgaria and Yugoslavia, his remarks more than once indicated the need for a still wider union which would embrace other Soviet satellites in Eastern Europe, as well as Greece when "liberated." [30]

On January 28, 1948, a small note on the last page of *Pravda* in-formed its readers (some of whom had supposedly been inquiring anxiously about *Pravda's* approving reports of a typical Dimitrov utterance on federation in Eastern Europe) that the editors of *Pravda* had printed the speech as a journalistic duty, but that they were far from supporting the whole idea. The note went on to re-mind the readers that the Eastern European countries should think about their independence and the strengthening of democracy rather than about the "problematical and artificial" schemes of federation. Thus, three short paragraphs marked the complete and irretrievable collapse of the main objective of Yugoslavia's foreign policy. Though it was Dimitrov who had to recant, the blow struck hardest at Tito and his Party.[31]

---

[30] The speeches of Dimitrov lead to the theory, discussed above, that the veteran Communist leader had attempted to form a federation of Eastern Communist states in order to free them from the influence of Moscow. What-ever the merit of such theorizing, it must be obvious that Dimitrov's speeches could not have been made, and publicized in the Soviet press, unless at the time when they were given they expressed the viewpoint of the U.S.S.R.

[31] See also Andrew Gyorgy, *Governments of Danubian Europe* (New York,

It will not be known for some time whether the Russians in sabotaging the plan for a South Slav federation (which may have been initiated by the Soviet Union), were suspicious of a union of their satellites or whether an expanded Yugoslavia was a prize to be withheld from Tito and his group but to be granted to another set of leaders of the C.P.Y. Before the deathblow given the federation, a reshuffling took place within the Yugoslav government. Hebrang, until then the head of the Economic Planning Commission and soon to be revealed as the leader of the anti-Tito faction within the Party, was demoted to a less important position. To the leaders of the C.P.Y. the substance and even more the manner of the Russians' treatment of the federation were to be important lessons in political behavior. Three years before they had emerged from the war as fanatical followers of Communism and the U.S.S.R. Their equally fervent nationalism led them to believe that the Russians would recognize them as their prize pupils and the dominant force in the Balkans. Now they saw Soviet agents at work within the Yugoslav army and the highest echelons of the C.P.Y., probing for a weak spot in Tito's regime. In addition, their most cherished foreign policies and economic plans were being sponsored or abandoned according to the interests and whims of Soviet policy. The stage was thus set for a more basic conflict.

1949), chap. VIII: "Alliances and Federation Projects in Danubian Europe"; and Samuel Sharp, "Federation in Eastern Europe," *The American Perspective*, March 1948.

CHAPTER 4

The Crisis

There are historical occasions that defy description. Their essence lies in a configuration of events and in a mood which once passed can hardly be reproduced by the most exacting research and accumulation of data. For it is precisely the feeling of the moment and the attendant passions, hesitations, and decisions which the passage of time blunts and which appear, even in the recollection of a participant in the drama, obscured and often distorted by the aftermath of the crisis. This is doubly so in a situation which has, in addition to a perplexing series of conflicts and clashes, the characteristics of an ideological crisis. For nothing is more difficult than to record and explain the state of mind which absorbs or rejects or begins to question religious or ideological convictions.

It may be thought that to characterize the break between Yugoslavia and Soviet Russia as ideological in nature is to anticipate or to beg the question. Yet by the summer of 1948, when an astonished world heard about the dispute, no single tenet of the Communist creed was as essential as the principle, engrafted on it ever since the late twenties, of the infallibility of the leadership of the Communist Party of the U.S.S.R. and the utter unthinkability of a public dispute between any bona fide Communist Party and its great leader and teacher at Moscow. Before 1948 occasions were not lacking when individuals and groups revolted against the rigor of Soviet control and left the Party amidst angry recriminations. Still more frequent was the process of purge applied to the supposed "Trotskyites," "Bukharinites," and other suspected or real deviationists, a process which led, in one case at least—that of the Polish Communist Party in 1938—to the suspension and temporary dissolution, at the orders of the Comintern, of the whole Party organization. Still, the spectacle in 1948 of a powerful and victorious Communist Party taking a resolute and uncompromising stand against the leaders of world Communism provided the most dramatic event in the history of the movement since Stalin's assumption of leadership. The drama and unexpectedness of the developments of the summer of 1948 were enhanced by the fact that the revolt was led by the very same people who only a few years before had demonstrated their boundless devotion to the U.S.S.R. and who had been the pioneers in the triumphant expansion of Communism in postwar Europe. Fantasy and hopeful speculation have embroidered the story of the Yugoslav-Russian dispute, and it is well to consider certain points which must have been in the minds of the men who in standing up against Moscow were defying not only one of the greatest powers of all times but also their own past and the belief which had been their only religion and occupation for most of their adult lives.

There have been many books of late recounting the experiences of those anti-Communists who after a period of devotion to Communism felt themselves betrayed and who gradually became revolted by the reality of Communism in action. The best known among these books, *The God That Failed*, recounts the experiences of several intellectuals who, because of their passion for action and protest, found themselves immersed in a movement which soon showed itself unmindful of their delicate moral and intellectual sensitivities. Yet what emerges, characteristically, from many of these accounts is the feeling of nostalgia and betrayed love and of the utmost difficulty in deciding to abandon the movement which for all its cruelties and absurdities appeared to be so universal in its aims and to set at rest so many of the most perplexing inner questions and problems. Turn from these people, who were for the most part amateurs and dilettantes in Communism, to a group of professional revolutionaries who had spent their lives hounded and imprisoned and hiding while fighting for a hopeless cause. The latter could yet be comforted by the thought that they were not alone, that more important than their dogma with its distant "inevitability," and more important than the handful of their supporters and sympathizers, were the existence and omniscience of the leaders of the Soviet Union. The belief in the U.S.S.R. was for them the most vital element of their creed and their sacrifices. Not long after the break between Tito and Moscow, when Tito's regime had already been loaded by the Russians and satellites with the most opprobrious epithets, one of the Yugoslav leaders could still speak of the U.S.S.R. with a passion which made him forget that the official line of his Party was that it had sprung to arms before Hitler's attack on Russia. Referring to Yugoslavia's reluctance to ask Russia for any help that would injure the economy of the U.S.S.R., Boris Kidrich said:

On June 22d 1941, we did not conclude that "happy times" had come when the U.S.S.R. would have to liberate our country from German, Italian, Hungarian, Bulgarian occupation, but on the contrary, we concluded that the time had come when it was necessary,—in the sense of international solidarity in the struggle against the fascist invaders, in the sense of that truly Marxist-Leninist internationalism which demands of every working man that he give all of himself at the fateful moment for the common cause of working and progressive mankind—to take up arms en masse and to sacrifice all, sparing neither life nor national wealth, nor children, nor the aged nor the honor of our girls and women, sparing nothing that is dear and sacred to everyone.[1]

Such is the self-proclaimed extent of the Yugoslav Communists' patriotic motives in taking up arms in 1941, and such is the residue of the emotion by which they were bound to the Soviet Union. It is small wonder that this emotion, because of its very intensity, could not last or had to turn, after a still further interval, to a most virulent hatred. But it was still present when the Central Committee of the Communist Party of Yugoslavia had to make the decision whether to defy or to capitulate to the Soviet demands.

In addition to the decision to cast themselves adrift from the Soviet Union, the Central Committee had to decide to face a world in which, by 1948, Tito's Yugoslavia literally did not have a single friend. The capitalist powers were not likely to support a Com-

---

[1] Boris Kidrich, *On the Construction of Socialist Economy in the Federal People's Republic of Yugoslavia*, speech delivered at the Fifth Congress of the C.P.Y. (Belgrade, 1948), p. 63.

munist regime, at least not without attaching certain conditions to their help; and, on the other hand, the Communist leaders of Yugoslavia in their 1948 frame of mind could not and would not ask for help from the side which they considered diametrically opposed to their social and political philosophy and whose assistance at this early stage of the conflict would have alienated from them a considerable body of their most faithful supporters, whose allegiance to the principles of Marxism was almost as strong as their loyalty to Tito and his lieutenants. The problem could not and did not exist in 1948 in the form which it was to take in the subsequent years. In 1948 the Yugoslavs were simply standing their ground. They probably did not foresee that the conflict would become a matter of life and death or that the U.S.S.R. would bar permanently and unalterably any road to reconciliation so long as Tito and his entourage remained in power. It did not enter their minds that, much as they would be attacked, their whole record of revolutionary endeavor, their services to the cause of Communism, and, indeed, their past as resolute opponents of the German invader would be equated with the blackest treason by the Soviet and satellite press and radio.

It must have been difficult for them to envisage a situation in which their erstwhile colleagues and friends would openly call for the overthrow of the Tito regime and would foment rebellion and intrigue within the Communist Party of Yugoslavia. It cannot be emphasized too strongly to what great extent the Yugoslav Communists tended in 1948 and even afterwards to view the world from the Russian-made point of view. The West was for them the camp of reaction and imperialism. That the day would come when they would look to the West hopefully for protection against Soviet aggression must have been a thought which the loyal supporters of the regime, and indeed its leaders, could at most entertain secretly and keep to themselves in the months immediately following the break. The possibility of a split with Moscow must have been faced by the regime, at least in 1948, not as a political maneuver which would bring allies to Yugoslavia and concrete economic and military help, but as a step which, if it proved irrevocable, would pit this small and backward country against the enormous power of the U.S.S.R. and its satellites with no chance of help from the outside world. How, then, could the leaders of the Communist

Party of Yugoslavia face unafraid the prospect of challenging the overwhelming power of their erstwhile protectors? How could they enter the road of defiance when all of their instincts, experiences, and the logic of the situation pointed to the hopelessness of the unequal struggle? There are two answers to the question. One must be found in the nature of the situation as it arose in 1948. The other is revealed in the character and mentality of the Yugoslav leaders.

It became very clear in the process of the dispute, perhaps as early as the spring of 1948, that for the very top leadership of the Communist Party of Yugoslavia, and probably for its intermediate leadership, the question of resistance to Soviet pressure was a matter of life and death. In 1937 Tito himself had been hand-picked by Moscow to reorganize the Communist Party of Yugoslavia. The entire leadership of the C.P.Y., including the Secretary-General, Milan Gorkich, was then purged and, it is not too much to assume, physically liquidated either in Russia or in Yugoslavia. Without doubt Tito and his more experienced lieutenants carried vivid memories of countless similar cases of Communist leaders who had in the past capitulated at Moscow's demand, gone to Russia to plead or to "explain," and then in the course of events found themselves either quietly "removed" or forced into obscurity and the bitter life of refugees and professional ex-Communists.

There has been up to now (December 1951) no attempt on the part of Tito and his group to identify themselves with the innumerable Communist leaders who in the thirties were liquidated as "Trotskyites" and "deviationists" of one variety or another, and in 1948 those unfortunates must still have been considered by the leaders of the Communist Party of Yugoslavia as traitors who had met their just deserts. But the self-protecting instinct of the Yugoslav officials must have warned them what would happen should they capitulate to the Russians, acknowledge their mistakes, and beg for forgiveness. When the dispute broke out in March 1948, the price the Russians would have exacted for a reconciliation would have included, at the very least, a change in the top leadership of Yugoslavia. Tito and his closest lieutenants, Rankovich, Djilas, and Kardelj, could expect to be deprived of effective control of the Party, the secret police, and the army, and to be replaced by Yugoslav Communists with the "international" viewpoint, led by Tito's bitterest rival within the Party, the former secretary of the Croatian Communist Party and head of the Planning Commission, Andrija Hebrang.

To be sure, the letters the Central Committee of the Communist Party of the Soviet Union addressed to the Yugoslavs in the spring of 1948 did not formally request a change in leadership of the Communist Party of Yugoslavia. But there is no doubt that had Tito acknowledged his errors and capitulated on the issues indicated by the Russians, he would have irrevocably lost his grip on the Party and encouraged the doubters and careerists within his organization to switch their allegiance to more promising prospects for eventual leadership.

The life of a successful Communist leader must be governed by two main motivations: he must believe in and follow implicitly, often with a great degree of idealism and naïveté, the Soviet Union and its leadership; at the same time, and without any inconsistency, he must prove his cunning by obtaining for himself a position sufficiently secure that any effort to dislodge him or to trip him (and no secretary-general of a Communist Party achieves his position without making mortal enemies who spare no effort to discredit him in the eyes of Moscow) would cause so much disruption and confusion that such action would appear uneconomical to his Soviet masters. In the past even such a position of relative invulnerability had not proved unassailable if attacked by a really determined Moscow. In the case of Yugoslavia, the Communist leader in question has also proved to be the undoubted master of the state, and therein lies the secret of Tito's success in defying the center of world Communism and of his determination in 1948 not to concede a point to the Russians. The slightest sign of weakness or indecision, after the Soviet attacks had become known, would have had an incalculable psychological effect upon the masses of Yugoslav Communists. The stand taken by the regime in 1948 was not primarily the result of an ideological disagreement or of nationalist resentment against the claims of a foreign power to have the decisive voice in Yugoslavia. It was the result, most immediately, of the realization of what a capitulation would mean. To capitulate, to concede, would have meant for the very top leaders, for Tito and his Politburo and "his" men within the Party hierarchy, almost certain physical extinction or exile, perhaps after a decent interval during which they would occupy various ministerial and Party positions of decreasing importance. For the Party and army leaders below the top level a shift in leadership to the pro-Russian faction would have meant a considerable purge, but they were, of course, in a much less exposed position. It is their loyalty to the regime and their affection for their wartime leader, both of which cannot be entirely explained by the efficiency of General Rankovich's secret police, which largely determined why, after the full implications of unaided struggle against the Soviet Union had become known in Yugoslavia, Tito and his group still remained in power and Andrija Hebrang and Sreten Zhujovich in jail.

The character of the leaders of the movement both at the highest level (the Politburo, federal ministers, and generals) and at the intermediate position (the Central Committee, ministers in the federal republics, higher officers, and so forth) furnishes yet another answer to the seeming ease with which the Yugoslavs picked up the challenge of a great world power. The sweep of a revolution almost invariably brings young men to the top. Tito's entourage during and immediately following the war contained a sprinkling of veteran "old Communists," but most of his followers were young people who had lived their formative years as Partisans under Tito's command. Their personal and political careers had been formed under the guidance of the Leader. Being young, they were perhaps especially susceptible to the emotional aspect of loyalty toward the man who had shared with them the danger of everyday struggle for liberation and Communism. They were also susceptible to the full bitterness of betrayed idealism and to wrath at the contemptuous and treacherous treatment which they felt they were receiving at the hand of the Russians. More important was the buoyant spirit of fanaticism and recklessness which, having carried them through the hardships of the underground in the old Yugoslavia and through their guerrilla war, was now acting against a "rational" appraisal of the chance Tito's Yugoslavia would have against Soviet Russia in a world which was likely to be hostile or suspicious but certainly not helpful to the weaker protagonist.

In many ways the group of people who became rulers of Yugoslavia in 1945 was unique. It consisted of men whose experience in politics was confined to agitation, guerrilla warfare, and Party congresses and conferences. Today, more than six years after the victory of Communism in Yugoslavia, one still reads of people in their late twenties, whose main claim to office lies in their record as Partisans, who have been appointed republican and even federal ministers—some of which positions require expert economic or administrative competence. Among the victorious elite of Yugoslavia in 1945 there were no Krassins or Chicherins to help the revolution with their business experience and administrative skill. The Ministry of Finance was entrusted to Sreten Zhujovich, whose qualifications consisted of a long record as a Communist fighter and who had been Tito's deputy during the war. Andrija Hebrang, another veteran Communist, who curiously enough became an enemy of Tito in the 1948 crisis, was for a while in charge of economic planning and in effect the economic boss of the country. Various industrial ministries were distributed to high Party officials who had distinguished themselves in the war but who were entirely innocent of administrative or economic experience. It is no wonder that economic planning and administration by the new regime, in a country economically backward and deficient in trained technical personnel, was soon bound to sink the economy of the state into a morass of confusion and inefficiency. The "planning" consisted primarily of doctrinaire measures taking no account of the actual economic potentialities of Yugoslavia. But the same naïve if touching spirit which persuaded the new masters of Yugoslavia in 1945 that their country was going to have heavy industry right away, since every socialist country must have heavy industry, and which made them refute every practical objection by copious quotations from Stalin's speeches, also inspired them with gallant unrealism concerning their position and their chances of economic and political survival even if totally isolated.

The same spirit is very much in evidence if we take the story of the attitude of Tito's regime toward the world from the beginning of the movement to about the middle of 1950. Mention has already been made of the utter and really tragicomic inability of Tito and his entourage during the war to view their own struggle and their own significance from the larger perspective of a world war. Tito's inability to understand why Mr. Churchill had to be informed about his visit to Moscow, while he, Tito, was not told about the Prime Minister's meeting with President Roosevelt at Quebec, is not merely a humorous episode but a very characteristic and revealing one.[2] Like the early leaders of the French Revolution and the more hotheaded Bolsheviks between 1917 and 1920, the Yugoslav Communists could not understand why, if their ideas were correct and invincible, the problem of their military and economic resources was to bar them from complete triumph and further expansion. And when Soviet Russia demonstrated her treachery, the immediate and natural instinct was to blame the attacks on Yugoslavia first upon the ignorance and then the wickedness of the ruling elite of the U.S.S.R., rather than upon the doctrine or the system of power inherent in world Communism.

In common with and even more characteristically than their Bolshevik prototypes after the November Revolution, the Yugoslav leaders were at first woefully unequipped to deal with foreign affairs. Most of the older generation, including Tito himself and a handful of people like Pijade and Zhujovich, had been professional Communist agents for most of their adult lives, alternating between jails and clandestine activities; their contacts abroad had consisted in participation in secret Communist conferences in Vienna or Prague, visits to Russia, and occasional stints of organizational or military work, such as during the Spanish Civil War. The very fact that in 1941 they were leaders in the much-purged Communist Party of Yugoslavia is sufficient testimony that they had never had the time or occasion to think independently about the Comintern's appraisal of the capitalist world or about the official Communist image of the Fatherland of Socialism. Their personal contacts with the Allied missions to the Partisans during the war did not affect the essence of their viewpoint about the capitalist West, though, as previously noted, their dealings with Russia demonstrated some unknown and unexpected features of Soviet policy. It appears, however, that Tito's interview with Churchill, during which he sullenly discounted any intention of communizing Yugoslavia by force,[3] and other similar encounters had no more meaning in changing or affecting the Communist viewpoint than did those wartime

[2] Fitzroy Maclean, *Escape to Adventure* (New York, 1950), p. 411.
[3] See Clissold, *Whirlwind*, pp. 194ff.

libations between Western statesmen and generals and their Russian counterparts on which so much was banked by sober observers and perspicacious commentators in the West.

The younger generation of Communist leaders, men who in their twenties and thirties had been Partisan generals and who following the victory took over the most important state positions, were, owing to their background and temperament, hardly capable of improving upon their elders' knowledge of the outside world. Most of them had been Communists since their teens. Socially they were a motley crowd. Alexander Rankovich, the rather fearsome Minister of the Interior and head of the secret police, had been a tailor before the war. There is, at the same time, a fair number of Yugoslav Communists whose origins lay in the ruling and professional classes of prewar Yugoslavia. Kocha Popovich, who after the war become the chief of staff, came from a millionaire's family. The father of Boris Kidrich, who in January 1948 succeeded Andrija Hebrang as the head of the Planning Commission, had been rector of the University of Ljubljana. But this diversity of backgrounds could not diminish the common element of Communist fanaticism which made its disciples view the world through the narrow lenses of Communist propaganda and which, combined with their equally intense emotion for their leader, made them support Tito in 1948 in defiance of the U.S.S.R. This fanaticism was still and paradoxically combined with distrust and hatred of the Western powers.

It is thus not difficult to see that the paradoxes and contradictions in Yugoslav foreign policy during and after the crisis of 1948 must be traced mainly to the background and character of the Communist leaders of Yugoslavia. The intervening years have taught the Tito regime a great deal. They have transformed a group of rather narrow-minded people, whose main motivations lay in their Communist ideology and the drive for power expressed in nationalism and expansion, into a group of sophisticated politicians who are learning rapidly how to look at and cope with the world on their own, and who can set their previous naïvetés, but not yet their beliefs, in a historical perspective. But it is wrong to attribute to the Tito regime of 1948 the experience and sophistication it possesses in 1951. It is well to realize that they rushed—or rather were thrown—into the conflict with the U.S.S.R. with but a very imperfect idea of what their defiance would imply, though they did have a shrewd notion of what would be the result of a capitulation.

The whole complex of events and personalities surrounding Tito's regime up to and through 1948 helps to explain why the first Soviet attempt to interfere with the personnel of the Yugoslav government consisted in the demand that two diplomatic officials, Velebit and Leontich, be dismissed as traitors. The two officials were persons of no political importance, but they represented, as we shall see, something very rare in the Yugoslav government of 1947 and 1948: they were men with some knowledge and understanding of the West, men who could at least begin to interpret the outside world to their masters. The presence of such people in Tito's entourage was, from the Russian point of view, extremely undesirable; hence the U.S.S.R. demanded their dismissal as "spies"— a flexible word in the Soviet vocabulary, including, in addition to its usual meaning, persons with the ability to see more than one point of view.

The crisis itself when it reached the breaking point in the summer of 1948, and when it was publicized in both Moscow and Belgrade, caught the world unaware. It had been possible to speculate, at least from January 1948 on, that something was wrong in the relations between Yugoslavia and the U.S.S.R., but it was impossible to conclude without complete knowledge of the background and personalities involved that the world would be treated to a full-scale dispute and then lasting hostility between Soviet Russia and her most prominent pupil among the the Communist Parties of Europe. It would have been easier to assume that the Polish Communists with their national grievances or the Czechs with their "Western" background would have been the first and most serious offenders against Soviet imperialism. Actually, any man who, prior to January 1948, would have predicted a break between Tito and Stalin would be entitled today to be honored as a prophet with occult powers of predicting the future but certainly not as an expert basing his prognosis upon factual evidence. We have explored here the long sequence of events which had tended to force the Yugoslav leaders and their Russian masters apart and which had slowly undermined the Yugoslavs' original boundless confidence in and admiration for Moscow. Yet, were the Yugoslav grievances more substantial than those which the Poles could raise against the U.S.S.R.? Couldn't every satellite, every Communist-sponsored government in Eastern Europe, duplicate and surpass the story Tito was to offer later of Soviet duplicity, espionage, and attempted economic exploitation? Didn't Soviet Russia manifest its belief in Tito's loyalty by withdrawing Soviet troops from Yugoslavia right after the end of hostilities? [4] That the juxtaposition of events would crystallize in a crisis could not be known before January 1948 for the simple reason that the main actors in the crisis could not conceivably foresee their future course of action. By January, however, things began to happen with fateful rapidity, and by March and April of that year the situation had gone the limit, though the world was not to know about it until two months later.[5]

More than three years have elapsed since the crisis shattered the solidarity of the Communist bloc and raised in the outside world a variety of hopeful expectations, some reasonable, others fantastic. Yet though the facts of the dispute have become much clearer, a mass of oversimplification and confusion still prevails about its origin and development. We cannot speak with assurance about many aspects of the Yugoslav crisis, but we know enough to identify its central issue and to determine the main factor which enabled Tito in 1948 to defy Stalin's Russia. The central issue was not collectivization, not the Serbo-Croat situation, not even nationalism in the sense in which it is used by many commentators. All those issues did play their part in the conflict, but they served as its embellishments, convenient talking and arguing points, and not as the central point of the dispute. The central point was: Who is to have political power in Yugoslavia? The Russians were not interested, primarily, in what the rulers of Yugoslavia were doing

---

[4] Soviet actions in this respect are often quoted as an instance of Tito's early "nationalism," which supposedly led him to demand the withdrawal. It is probably true that the Russians withdrew partly in order to soothe the suspicions of their allies. But it is not too much to state that the withdrawal would not have taken place with such rapidity had they not been satisfied that Tito was completely reliable and that he no longer needed their help to consolidate his power.

[5] Hamilton Fish Armstrong mentions as a great coup of the American Embassy in Belgrade that they predicted the break on June 18 (*Tito and Goliath* [New York, 1951], p. 88).

with their absolute power, whether they were collectivizing rapidly or slowly, whether they were pursuing a pro- or anti- Great Serbia policy, whether the Communist Party of Yugoslavia was run according to its statute or not. By 1948 the Russians' main if not only interest was to replace Tito and the elite surrounding him by their own men. This is not to say that the ideological and political charges preferred against Tito by the Central Committee of the Communist Party of the U.S.S.R. were entirely fabricated and insincere. But they came as a superstructure; they represented a rationalization, probably sincere, of the original and most important belief that Tito was a traitor since, more because of his position than by his choice, he could not be a pliable instrument in the hands of Moscow.

The source both of Tito's strength and of his annoying effect upon the Russians was his position as undoubted dictator of a Party which was the sole master of Yugoslavia in 1948. The Russians found the situation in Yugoslavia intolerable: they could not exercise enough leverage within the C.P.Y. to have their wishes carried out without negotiation; indeed, the Yugoslav Communists seemed able to rule their country with an iron hand, quite free from the pervasive power of the Soviet Union. It was imperative that Tito agree to relinquish the effective instruments of his control—the secret police, the Party organization, and the army—to those who took their orders directly from Moscow. If he agreed, he would be permitted to stay in his elevated position as Premier and Secretary-General of the Party a little while longer, stripped of his powers, of course, and a figurehead rather than a dictator. If he didn't agree, Moscow decided, he had to go right away.

The nucleus of political power in Yugoslavia in 1948 consisted of relatively few men. The Politburo of the Party contained in the spring of 1948, and so far as is known still contains today, the following officers in addition to Tito: the two secretaries of the Central Committee, Alexander Rankovich (also Minister of the Interior and head of the security police) and Milovan Djilas (also Minister of Propaganda); Mosha Pijade; Blagoje Neshkovich, Premier of Serbia; Edward Kardelj, Minister of Foreign Affairs and Deputy Prime Minister; Boris Kidrich, chairman of the State Planning Commission; Ivan Goshnjak, now Deputy Minister of War; and Franz Leskoshek, Minister of Heavy Industry. Nationally, the Politburo has been admirably balanced, containing two Croats, three Serbs, three Slovenes, and one Montenegrin (Djilas). Politically, it contains men who have been long-time friends and collaborators of Tito. The friendship between Tito and Mosha Pijade, for instance, extends back to the years the marshal spent in a Yugoslav jail before the war. And the young men of the Politburo, who were Partisan generals and officials during the war, have been literally "made" as political figures by Tito. In addition to these people, and probably equally important as members of the ruling elite of Yugoslavia, are various provincial Party and government bosses like Vladimir Bakarich, Prime Minister and Secretary-General of the Communist Party of Croatia; Lazar Kolishevski, who holds the same position in Macedonia; high army officials like Kocha Popovich, chief of staff of the Yugoslav army; and a handful of others. They have been, almost without exception, personally selected for their jobs by Tito; and they are linked to him by the strongest ties of self-interest and, in many cases, no doubt, of personal affection, for he is to them the man with whom most of them shared the dangers of war and conspiracy.

In January 1948 two events took place which mark the opening of the decisive phase of the conflict between Russia and the Communist Party of Yugoslavia. As we have seen, the Russians at that time vetoed the plan for the Balkan federation, which was the fondest and most ambitious aspiration of Tito's foreign policy. A few days previously Andrija Hebrang, until then in charge of the national economy as chairman of the State Planning Commission, had been demoted to an inferior ministerial post (the Ministry of Light Industry), his previous office going to Boris Kidrich. Hebrang deserves some attention, since he has been denounced by the regime with so much vehemence and hatred that there is little doubt that he was the pivot of Soviet plans to undermine Tito within his Party, just as General Arso Jovanovich was entrusted with the same role in the Yugoslav army. Before 1941 Hebrang had been an important figure in Yugoslav Communism. In July 1948 Tito had the following to say about Hebrang's wartime role:

A rather unhealthy situation was created in Croatia after the return of Hebrang from the concentration camp when he became Secretary of the Central Committee of the Communist Party of Croatia. Hebrang not only had an incorrect attitude toward the other leading comrades in the Central Committee but also took an incorrect stand toward the Serbs in Croatia . . . Here is what Comrade Kardelj, who was at that time visiting various places in Croatia, wrote to the Central Committee [of the Yugoslav Party]: "In the first place, things will not go well in Croatia as long as Andrija Hebrang is secretary of the Central Committee of the Communist Party of Croatia, that is, as long as he is there at all. His mentality and his character are such that they represent a constant tendency toward the weakening of Croatia's connection with Yugoslavia." . . . These and other mistakes came to the fore in Croatia and created an unhealthy atmosphere in the Party there, so that the Central Committee of the Communist Party of Yugoslavia decided to displace Hebrang and to remove him from Croatia altogether.[6]

Hebrang was further described with less detail but more vigor, by Alexander Rankovich at the Fifth Congress as "a hypocrite, harmful element, traitor, and tool of the class enemy."[7] Subsequently, Tito and his lieutenants more than once declared that all during the war Andrija Hebrang had been a paid agent of the Gestapo, the ultimate proof of his guilt being his release from the concentration camp.[8] If the Yugoslav leaders are truthful, then they entrusted, following the war, the most important economic post in the country to a man whom they knew to be a "fractionalist" and "deviationist" if not a traitor. But, whatever the facts of Hebrang's administration of the Communist Party of Croatia, he must have been a leader of considerable following in the Party, or a protégé of the Russians, or both, if he, not a "Tito's man," was given a position of such importance. Even in January 1948 he was not yet eliminated, but only "transferred." Andrija Hebrang must have gone to his new office with the same uneasy feeling that H. G. Yagoda undoubtedly experienced upon his transfer from the N.K.V.D. to the Ministry of Posts during the great purge in Russia in the thirties, and that Kostov, Rajk, and Gomulka were soon to share under similar conditions in their countries when their new lesser ministerial and official positions were but the first steps on the road to complete disgrace and arrest.

The progress of the Yugoslav Party purge can be traced to some extent from the statement issued by Sreten Zhujovich, the other

[6] Tito, *Political Report of the Central Committee*, p. 103.
[7] Rankovich, *Report . . . on the Organizational Work of the C.P.Y.*, p. 86.
[8] See Chapter 1, above.

member of the Central Committee purged in the spring of 1948. Zhujovich's case is markedly different from that of Hebrang. His treatment by the regime would warrant a supposition that he was considered more a dupe of the Russians than their full partner in the attempt to displace Tito. Unlike Hebrang, he was in Tito's entourage during the war. "Crni" Swarthy—which was his sobriquet during the war—appears often in Stephen Clissold's book *Whirlwind* as a resourceful Partisan leader. He was in fact Tito's deputy commander in chief and heir apparent during the Partisan days. A veteran Communist who had fought in the Spanish Civil War, Zhujovich, despite his position, obviously did not belong to the inner circle around Tito. Following the liberation, Zhujovich became Minister of Finance, but, as in the case of Andrija Hebrang and Arso Jovanovich, his high official position was not matched by a correspondingly high Party post. It must have been a galling situation for a man, once second in command of Yugoslav Communism, to be outranked by a group of much younger men, and so Sreten Zhujovich took to frequenting the Soviet Embassy in Belgrade.

Two and a half years after his arrest, Sreten Zhujovich was "rehabilitated" and released from prison. He had never been attacked by the regime with a vehemence equal to that leveled against Andrija Hebrang. Although Zhujovich was characterized by Rankovich at the Fifth Party Congress as an "obdurate fractionalist and hypocrite, slanderer and enemy of our Party and country," [9] compared with what was said about Hebrang at the same Congress, this castigation sounds almost complimentary. The charge of actual treason and complicity with the Ustashis and Germans, which has constantly been made against Hebrang, has never been preferred against Zhujovich. His release and recantation in the fall of 1950 was an astute move on the part of Tito's regime and one likely to prevent or minimize potential dissatisfaction among the old-line Serbian Communists, who remain the least reliable element in the Communist Party of Yugoslavia.[10] Zhujovich's recantation, as printed in *Borba*[11] and repeated in part in his interview with foreign and domestic correspondents,[12] throws considerable light on the events

[9] Rankovich, *Report . . . on the Organizational Work of the C.P.Y.*, p. 87.
[10] See, for example, pp. 227–228.
[11] November 25, 1950.
[12] See *Borba*, December 2, 1950.

of the spring of 1948 and the general background of the Soviet-Yugoslav dispute, though some of its points have to be treated with extreme caution.

At the time of the crisis, and until his prison education and meditation convinced him otherwise, Zhujovich's main beliefs had been as follows: Yugoslavia would become eventually a part of the Soviet Union, and in the meantime the Communist Party of Yugoslavia had to prove worthy of its ultimate merger with the Russian Communist Party. Likewise, there could be no question about the correctness of the views and interpretations expounded by the Communist Party of the U.S.S.R., because this Party and its leader were the living embodiments of Marxism-Leninism. There is no reason to question this avowal of faith by Zhujovich, but it is important to add that the whole history of the Yugoslav Party is an incontrovertible testimony to the fact that Zhujovich's beliefs were shared by the Party hierarchy until it dawned upon them that in the process of "becoming worthy" of the merger with the Union of Soviet Socialist Republics their own positions and eventually their own necks would have to be sacrificed; and until it dawned upon them that their own national interests and pride were being sacrificed not to the ideal of world Communism, to which they were ready to consent grudgingly, but to the pure power interest of Soviet Russia. Zhujovich's grievances against his colleagues, and perhaps his Communism, which was of a longer standing than theirs and not as emotionally colored by the attachment to their leader and wartime commander, prevented him from following them into what was to be called, with but partial truth, "national Communism."

Zhujovich's recital confirms the assertion made by the Yugoslavs (and previously admitted by the Russians) that between 1945, when he met Molotov at San Francisco, and until and through March 1948 he acted as an agent of the U.S.S.R. within the Central Committee of the C.P.Y., reporting to the Russians faithfully, usually through Lavrentiev, their ambassador in Belgrade.[13]

On March 1, 1948, the Central Committee of the Communist

---

[13] The Russians admitted in a letter from the Central Committee of the C.P.S.U. that Zhujovich did communicate with their ambassador, Lavrentiev (see *The Soviet-Yugoslav Dispute*, p. 49).

Party of Yugoslavia held a meeting. It appears almost certain from Zhujovich's somewhat confused narrative that the whole issue of Russo-Yugoslav relations came up for discussion. Andrija Hebrang was thrown out of the Central Committee.[14] According to Zhujovich's recantation, he, already a marked man, ran immediately after the session to the Soviet ambassador and told him all about it, offering to talk with Tito or Kardelj in order to try to repair the growing breach between the Russians and Yugoslavs. If this is true, then the gallant Partisan and revolutionary leader exhibited himself as a man of limited intelligence; though skilled in conspiracy and warfare, he was yet unable to comprehend the full implications of the situation.[15]

Zhujovich's turn came in April, at the plenum of the Central Committee which preceded the definitive defiance of the U.S.S.R. contained in a letter of April 13, 1948, from Tito and Kardelj to Stalin and Molotov.[16] Zhujovich's activities had, of course, been well known before, and his assiduity in attending the Soviet Embassy had aroused some rather ominous comments from Djilas. One important and most probable detail is revealed by Zhujovich in connection with the April plenum: the correspondence which had been going on between the "Central Committees" of the Communist Parties of Yugoslavia and Russia was in fact unknown to the members of the Central Committee of the Communist Party of Yugoslavia; Zhujovich had learned about it only from Lavrentiev. The only men who were supposed to know what really was happening were members of the Yugoslav Politburo.[17] It was at the April session that Zhujovich was expelled, his arrest following a few days later; thus were ended once and for all his conversations with Lavrentiev and his attendance at the movies at the Russian Embassy.

In her book, *Revolution in Eastern Europe*,[18] Miss Doreen Warriner makes a valiant argument for her thesis that the basis of He-

[14] Zhujovich's statement to *Borba*, November 25, 1950.

[15] Our credulity is still more strained when we are told that Lavrentiev had to remind Zhujovich not to tell anybody about his conversations with him (*ibid.*).

[16] *The Soviet-Yugoslav Dispute*, pp. 18ff.

[17] There is no reason to doubt the authenticity of this detail since it, in fact, reflects adversely upon the Yugoslav leaders and could not have been interpolated by them into the confession.

[18] London, 1950.

brang's and Zhujovich's disgrace is to be found in their realism on matters of economic policy and their opposition to "romantic planning" sponsored by Tito's group. Miss Warriner finds the source of the Soviet-Yugoslav dispute in this disagreement and in the accompanying argument between Hebrang and Tito about collectivization.[19] This argument would reduce the whole dispute to an economic issue, consisting basically in Tito's unwillingness to achieve full socialism and at the same time in his adventurous and ultra-left industrial policy. Even when so stated the argument is clearly inconsistent; and when the facts are examined it becomes crystal clear that no other satellite country, except perhaps Bulgaria, attempted to reach socialism between 1945 and 1949 as fast and as unrealistically as did Tito's Yugoslavia. Even in collectivization Yugoslavia's achievement, as we shall see, was second only to Bulgaria and greatly surpassed the feeble efforts made in this direction by the Polish, Czechoslovak, or Hungarian Communists.

Now what of the "economic realism" ascribed to Hebrang and Zhujovich and its meaning as the basis of the inter-Party quarrel? All of the evidence on that score is provided by the present leaders of Yugoslavia themselves. Kidrich's economic report at the Fifth Party Congress is one long philippic against the two "deviationists."[20] Why? Because in their 1948 frame of mind, which was still that of fanatical Communism, the Yugoslav leaders could not find anything which would be more discrediting to their imprisoned rivals and more likely to destroy their prestige among the rank and

[19] "Hebrang was one of the few surviving pre-1941 Communist leaders, the only powerful mind in the government; Zhujovich had been a leading partisan General. They were the rationalists . . . When the Cominform decision to undertake collectivization was reached, it was clear to Tito that Hebrang and Zhujovich would get support from the other Communist parties, and their opposition then became a challenge to Tito's own power" (*Revolution in Eastern Europe*, p. 53).

[20] For example: "Like the pernicious attitude of all enemies of our people, their attitude first makes its appearance in the form of profound disbelief. They did not believe either in the economic strength of our country or in the creative strength of our working class and working people, or in the possibilities of the construction of socialism in our country . . . Hebrang and Zhujovich were unable to prove with arguments the helplessness of our economic forces and the lack of possibilities for the construction of socialism in our country . . . For this reason, as the result of iron logic which applies to all enemies of the people, they began to sabotage the economic measures of our Party" (Kidrich, *On the Construction of Socialist Economy*, pp. 46 and 47–48).

file of the Yugoslav Communists than the charge that the two men had been dubious of the possibility of rapid transformation of Yugoslavia into an industrial and socialist country. There is no doubt that Hebrang and Zhujovich had been charged with an impossible task, and there is no doubt that there had been serious arguments about Yugoslavia's economic course. But the economic issue has throughout been subordinate to the political one, and it is because of the latter that Hebrang and Zhujovich found themselves in their predicament.

With the arrest of Hebrang and Zhujovich, and with the decisions announced at the Party conferences of March and April 1948, Tito and his group step into the pages of history in a new character. The one-time servants of the Comintern and Soviet Russia had chosen the course of defiance. This course in the spring and summer of 1948 did not yet mean with absolute certainty a complete rupture with the Soviet Union. But the possibility of such a contingency must have entered the minds of the Yugoslav leaders. If the letters which were exchanged between the two Central Committees—that of the C.P.S.U. and that of the Yugoslav Party— are analyzed, it becomes apparent that neither side could quite believe in the completeness and irreversibility of the breach. The Yugoslavs seemed to cling tenaciously to the hope that somehow the Russians—somebody in Russia—would "understand" them. At one point they almost plead for someone in the Russian Central Committee to come down to Yugoslavia to see with his own eyes how they had been maligned and what an exemplary Stalinist Party they are. On the Russian side, there is perhaps discernible an element of wishful thinking: once Soviet displeasure had been announced publicly, the Yugoslavs would without doubt fall to their knees and eliminate the Evil Four—Tito, Djilas, Kardelj, and Rankovich—who had been causing all the trouble.

As examples of the epistolary art, the letters are not remarkable. What is most noticeable about their form is the incredible contempt and harshness with which the Central Committee of the Communist Party of Russia speaks to the people who are rulers of a supposedly independent country and, at the time of the writing, still their ideological brothers. In the letters of the Central Committee of the Communist Party of Yugoslavia one looks in vain for any assertion that what goes on in Yugoslavia is their business but not the Russians'. Tito and Kardelj explain their position with determination but not without a note of reverence and humility toward their Russian colleagues. There may have been a note of deliberation in the Yugoslavs' modesty; they were to publish most of the correspondence, and the contrast the letters present is very telling: the irritated and brutal tone of the Russian Communists grates harshly against the air of injured innocence and quiet dignity with which Tito and Kardelj attempt to refute the charges. But it is equally likely that the Yugoslavs, despite their determination, still could not shake off the feeling of awe and respect when they addressed themselves to their erstwhile idols and highest superiors, Stalin and Molotov.

When we inquire who were the real parties to the correspondence, we run into a slightly Chestertonian situation of mystery and fiction. Officially, the letters were exchanged between the Central Committee of the Communist Party of Yugoslavia and that of Soviet Russia. Nobody knows whether or when the Central Committee of the Communist Party of the Soviet Union has met in recent years. Insofar as the Yugoslavs are concerned, Sreten Zhujovich's confession, which was released in November 1950 with an official imprimatur of the regime, shows clearly that he did not know of the Russian letter of March 27, 1948, until it was shown to him by the Russian ambassador early in April, and consequently that he probably did not know about the Yugoslav letters of March 18, which has never been published, and March 20, which, though signed by Tito, carried the heading: "Central Committee of Communist Party of Yugoslavia to Central Committee of Communist Party of Soviet Union." And Zhujovich was a member of the Central Committee until his expulsion in April.[21] It was only at the April plenum of the Yugoslav Central Committee that the correspondence was revealed. Zhujovich in performing his last spying job for the Soviet ambassador informed him that the Russian letter of March 27 was read at the April plenum, which surprised Lavrentiev a great deal.[21] In fact, the correspondence probably took

---

[21] See Zhujovich's statement in *Borba*, November 25, 1950, and *The Soviet-Yugoslav Dispute*, p. 9.
[22] See Zhujovich in *Borba*, November 25, 1950.

place between the two Politburos. The Russian letters are written with vigor and with a certain fondness for military and historical comparisons. One of them contains the striking statement, "In his time Trotsky also rendered revolutionary services."[23] It is unlikely that anyone but the highest authority in the Soviet Union would have dared to make such a pronouncement.

The crux of the dispute from the Soviet viewpoint in 1948, when it had not yet been "discovered" that Tito was an agent of the Gestapo and the imperialist powers, consisted in three classes of grievances. There was, first of all, the feeling that the Yugoslavs refused to divulge to the representatives of the Soviet Union economic and other information to which the Russians felt they were entitled. Connected with this complaint were the facts that Soviet experts and representatives in Yugoslavia were surrounded by spies and informers, and that the Yugoslav regime did not treat Soviet Russia deferentially but seemed to consider it a "bourgeois power" rather than the "friendly power which had liberated Yugoslavia from the German occupation."[24] That the Soviet experts, military specialists, and so forth merited the privilege of being maintained by a fellow socialist country at a great cost, and that they had the unquestioned right to go snooping around and attempting to subvert the regime, appeared to the Russians as the most natural thing in the world. The Soviet ambassador "not only has the right but is obliged from time to time to discuss with the Communists in Yugoslavia all questions which interest them."[25] The Russians also had the right to choose the officials they had to deal with in Yugoslavia. Thus Tito and Kardelj failed in their duty when they did not remove Vladimir Velebit, Deputy Minister of Foreign Affairs, despite Molotov's statement that Velebit was an English spy. The same was true of the Yugoslav ambassador in London, Leontich.[26]

The first and most obvious series of Russian grievances is far from being unimportant despite the petty character of the complaints. They disclose, in fact, the initial reason for Soviet dissatisfaction with Tito's regime, and those writers who have chosen to

[23] *The Soviet-Yugoslav Dispute*, p. 52.
[24] *Ibid.*, p. 35.
[25] *Ibid.*
[26] *Ibid.*, pp. 33–34. Both Velebit and Leontich were transferred to other positions in June 1948.

look much deeper for the "real" causes of the Soviet-Yugoslav crisis have unwittingly fallen into a trap of their own making. The Yugoslav regime in 1945 was more pro-Russian than any other Communist-dominated government in Eastern Europe. None of the complexities which the Russians encountered in strengthening their hold in Poland or Czechoslovakia seemed to exist in Yugoslavia. On all the major issues the Yugoslavs were behind them. But when it came to the small things—arranging a "joint" Russo-Yugoslav trading or industrial company, or getting rid of an official personally obnoxious to them—the Russians encountered difficulties. The difficulties were not due solely to the Yugoslavs' pride in their sovereignty. The Yugoslav leaders, hardened revolutionary fighters and conspirators that they were, were remarkably innocent of the facts of life when it came to international politics and economics.[27] When the issue was an economic deal with Russia which would put them at a disadvantage, or when they were asked to destroy a deserving official because the Russians insisted upon it, the Yugoslavs were likely to ask themselves: "But what does it have to do with Marxism or our love for the Soviet Union?" Their innocence, as is often the case, was interpreted by the Russians as a sign of perversion, and it was soon easy for them to feel that Tito must be engaged in some horrendous anti-Russian intrigues.

One specific Russian charge requires some comment. Vladimir (Vlatko) Velebit had been continually accused by them of being an English spy. The Yugoslavs finally did remove Velebit from the Ministry of Foreign Affairs, but they kept asking—an unheard-of thing—for definite proofs of Velebit's guilt. The answer they got was characteristic: "Why so much consideration for an English spy, who at the same time is so uncompromisingly hostile toward the Soviet Union?"[28] Velebit was a man of no political consequence in Yugoslavia. He was, however, in 1948, one of the very few men in Tito's entourage who seems to have known and understood the West. A lawyer by profession, he had during the war performed a variety of confidential and diplomatic missions for the Partisans.[29]

[27] Or, rather, they were doctrinaire Communists to such an extent that their native shrewdness was in those matters obscured by their fanaticism.

[28] *The Soviet-Yugoslav Dispute*, p. 34.

[29] See Clissold, *Whirlwind*, pp. 151 and 181, and Maclean, *Escape to Adventure*, pp. 342 and 346.

Such a man was, from the Russian point of view, most undesirable as an official of the Yugoslav government. He had visited London during the war and had made a good impression on the British. That was his treason, and no further proof was required.

In a letter of May 4, 1948, the Central Committee of the Communist Party of the Soviet Union undertook another line of attack upon the Yugoslavs. This line has been most emphasized by those analysts who believe that there must be something deeper in the dispute than the question of political power and personalities— that there must be an "ideological" explanation. The letter, written under the heading, "On the incorrect political line of the Politburo of the C.C. of the C.P.Y. in regard to the class struggle in Yugoslavia," [30] proceeds to castigate social policies of Tito's Yugoslavia. The issue turns largely on the extent and character of the collectivization drive in Yugoslavia and its real or feigned meaning as the reason for Russia's displeasure with Tito. A historian or social scientist abhors very often a simple solution, and it has been easy for many even non-Communist commentators and writers on the Yugoslav problem to envisage Soviet Russia—the guardian of Communist morality and ideology—turning its solicitous gaze upon Yugoslavia where "the capitalist elements are increasing in the cities and the villages." [31] and demanding a radical change in the policy of the regime. What are the facts?

The Russian charge was summarized in the communiqué of the Cominform of June 28, 1948, which stated that in Yugoslavia, where "individual peasant farming predominates . . . [where] the land is not nationalized, where there is private property in land and where land can be bought or sold, where much of the land is concentrated in the hands of the kulaks . . . there could be no question of correct Marxist policies being applied." [32] But the question obviously cannot be judged in absolute terms; it must be considered from two separate angles. First, was the extent and nature of collectivization considered by the Russians as the main criterion of their satellites' loyalty and Marxist "correctness" in the period from 1945 to 1948? And, secondly, was Yugoslavia's stand on col-

[30] *The Soviet-Yugoslav Dispute*, pp. 41–43.
[31] *Ibid.*, p. 41.
[32] *Ibid.*, p. 63.

lectivization less Marxist than that of the other satellites? The answer to the first question must be emphatically in the negative. As we have already seen, Soviet Russia's interest during the years from 1945 to 1948 consisted in building up strong pro-Soviet regimes in the satellite countries, governments which were allowed and encouraged to develop considerable flexibility in their social policies in order not to alienate the support of the peasants and lower middle classes. The Russians, with the terrible experience of their enforced collectivization of the early thirties in mind, were not likely to insist, prior to the crisis of 1948, on a rigorous policy of collectivization in their satellites, for such a course would have threatened their economic recovery and the progress of political consolidation by the Communists.

As to the second question, there is ample ground to believe that the rulers of Yugoslavia, out of their Communist fanaticism and economic naïveté, before 1948 pursued a faster pace in the collectivization of agriculture than any other country in the satellite area except, perhaps, Bulgaria, where the same characteristics motivated its Communist government. Doreen Warriner, who is far from friendly toward Tito's regime, admits that the pace of collectivization has been faster in Yugoslavia than elsewhere.[33] Miss Warriner's qualification that the collectives are not true ones (that is, not analogous to the Russian *artel*), but simply producer coöperatives somewhat like the Russian *toz*, echoes a similar point made by the Cominform press. But this objection, as a basis of criticizing Tito for betraying the principles of practical Communism, is effectively refuted by Miss Warriner herself when, in speaking approvingly of collectivization among the satellites (which was begun in earnest largely as an aftermath of the Tito affair), she writes: "To win over as many as possible of the middle peasants for collective farming, a form of cooperative organisation has been chosen which is not a full collective, but a transitional form, known as the labour production cooperative."[34] It is very difficult to see a genuine reason in the Cominform's accusation of Tito's agricultural policy as antirevolu-

[33] "By August 1949, the Government claimed that there were 4000 of these [producer coöperatives], including twenty percent of the peasantry, which if true, means there are more collectives in Yugoslavia than in any other East European country" (Warriner, *Revolution in Eastern Europe*, p. 56).
[34] *Ibid.*, p. 152.

tionary and helpful to the growth of capitalism in the villages, when he in effect had been doing before 1948 what most of his accusers were ready to undertake, and on a less ambitious scale (largely because they viewed more realistically the economic and social aspects of collectivization), only after 1948. The whole line of allegations that the Soviet offensive against Tito's Yugoslavia has been caused by the social and economic policy of the regime cannot confront the facts of the case.[35]

Has then the displeasure of Soviet Russia and the Cominform been incurred by the incautious character of Yugoslavia's economy and by the extra-leftist character of its economic laws? [36] It is very difficult to see how this criticism, which appears to be perfectly sensible, fits in with the accusation that the Yugoslav leaders have not gone far enough in socializing their country and in paying attention to Russia's advices. Tito and his group cannot be both lacking in the Marxist fervor and perpetuating capitalism and ruining the economy of their country through a variety of doctrinaire Marxist measures. The Cominform's criticism of Yugoslavia's economic plans brings out very clearly that the Yugoslav Communists have erred in their economic policy. Their errors found their source in the uncritical acceptance of the most naïve premises of Communism and could not, originally, figure one way or another as the basis of the Soviet-Yugoslav dispute.

It must not be thought, however, that the economic and social part of the Soviet accusation against Tito is insincere. As the tone of these accusations suggests, and as the sequence of events in the Cominform countries confirms, the Russians managed to convince themselves that Tito's reputed intransigence was not merely an act

[35] The extent of actual collectivization in Yugoslavia has been variously estimated. The regime claims that something near 40 per cent of the land has been collectivized; other estimates range from 20 to 30 per cent. See Irwin T. Sanders, "The Changing Status of the Peasant in Eastern Europe," *Annals of the American Academy of Political and Social Science*, September 1950, especially pp. 86–87; and Armstrong, *Tito and Goliath*, p. 120.

[36] "Recently, even after the Central Committee of the C.P.S.U.(b) and fraternal parties had criticized the mistakes of the Yugoslav leaders, the latter tried to bring in a number of new leftist laws. They hastily decreed the nationalization of medium industry and trade, though the basis for this is completely unprepared" (the Cominform communiqué, quoted in *The Soviet-Yugoslav Dispute*, p. 66).

of personal treachery but that it was deeply connected with a basic anti-Marxist tendency of his social and economic policy. Perhaps the most frightening and significant feature of the correspondence is that it reveals the ease with which doctrinal considerations can often color and distort the analysis of a political situation. Russian Communism stands revealed as being influenced by the habits of thought and speech, if not properly speaking the ideology, of its creed.

"We are disturbed by the present condition of the C.P.Y."[37] Here is the third line of attack pursued by the Russians against the Tito regime. The Yugoslav Communist Party is run dictatorially. New members for its Central Committee are coöpted instead of being elected. The Party itself is content to remain hidden behind the façade of the People's Front. Its lack of intra-Party democracy is underlined by the fact that one of the secretaries of the Central Committee (Alexander Rankovich) is not only the Minister of State Security but also the Personnel Secretary of the Party.[38] In short, according to the Russian charge, the Party, instead of being a democratic organization run by the rank and file of its membership, is a closed private preserve of a few leaders who constitute its Politburo and is in fact run dictatorially by its Big Four: Tito, Kardelj, Djilas, and Rankovich. That such a charge could be raised by the leaders of a Party which, at the time the accusations were being presented, had not had a Party Congress for nine years, whose highest officials had been purged at the orders of a dictator and in a manner which makes the purging of Hebrang and Zhujovich mild by comparison, and whose history for the past twenty years had been one long record of complete denial of its basic organizational tenets, is testimony to the extent to which self-indoctrination and absolute power may lead in the destruction of all sense of proportion and capacity for introspection. The Communist Party of Yugoslavia was thus accused of having imitated successfully the main organizational and personal features of the Communist Party of the Soviet Union.

There must have been many reasons why the Russians, even before 1948, were disturbed about the situation in the C.P.Y. It was

[37] *Ibid.*, p. 15.
[38] *Ibid.*, pp. 15–16.

a Party which exhibited all the characteristics that make its successful manipulation from the outside quite difficult. The Russians
prefer a situation in which no single leader or group of leaders, no
matter how great their attachment to the Soviet Union and Communist fanaticism, are in the position of complete authority. Tito's
position was different from that of Gomulka in Poland, or Gheorgiu-
Dej in Rumania, or even Rakosi in Hungary, in that he was the
undoubted master of both the state and the Party. Unlike Rakosi or
Dimitrov, he was furthermore a man covered with a panoply of
military honors, the national hero to many of his countrymen,
and, alone among the Communist Party leaders of Eastern Europe,
in complete command of his army. Such a combination of attributes
would have made even the most humble and devoted servant of
Communism a very difficult man to deal with, and the dictator's
personality is not marked by an excess of humility. It is not difficult to perceive in the letter of the Russian Central Committee a note
of scorn and exasperation; the Russians had not really accustomed
themselves to the idea that Tito was no longer a rather inferior agent
of the Comintern and that the "Comrade Walter" who used to report dutifully to the Comintern was now the leader of his state and
a man to be argued with.

The solidarity of the high command of the C.P.Y. must have
also worried the Russians right from the beginning. Early in 1945
Milovan Djilas made some disparaging remarks about the behavior
of the Russian troops in Yugoslavia, contrasting unfavorably some
actions of the Soviet officers with the behavior of the British officers attached to the Partisans. Djilas' remarks were made at a
session of the Central Committee of the C.P.Y., yet they became
known immediately to the Russians and provoked a telegram from
Stalin to Tito.[39] Djilas personally apologized to Stalin, but the fact
that he was allowed by Tito to remain in a position of high importance and power was an unpleasant lesson to the Russians. That
the Minister of Propaganda was, until the Soviet-Yugoslav break.
the person most renowned in Tito's entourage for his violent anti-
West tendencies and his fanatical Communism was evidently of
little consequence in comparison with his one outburst of bad temper. He became, in fact, a marked man to the Russians, and three

[39] *Ibid.,* pp. 38–40.

years afterward they were to see in that rather trifling incident a significant proof of the anti-Soviet tendency of the regime. But Djilas' case is a fine example of the working of the despotic mind, which balances the lifetime of devoted service against one incautious remark.

Within the Communist Party of Yugoslavia the Russians encountered, in brief, a strong and united nucleus of leadership. These leaders had stood the test of the postwar years, and official honors had been heaped upon them. Taught by their own Party history, the Russian Communists may well have expected dissension to arise within the central organs of the Yugoslav Party and state. Yet aside from Hebrang and Zhujovich, the Russians obviously failed to recruit any Communist leaders of the first rank in Yugoslavia. The ideological tie which bound together the Yugoslav hierarchy was reinforced by an extraordinary feeling of solidarity, born of the war, and a most common-sense notion of self-interest. The Russian Communist Party after the Bolshevik Revolution had had as its elite a group of "prima donnas," people who intellectually and temperamentally had often very little in common, and who had been harnessed to the common task only through the extraordinary personality of Lenin. To some extent the same situation was reproduced after World War II in Eastern Europe, where the Communist Parties found among their leaders people of the most diverse backgrounds and temperaments: old revolutionaries and underground fighters confronted the intellectual type of Communist who had spent his war years in Moscow. It was only in Yugoslavia that the hard core of leadership consisted of a veritable "band of brothers" who, having survived the common danger, were now securing their hold upon the country with the same mixture of implacable fanaticism, naïveté, and cunning which had characterized them during the war.

Against that background the Soviet agents were busily employed, but with little success, in trying to subvert this or that general or Party official. It is perhaps a tribute to General Rankovich's secret police that the Soviet efforts were to yield such a meager result. It is also significant, and a rather unusual circumstance, that most of the wooing had to be done by the Soviet ambassador, since he was the only man who could meet Yugoslav ministers and high officials without arousing too much suspicion. This combination of the solidarity of the top leaders and the supervision of every official not within the charmed circle yields, of course, a great deal of credence to the Soviet assertion that the Yugoslav Party was not run democratically. The Central Committee of the Party had, at the time of the exchange of letters with Moscow, twenty-six members, a surprisingly small number for a Communist Party in power.[40] The Yugoslav Party had not held a Congress since the war, not, as a matter of fact, since 1928. In this, of course, it was in a sense following the example of the Communist Party of the Soviet Union, which has not held a Party Congress since 1939. All the important and key Party posts were held by handpicked nominees of Tito and his group.

It is interesting to note that in the three years which have intervened since the crisis several purges of "Cominformists" have taken the toll of a few federal and republican ministers and some generals and diplomatic officials; but no key Party official has been purged since Hebrang and Zhujovich. But if the Party was in 1948 (as it undoubtedly still is today) organized on the basis of very strict control by a few people, it does not follow, as the Russians fondly imagined in the spring of 1948, that an announcement of their displeasure would bring the whole edifice tumbling down. Their own one-time pupils and agents—the leaders of the C.P.Y.— had learned their lessons too well. In July 1948 the Communist Party of Yugoslavia finally held its Congress, and the regime, despite its ambiguous position, made the occasion a triumphant display of the solidarity of the Yugoslav Communists and of their affection for their leader.

The characteristic that has made the Communist Party of Yugoslavia strong, first as an instrument of revolutionary struggle and later as the means of holding on to power, is the same that has made it weak as a political party, in the proper sense of being qualified to discharge the tasks of administration and planning which must be performed in a modern state. That characteristic is its habit of secrecy and the conspiratorial psychology which pervaded the Party long after it had become the sole ruler of Yugoslavia. It has given the leaders of the C.P.Y. the feeling of solidarity, the feeling that there

[40] *Ibid.,* p. 24.

was nothing they could not accomplish by fighting for it, but it has also left them with a sense of political and economic romanticism which has been largely responsible for their administrative ineptness and political naïveté. An incidental product of the habit of secrecy is seen in the fact that between 1945 and 1948 the Party could not shake off the vestiges of its clandestine origin and activity. The tradition of anonymity of the Party's officials, which during the war baffled the Allied missions with the Partisans, was kept through and beyond the victory.[41] The Party preferred to hide behind the fiction of the People's Front, and until the Fifth Congress in July 1948 it was impossible to say with certainty who were the Party's officials or even its secretary-general. Likewise, until 1948, the Party was never referred to in the official Yugoslav documents.[42] The Russians were prompt to seize upon the Yugoslav Party's bashfulness and to proclaim it to be another aspect of the anti-Marxist and anti-Communist attitude of Tito and his clique.[43]

The exact reason for the Yugoslav policy of concealment of the Party before 1948 must still remain rather obscure. But it is most unlikely that the reason for it was the one alleged by the Russians: that the Yugoslavs were "hiding" their Communist Party because they were not genuine Marxists. The nature of the reforms they undertook in their country between 1945 and 1948 is in itself an excellent indication of whether the Yugoslav Communists were afraid to display their true character. It is laughable to accuse them of trying to appease their countrymen or the West by not raising the specter of Communism. They were not afraid to liquidate brutally the opposing elements in the country, whether in the

---

[41] See, for example, Clissold, *Whirlwind*, pp. 233–234.

[42] Jacob B. Hoptner, "The Foreign Policy of the National Liberation Movement of Yugoslavia" (unpublished M.A. thesis, Columbia University, 1950), p. 95.

[43] "In this lies the greatest error of the Yugoslav comrades. They are afraid openly to acclaim the Party and its decisions before the entire people so that the people may know that the leading force is the Party, that the Party leads the Front and not the reverse . . . But the Politbureau of the C.C. of the C.P.Y. is afraid to admit this openly and proclaim it at the top of its voice to the working class and all the people of Yugoslavia. The Politbureau of the C.C. of the C.P.Y. feels that if it does not emphasize this factor, the other parties will not have occasion to develop their strength in their struggle" (the C.P.S.U. to the C.P.Y., *The Soviet-Yugoslav Dispute*, p. 44).

Catholic or the Orthodox Church, or their wartime allies like Dragoljub Jovanovich and Milan Grol. Their social policy was prompted by unnecessarily severe and rigid doctrinaire Marxism. The device of the People's Front or of a nominal coalition of political parties veiling but thinly the reality of Communist dictatorship has been used in all the satellite countries, and the Yugoslavs, even before their break with Moscow, "improved" upon by the formula by gradually liquidating the remaining political parties save one. Also, the Communists in Yugoslavia never masqueraded under a different name as did their Polish or Bulgarian colleagues, who preferred not to use the word "Communist" in the formal description of their parties.

Yet a certain amount of mystery remains attached to the obvious reluctance of the C.P.Y., during the first three years of its domination of the state, to reveal to the public its role and structure. Here, only a very tentative and speculative answer is offered to the question, since we do not possess enough facts to be able to speak with assurance.

This tentative explanation is as follows: Even after their victory, paradoxically, the Yugoslav Communists retained the psychology of conspiracy about their Party. Their leaders had been masters at conspiracy, and the C.P.Y. under Tito had been the only Communist Party in Eastern Europe to have a full and functioning Party apparatus inside the country prior to the German attack. Furthermore, their conspiracy had consisted not only in illegal Communist activity but also in activity on behalf of a foreign power—the U.S.S.R. Whatever the authenticity of the secret instructions of the Comintern which Tito received in 1941—instructions which provided for the eventual amalgamation of Communist Yugoslavia in a greater union of Soviet Socialist Republics—the fact remains that the prewar Yugoslav Communist Party had considered itself, with pride, as an extension of the Soviet Union.[44] Now, through the war and in the years immediately following, a variety of conflicts developed between the leaders of Yugoslav Communism and the Soviet Union.

[44] The instructions are reproduced in Clissold, *Whirlwind*, pp. 238–241; they are also quoted in Bogdan Raditsa's article, "The Sovietization of the Satellites," *Annals of the American Academy of Political and Social Science*, September 1950, pp. 124–126.

The power interests of the Yugoslavs and the consequent growth of nationalism led them increasingly to oppose various Soviet moves within Yugoslavia which affected the country as a state. Yet, whether consciously or unconsciously, they did not lose the feeling that eventually, even if in the distant future, Yugoslavia would be absorbed into one Communist federation of Europe; and, consequently, they felt that the psychology and atmosphere of secrecy should surround some aspects of the C.P.Y. until the day of the amalgamation.

This theory may well appear paradoxical, but it finds support in the words of Sreten Zhujovich, already quoted here, when he refers in his recantation to his basic belief at the time of the 1948 crisis that Yugoslavia should ultimately, having proved "worthy" of the honor, be admitted into the U.S.S.R. and the C.P.Y. be merged with its great prototype. Zhujovich was, for the Tito group, a traitor and intriguer, but there are indications that some of Tito's most faithful lieutenants were not differently minded prior to 1948. Thus, the following curious incident is related in a letter written by the Russians to the C.P.Y. on May 11, 1945. In 1945 Tito made a speech in Ljubljana in which he asserted that Yugoslavia would not agree to be partitioned into "spheres of influence." The speech was directed mainly against the Western powers, but the Russians even then thought that it was an oblique attack upon them.[45] The Russian ambassador was told to protest, and he reported back that Kardelj, with whom he conferred in this connection, agreed with the Russian interpretation of the speech and criticized his own leader. Lavrentiev stated that Kardelj had been quite explicit:

[Kardelj said that] Tito had done great work in liquidating fractionalism in the C.P. and in organizing the people's liberation struggle, but he was inclined to regard Yugoslavia as a self-sufficient unit outside the general development of the proletarian revolution and socialism. Secondly, such a situation had arisen in the Party that the Central Committee does not exist as an organizational and political centre. We meet by chance, and we make decisions by chance . . . Kardelj said he would like the

---

[45] Actually, though the Yugoslavs had even before been suspicious about the possibility of a "deal" over Yugoslavia between Churchill and Stalin, the speech in question was directed very clearly against the West, and it took a degree of morbid sensitivity and some bad conscience for the Russians to fuss over it. See Armstrong, *Tito and Goliath*, p. 65.

Soviet Union to regard them, not as representatives of another country, capable of solving questions independently, *but as representatives of one of the future Soviet Republics, and the C.P.Y. as a part of the All-Union Communist Party, that is, that our relations should be based on the prospect of Yugoslavia becoming in the future a constituent part of the U.S.S.R.*[46]

The Russians add in pious horror that Comrade Kardelj's reasoning about Yugoslavia as a future part of the U.S.S.R. was of course "primitive and fallacious." The Yugoslavs on their part, in the commentary to the correspondence issued in 1948, state emphatically that Tito's Ljubljana speech was directed exclusively against the West and that it was so interpreted in Yugoslavia.[47] On the other hand, the Yugoslavs have not commented on the alleged criticism of Tito by Kardelj or on the latter's supposed opinion about the future of Yugoslavia as a part of the Soviet Union. It is possible that they did not think it fit to dignify by a denial an obvious slander, but it is probable that the Russian ambassador's report, or its 1948 version, did actually contain an element of truth together with an element of invention, and that Kardelj really did say something about Yugoslavia's joining eventually in a greater Soviet Union. The point, however, is this: such sentiments as expressed by Kardelj in 1945 would not have been damning from Tito's point of view (as the reputed criticism of Tito would have been) at that time, and indeed throughout 1948, for, despite all their grievances against Moscow, the rulers of Yugoslavia could never define clearly the future relationship of Communist Yugoslavia with the Soviet Union. In their actions they began diverging from the wishes of Moscow, but in their beliefs they could not divorce themselves from the anachronistic concept of the ultimate union of all Communist states. Hence the Communist Party of Yugoslavia had to be kept under cover, so to speak, until the day of the merger. If this explanation appears far-fetched, then one must point out that for two years after their break with Moscow the Yugoslav Communists continued to think about and to describe the West in terms which could have been taken literally from *Pravda* or *Izvestiya*. The evidence in support

---

[46] *The Soviet-Yugoslav Dispute*, pp. 37–38. My italics.
[47] *Pisma C.K. K.P.J. i pisma C.K. C.K.P.(b)* (Letters of the Central Committee of the C.P.Y. and Letters of the Central Committee of the C.P.S.U.(b); Belgrade, 1948), p. 4.

of this thesis is far from overwhelming, but it contains a psychological observation which is applicable to more than one action of the reputed "deviationists" and "traitors to Marxism."

The line of allegations pursued by the Russians in their letters to the Yugoslav Central Committee suggests strongly that, in addition to their reasoned and specific dislike of Tito and his group, the Russian Politburo must have been motivated in the beginning of the crisis by a basic misunderstanding of the nature and psychology of Yugoslav Communism. The Yugoslav Communists had two alternatives: either the Hebrangs, Zhujoviches, and Arso Jovanoviches, having received Soviet anointment, would assume command in Yugoslavia, or Tito and his followers would defy the Russians and face a friendless world. From the personal point of view, Tito and his colleagues would have to repudiate their association with the center of world Communism, the association which had absorbed all of their adult lives and without which, even though they were now masters of a country rather than agents of the Comintern, they were likely to experience a certain lack of direction and assurance in their policies. It is important to realize that the reason for Tito's reluctance, which extended for more than a year after the exchange of letters, to admit the finality of the rupture with Moscow, and his corresponding unwillingness to take any steps toward the West, lay not only in the need for a gradual transition which would not befuddle his Communist followers too much, but also in the genuine inability of the Yugoslav leaders themselves to reappraise the world and to fit themselves into their new and strange position.

But the die was cast, and the alternatives confronting the Yugoslavs in April 1948 were capitulation or defiance. For the record, they asked in their letter of April 13 that an investigating commission of the Russian Central Committee visit Yugoslavia and see with their own eyes the proofs of Tito's attachment to the U.S.S.R. and Communism.[48] Yet they must have known that once Moscow had made up its mind, it did not work through investigating commissions. The Russian counterproposal envisaged a discussion before the Cominform—hardly an impartial body.

Throughout April and May the Russians kept the Politburo of their satellites informed of the progress of the dispute, and thinly

[48] *The Soviet-Yugoslav Dispute*, p. 30.

veiled references to Tito's imminent disgrace began to appear in the Russian and satellite press. The Cominform journal carried editorials on June 1 and 15 echoing the Soviet charges. A naïve person might easily have concluded upon reading the editorials that *For a Lasting Peace*, then still published in Belgrade, was in fact referring to the Communist Party of the U.S.S.R., for its strictures referred to the inadmissibility of personal dictatorship within a Communist Party and to the evil practice of having Party officials nominated rather than appointed.

Within the Communist Parties of the satellites the news of the conflict must have induced a state of panic. Which one of them was not guilty of many of Tito's sins: of hiding behind a national or people's front, of appeasing peasants and the lower middle classes? What was it exactly that the Russians wanted, and who was to be the carrier of the disease of "nationalism" and "deviationism" in their own Party? And then on June 28, from a conference in Bucharest, the Cominform issued its blast at Yugoslavia and the incredulous world had an authoritative confirmation of the rumors. The statement [49] followed very closely the main line of the Russian accusations, with more emphasis being put on "an undignified policy of defaming Soviet military experts and discrediting the Soviet Union" allegedly indulged in by the rulers of Yugoslavia. Noticeable, also, was the open invitation to Yugoslav Communists to replace their leaders, four of whom were singled out in the resolution: Tito, Djilas, Kardelj, and Rankovich.[50] In contrast, the resolution extolled the behavior of Zhujovich (whose name is misspelled in the English version of the resolution) and Hebrang.

The dignitaries at the Bucharest meeting included Traicho Kostov, who led the Bulgarian delegation, but who was soon to be liquidated by his colleague on it, Vulko Chervenkov; and Andrei Zhdanov, for whom the meeting meant his last official appearance as the mentor of the Cominform, for two months afterward he was dead. Notable by their absence were Wladyslaw Gomulka, Secretary-General of the Polish Communists, then probably under house arrest, and Georgi Dimitrov, the man who, as former head of the Comintern and now Tito's counterpart in Bulgaria, could best en-

[49] Reproduced, *ibid.*, pp. 61–70.
[50] *Ibid.*, p. 62.

lighten the conferees about the Communist Party of Yugoslavia and about Tito. The assembled leaders may well have reflected that they were putting a seal of approval upon open and public dictation of their policies by the Soviet Union. They simultaneously destroyed the fiction that the Cominform was an organization based upon the principle of equality, as had been asserted less than one year before by Andrei Zhdanov. It now fell to Zhdanov to lead in the denunciation of Tito and to frame what amounted to a most peremptory directive to the Communist Parties of the satellites.

And so the conflict was on. Soon it appeared as if the Communist Parties, the armies, and the governments of Eastern Europe were filled with destructive and demoniac spirits. In Yugoslavia they were called "Cominformists," in the satellites "Titoists." They shared in the general characteristics of treachery, long-standing espionage which often extended back to their activities on behalf of the Germans during the war, and a general wrecking activity designed to sabotage the national economy and to comfort the class enemy. For all their diabolical cunning, which had enabled them to dupe the Party and the people for decades, they were now speedily apprehended by the security police and their alert colleagues, and more often than not confessed the full enormity of their crimes in great and elaborate detail.

In Yugoslavia the revelation of the crisis failed to bring about the *Götterdämmerung* which the Cominform and the Russians had expected. The Russians had probably been misled by their agents about the extent of the opposition to Tito within the Yugoslav Party and army. With Hebrang and Zhujovich in jail, the leadership of the Party remained solidly behind the dictator. The very vehemence and contemptuous tone of the Russian's statements became the best propaganda weapon of the Yugoslav regime, and all Soviet pronouncements were eagerly seized upon and officially circulated in Yugoslavia. To the Yugoslav people the somewhat tarnished servants of the Comintern were now revealed as the defenders of their national independence. To the rank and file of Yugoslav Communists, Tito and his group could say, "Read and see for yourselves whether we have been guilty of all the things the Russians are accusing us of." The two traitors had their biographies dutifully embellished:

Hebrang, who during the war had been thought valuable by the Partisans, who had been exchanged for high officials of Pavelich's puppet government in Croatia and thus rescued from a German concentration camp, was now described as a wartime traitor and collaborator set free by the Gestapo to do his dirty work within the Party. Zhujovich, who had fought at Tito's side during the war, now became a coward and fractionalist, with a record of anti-Party activity going back to before 1937. There were no high Party officials willing to follow in their footsteps. There were a few minor purges in the Central Committees and governments of the provinces (federal states). A disgruntled general, Arso Jovanovich, was to end his career in the manner already described. A major general, Pero Popivoda, fled the country in August 1948. The escaped warrior has since been reported by the Russian and Cominform press as witnessing various purge trials in Hungary and elsewhere, always ready to draw a suitable and quotable analogy to the future fate of his erstwhile commander in chief. By and large, the Communist Party of Yugoslavia has been purged less in the three years which have elapsed since the beginning of the conflict than have any of the satellite Parties.

What counted at the time of the crisis was that the Party, and the army, and the other instruments of power be retained firmly in the hands of the dictator and his group. The Fifth Congress of the Communist Party of Yugoslavia took place in July 1948. Most of the delegates were still probably befuddled by what was going on, but there was no hesitation, even if there was some confusion, in the speeches of the leaders. To fight was natural for them. The struggle which faced them now was still confused, and to the Yugoslav leaders it still appeared somewhat unreal, but it could be resolved peacefully only if *they* were to be fully vindicated. "We hope that the comrades, leaders of the C.P.S.U.(b), will give us an opportunity to show them here, on the spot, everything that is inaccurate in the Resolution [of the Cominform]. We consider that it is possible to arrive at the truth only in such a case and in such a way." [51] It was unwise at this stage to say that the conflict was already irrevocable, and perhaps the leaders could not yet bring themselves to face this

[51] Tito, *Political Report of the Central Committee*, p. 136.

possibility. The power motive inherent in Communism was to triumph in Yugoslavia, as it had triumphed in Russia, over the tie of the ideology, and there was a deep if unconscious insight, as well as irony, in the chant the Congress took up at the conclusion of Tito's and Rankovich's speeches: "Stalin—Tito—Party!"

CHAPTER 5

Titoism

Yugoslavia's defection from the seemingly monolithic Soviet bloc was greeted by the world either with complete incredulity or with exaggerated hopes. At first some felt—and this feeling continues to persist, encouraged by those circles which have most to lose if it is established that a Communist country can break away from the Soviet camp—that the whole thing was a gigantic hoax perpetrated to dupe the gullible West and to open a line of supplies and credits to Russia's allies. It was still easier to adopt the opposite view and to see the Tito affair, with a few qualifications, as a telling sign of the mortal weakness of Soviet imperialism and as the first indication of the impending revolt of nationalism in Eastern Europe against Soviet power. The latter view has yielded a variety of embellishments which, depending on the writer's attitude, have been added to fit the situation in the given Communist-dominated country. For example, one of Tito's main sins was his undue dependence on the peasants, and it was easy to draw a wishful parallel to the Chinese Communist Party, which is largely peasant in its composition and appeal. The hunt was on for budding Titos and incipient Titoisms. The bill of accusation against the Yugoslav Communist Party, produced so laboriously and with so much ingenuity by the Russians, was eagerly studied in the West and compared gleefully with the situation prevailing in other Communist Parties. To some in the West, Titoism has become a weapon of self-destruction obligingly forged by Communism to spare the West the unpleasant task of studying and developing a policy toward the Soviet Union and her satellites.

In the welter of confusion and wishful thinking, the basic facts about the Soviet-Yugoslav dispute have become obscured and neglected. Largely lost has been the essential insight that Titoism is not a matter merely of nationalistic inclination or a dislike of the Russians by a group of Communists, but mainly a function of the psychology of power combined with a situation in which a defiance of the imperialist power is both practical and, in a sense, inevitable for a group of Communist leaders who cherish their position of unchallenged authority in their own country. It is no reflection on the current nationalism of Tito and his lieutenants to say that until they realized that the object of Soviet policy was their eventual removal and replacement by more "internationalist" Communists they did not see a great deal of contradiction between their Yugoslav patriotism and their loyalty to Moscow. It is, also, unwise to see *all* of the leaders of the satellite countries as unthinking tools of Soviet imperialism rather than, as some of them must be and give every indication of being, opportunistic politicians who realize, perhaps regretfully, that neither their own position within their Parties nor the situation of their country vis-à-vis the Soviet Union warrants an emulation of Yugoslavia and Tito. The great purge in the Communist Parties of the satellites which began in 1948 happened to coincide with, and was largely accentuated by, the Yugoslav defection from the Soviet camp. There is no doubt that the purge would have taken place with or without Titoism. Yet its character was strongly influenced by what was happening in Yugoslavia.

There is, after all, a substantial excuse for the variety of misconceptions about Titoism current in the West. It has only to be reflected that the real experts on this issue—Marshal Tito and his advisers on the one hand, and the Russians and their friends in the satellite countries on the other—have succeeded in convincing themselves that struggle for power was but a secondary issue in the dispute and that the real causes are to be found in problems of nationalism and ideology. Titoism has become a term which now embraces all varieties, whether real or invented, of anti-Russian behavior within world Communism. Insofar as it expresses an attitude of disillusionment with the current situation in the U.S.S.R., it bears a superficial resemblance to Trotskyism, a term which has been likewise used and abused as a common denominator of Communist opposition to the U.S.S.R. But Trotskyism, unlike Titoism up to the present moment, grew from a clash of personalities into something vaguely resembling an ideology.

Sooner or later Titoism will also acquire an ideology, for the simple reason that it is impossible for people or nations to disagree over an extended period of time without devising a theoretical structure for their disagreement. Already the Tito of 1951 is not the Tito of 1948, who was a "Stalinist" in every respect save in his unwillingness to put his head into a noose when so requested by Moscow. By a rather characteristic irony of history, the Yugoslav regime of 1951 is beginning to exhibit some of the characteristics of which it was wrongly accused in 1948: it is moderating its collectivization and agricultural policy; it is more willing to recognize the realities of economics when it comes to the reorganization of the national economy, even though such realism may be "nonsocialist"; and it begins to view the West as not exclusively imperialist and bent upon capitalist-inspired war. To a Russian Communist the Yugoslav development is easily explicable as following "the law of history," which decrees that whoever leaves the camp of the Soviet Union must wind up among its bitterest enemies. The present course of Yugoslavia is a direct confirmation of the wisdom of the Central Committee of the Communist Party of the U.S.S.R., which could see the seeds of treachery in the behavior of the Yugoslav Communists when none were visible to an ordinary Communist. Actually, the Yugoslav Communists behave today as if they were slowly waking from a hypnotic trance and had to act for the first time fully on their own.

One of the outstanding features of the continuing crisis between Yugoslavia and Russia has been the remarkable difficulty the Yugoslav Communists have experienced in reorienting some of their ideas and habits of thought. Surely no better laboratory case of the pervasive influence and power of complete Communist indoctrination has ever been uncovered than that of the Yugoslav Communist leaders in the slow and bewildered process of transformation, in the groping for a systematic answer to the world, through which they have been going during the past three years. They have traveled a long road from their early, almost childlike, faith in the Soviet Union and Stalin, depicted so vividly in Dedijer's diary, to their present somber appreciation of the power, of the ruthless determination to brook no opposition, embodied in Russia. Their own Titoism is therefore of a different nature than the usual manifestation of the same phenomenon found elsewhere in the satellite countries. Since the Yugoslavs' attachment to Soviet Russia had been deeper and had had fewer reservations than that of Communists elsewhere in Eastern Europe, their reaction against Soviet imperialism and to their own lost illusions and beliefs has had to be more violent and spontaneous. It has been the reaction of betrayed love, but it has not hardened into cynicism and a complete disregard of ideological values: for Tito and his colleagues remain Communists still; they still adhere to the basic social and political motivations of their creed. But there is now perceptibly less assurance in their policies and a certain impression that they are merely going through the motions. In time, if they are allowed time, the Yugoslav Communists may find their own systematic theology. Until now their main effort in this direction has consisted in a rather dreary exegesis of Marxism and Leninism and—a faint echo of their once buoyant belief in their role as the pioneers of a new wave of Communism that would sweep the world after World War II—in the often repeated conviction that the spread of Communism will of itself destroy the devices of Soviet imperialism.

To Tito has been attributed the ambition of becoming a rival leader of world Communism, or, even, of inheriting Stalin's mantle. But if Tito does possess such an ambition, then it must be reasoned that he and his advisers have learned nothing of political realism and that they have failed to analyze their earlier infatuation with the Soviet Union as being based not only on Communism but also on a belief in the limitless power and resources of the U.S.S.R. As a matter of fact, a new and plaintive note has crept into the public pronouncements of the Yugoslav government. The rulers of Yugoslavia are now fond of emphasizing that theirs is a small country and that their cause is the cause of every small nation bent upon the preservation of its sovereignty and dignity. The most cherished notion of the rulers of Yugoslavia is to preserve their power and to eschew any political and international adventures. Their earlier lust for territorial expansion, in the days when they envisaged themselves as the deputies of Soviet Russia in Eastern Europe and as unifiers and rulers of the Balkans, has been considerably reduced. For some time now they have been working to become good neighbors of Italy and Greece, a startling change from their pre-1948 attitude. To see the same people who only a few years ago were full of bluster and fire, practically ready to take on the whole capitalist world if told so by Soviet Russia, now singing the praise of international understanding, neighborliness, and national sovereignty is to reinforce one's faith in the power of education. But it has been an unusual process of education.

It is clear that the rulers of Yugoslavia cannot qualify as very active propagators of Titoism elsewhere in the satellite area. They are not afraid to stand up against the Soviet Union. Their record shows them to be extremely courageous men, naïve in many things, but extremely cunning and ruthless when it comes to perpetuating their own power against external or internal challenge. But they are now aware that Yugoslavia is a small power. While they have a superb understanding of the methods of Soviet policy, their analysis of the basic reasons for and motivations of Russia's political behavior has proved at times as fallacious as that of many experts in the West. It is unlikely that the present rulers of Yugoslavia will ever give up their Communism or modify the essence of their rule, which is the standard one of the one-party police state with all the appurtenances. Their Communism—the only meaningful definition of the term being at present the pattern of social change adopted in Russia over the last thirty years—is the only social philosophy in the terms of which they can think or act. Some features of Russia's economic development may be omitted or postponed in Yugoslavia, but the idea of the socialist state in which every aspect of the economic life is controlled by the state, and in which the state has no competitor in people's loyalty, religion, or education, is still the goal of the Communist Party of Yugoslavia. The basic features of a one-party state are also unlikely to disappear. There is a very real question whether the regime could survive should it introduce even the incipient forms of political democracy. It is understandable that the present nationalistic attitude of Tito's regime has given it certain over-all popularity which, in combination with the consciousness of national danger, has enabled it to discard some purely repressive measures and to talk about the rights of the individual, decentralization, and so forth. Such concessions can be proudly displayed and contrasted with the conditions in the Soviet Union and the satellites. They do not affect the basic facts that Tito's government could not afford to introduce the elements of democracy in Yugoslavia—the notion of competing political parties, a free press, judicial independence, and so forth; that it would not want to do so even if it could afford to; and that it would not know how to go about introducing democracy even if it wanted to.

If the description above fits Titoism in December of 1951, then what was its meaning in the summer of 1948? It was not, as has often been asserted, the notion of national Communism. True, the Yugoslavs have written, "No matter how much each of us loves the land of Socialism, the U.S.S.R., he can, in no case, love his country less, which also is developing socialism." [1] But the burden of the Yugoslavs' case has been their insistence that though they loved the U.S.S.R., were willing to follow its directions and accept unquestioningly its foreign policy, they were not willing to pursue the course abjectly to the point of self-destruction. It has already been pointed out that there was no bona fide issue about the economic or social policy of the Yugoslav regime. The argument turned really on the character of the Communist Parties and their state appendages in the People's Democracies. Were they to be autonomous units with some leadership and cohesion of their own, following the Communist Party of the "Land of Socialism" but preserving internal autonomy, or were they to be as dependent on Moscow as they had been when out of power and illegal? It was natural that nationalism was a side issue in the power struggle, but that, once the conflict became a public property, the issue of nationalism was allowed to dominate the public debate; however, one can assert without quibbling that the source of the dispute between Stalin and Tito consisted in the Russian attempt to seize the instruments of political and military power in Yugoslavia.

Now, the precise difference between the type of Titoism prev-

[1] *The Soviet-Yugoslav Dispute*, p. 19.

alent in Yugoslavia and the similarly described phenomenon in the rest of the satellite countries was this: elsewhere in the satellite area there was no solidly united group of native Communist leaders who controlled the army, the secret police, and the Party apparatus in their country. The Russians still had their own troops in some of the satellites in 1948. They often controlled the higher echelons of the army, and their men, even if they happened to be of the given ethnic origin, held strategic positions in the Party and state apparatus. Most important of all, no Communist Party in the satellite area could boast a Tito, that is, a man who held undisputed sway over his Party and government and commanded the great emotional loyalty of the Communist hierarchy. Furthermore, the Communist Parties in the satellites, except perhaps in Bulgaria and in a different sense Czechoslovakia, were weak. Without the tremendous weight of the Soviet Union behind them, they could not expect to hold on to power long. It is paradoxical but true that successful Titoism in Yugoslavia was possible only because, of all the Communist-ruled satellites in Europe, Yugoslavia was the only one which approximated the Stalinist pattern of the state and the Party. And not only that. We have seen how close were the ties which bound together the Communist leaders of Yugoslavia. They were the ties of temperament, of dangers faced and survived together, and of common interest. How different it was and still is in the Communist Parties elsewhere in the People's Democracies. There the Kolarovs, Rakosis, and Zambrowskis—the men who, separated from their countries, had spent long years in Russia during the war—returned at war's end to share the power with the Kostovs, Gomulkas, and Rajks. The latter had grown from obscurity to Communist prominence during the war and were, more often than not, out of touch with the realities and attitudes of Soviet policies. The men who between 1945 and 1948 sat in the Politburos of the Communist Parties of Poland, Bulgaria, and Hungary had often very little in common save the label of Communism. Groups as mixed as they in background and personality could not be expected to show the resolution and resourcefulness displayed by the Yugoslav Politburo. Even if the Politburos of the other satellites had been in a position in 1948 to duplicate the Yugoslav defiance, the odds are great that they would not have done it.

The reaction of the Communist leaders in Eastern Europe to the public announcement of the Tito affair must have been a mixed one. The Yugoslav leader could not have enjoyed great popularity in the Balkans, which before 1948 were considered by the Yugoslav Communists, with the apparent approval of Moscow, as their *Lebensraum*. Albania was at that period a satellite of Yugoslavia, and after the outbreak of the Russo-Yugoslav dispute the Albanian Communist Party was to undergo a drastic purge before the country was allowed to advance to the status of a direct satellite of the U.S.S.R. The Bulgarian Communists had been, before January 1948, when a fiat of Moscow ended the whole business, mercilessly prodded by the Yugoslavs to merge Bulgaria in the South Slav federation, in which Tito and his colleagues would obviously play the leading part. The Yugoslavs' blustering ways, their constant reminders that the Communist Party of Yugoslavia had achieved power mostly by its own exertions, unlike some other Communist Parties, and their boasts about the extent of socialism already realized in Yugoslavia could not have made Tito and his colleagues too popular among the higher echelons of the Communist Parties of the satellite states.

At the same time, there was an obvious community of interests, in a very special sense, among the satellite governments. If one of them was to be pressed hard by Moscow, what could the others expect? Initially, there must have been a strong tendency to hope that the Russians and the Yugoslavs would reach a compromise, would avoid a breach in the Communist front, and would, incidentally, set a precedent for a modicum of autonomy for the satellites. This failure to understand Soviet policy, moreover, led Wladyslaw Gomulka, during his recantation, to describe thus his first reaction to the news of the dispute: "I thought at first that the measures applied to deal with C.P.Y. were too severe. I thought one should have talked with the leadership of the C.P.Y., sent a delegation [to Yugoslavia]; one should have explained, and pleaded, and perhaps conceded something [to Tito]." [2] But Gomulka, like Tito before 1948, though in a different way, did not understand the psychology of the people for whom and with whom he had worked most of

[2] From his speech at the September plenum, recorded in *Nowe Drogi*, September–October 1948, p. 141.

his adult life. Gomulka's first reaction was probably not atypical. Whatever the Communist notables thought about Tito, he was one of them; and if he was to be purged, none of them was safe. Some of them may even have been envious of Tito's courage in standing up against Moscow; they may have wished him success in his enterprise.

It was probably the last-mentioned factor that was potent in Moscow's decision to make its conflict with Yugoslavia irrevocable, even after it had become obvious that the Yugoslav regime would not collapse at the first blast of the Cominform's trumpet. Better lose Yugoslavia, for a time at least, than create the impression that the Soviet Union was losing its uncompromising vigor and its passion for infallibility. Concede, on the other hand, and the charm was broken. Hence the original issue in the dispute had to be exaggerated and distorted. Tito's insubordination could not be an isolated incident. It had to be connected with a long record of un-Marxist behavior, and then with treachery and outright dealings with the imperialist West.

Once the full extent of the conflict had become known in the satellite countries, along with the determination of the Russians to brook no compromise, the attitude of satellite Communist leaders must have undergone a curious change. Tito and the existence of his regime now appeared as the direct menace not only to their remaining autonomy but even to their personal safety. Whether they believed the Russian charges or not (and it is unlikely that the more intelligent among them could believe that Tito during the war had been working with the Gestapo and was now merrily carrying on with the British and Americans), they were well aware of the curious wave effect which a purge produces within the body of organized Communism. Because a purge took place in the Communist Party of the U.S.S.R. in the thirties, hundreds of foreign Communist leaders were purged and liquidated. Now again it was as if an angry god was to be appeased and propitiated. The chorus of bitter denunciations and hysterical abuse poured upon Tito in the press of the satellite Parties was largely sincere and spontaneous.

Titoism in the satellites was likely to take on a different aspect from that which it had in Yugoslavia. It could not be a reaction of a unified power system fighting against an attempt to subvert it or to subordinate it from abroad. The "national Communists" who wanted to emulate Tito in their own countries had, first, to seize control of their Parties and governments before they could even think of standing up against the U.S.S.R. As a matter of fact, Titoism in the sense described above—the only sense in which it is the "real" Titoism, paralleling the development in Yugoslavia—did not arise in any of the satellite countries. Some of the purged leaders stumbled into the deviation. Their resentment against this or that aspect of Soviet domination or Soviet-sponsored policy for their country left them exposed and vulnerable to attack. Many of them could not or would not adjust themselves to the rapid transition from the policy of gradualism and toleration which had prevailed before 1948, with Soviet approval, to the new policy of ostensibly rapid advance toward the Communist state ordered by the Cominform resolution of 1948. That quality of organized Communism which makes it plunge feverishly into any policy pursued at the given moment has often the side effect of leaving after every radical change of policy a small residue of leaders ideologically suspended in the air. The policies propagated with Moscow's blessings in 1946 became by the summer of 1948 equivalent to treason against Communism. Then many a case of personal rivalry, of inefficiency, or simply of gossip, resulted in a purge which has been fitted into the story of never-ending treachery, Titoism, and general manifestation of the class enemy.

How a relatively trivial incident can become the basis of a man's disgrace is best illustrated by the example of Milovan Djilas, one of the most important leaders of the Communist Party of Yugoslavia. Djilas as the minister in charge of the Yugoslav press and propaganda between 1945 and 1948 earned deservedly the reputation of being a fanatical Communist whose vituperation and hatred of the West were matched only by his admiration of Communism and the U.S.S.R. Yet, as we have seen in the Soviet-Yugoslav correspondence, Djilas was most emphatically disliked and suspected by Moscow. Had Tito capitulated in the summer of 1948, Djilas, it is reasonable to assume, would have been among the first to be purged in Yugoslavia. Now the basis of Moscow's anger with Djilas was one hotheaded remark, made in the supposed secrecy of the Central Committee, in which he criticized the behavior of the Russian troops in Yugoslavia in 1945. It is a startling evidence of the morbid instinct of suspicion which permeates Soviet Communism that one incautious remark was allowed to destroy a lifetime of devoted service to Communism and to condemn irretrievably a man who by temperament and conviction was an ideal follower of the U.S.S.R. There must have been many people in the highest Party and governmental circles in the satellite countries who, despite their devotion to Soviet Russia, had cried out at one time or another against an incident of Soviet brutality or economic exploitation of their country. It cannot be known now how many of them were liquidated, especially after 1948, amidst lurid tales of sabotage, of espionage for the Western Powers, of Titoism, while the initial source of their disgrace may have been a rude remark to a Russian official or an incautious comment about the Soviet Union imparted to a trusted Party colleague.

Apart from purely personal factors involved, there is another and almost functional reason for the purge of the Communist Parties of Eastern Europe. Every political system must have in it a mechanism of change which will allow it to shift its course occasionally and to unload the burden of unaccepted policies and popular frustrations. In an authoritarian system, where the power element is so highly personalized and veiled in emotional intensity, a change of directions or an internal or external crisis is apt to be accompanied by a purge, the object or objects of which become the personifications of all the hateful forces requiring repression and privations. A political purge in Soviet Russia or the satellites often transcends the immediate importance of the few persons involved in a trial or under disgrace. It becomes very often a living drama depicting a struggle of the regime with all the dark forces opposing it. By the same token, a defection within Communist ranks, no matter how personal or apolitical may be its background, sends a tremor throughout the whole system. Pressure is exerted at every level of the Party and government, and those having personal ties with the accused, or perhaps even a similar background, become automatically suspect and liable to political destruction. It is the potential, as well as the actual, opponents of the regime and the deviationists who suffer from periodic purges. In a sense, one can think of a Communist Party or a Communist regime as defying, by its rigidity and its aura of infallibility and restless activity, the normal pattern of political behavior. Everything in normal political processes urges the regime to relax and to soften its repressive and exacting characteristics, and it is only the intermittent waves of euphoria and hysteria which provide the dynamism for the restlessness that is so characteristic of a Communist Party in or out of power. A periodic purge becomes a necessary feature of political life.

The emergence of Communist Yugoslavia as an opponent of the U.S.S.R. and the Cominform has illuminated a phenomenon of opposition and dissension within the Communist camp. But Titoism, as that phenomenon has been called, embraces a wider variety of causes and manifestations than has been apparent in Yugoslavia. It ranges from cases where nationalism, as a reason for the disgrace of a Communist leader or for his opposition to the Cominform, appears less diluted by the power motive than was the case with Tito, to situations where no nationalism and no opposition to Moscow is evident, but where the purged leader has been damned by an intra-party intrigue or personal quarrel and then had affixed to him the now common label of treason and anti-Soviet activity.

II. CRISIS IN THE POLISH COMMUNIST PARTY

Polish Communism in its very genesis embodied certain ambiguities and contradictions of which its history is a long record. When in the summer of 1948 the Secretary-General of the Polish Workers' Party, Gomulka, was being purged for reputed Titoism, his disgrace was connected to a "faulty" historical analysis pronounced by him on the origins and sources of Communism in Poland. A distant historical dispute was made the symbol of the struggle which threatened the Polish Communists with a split. Men and issues were not judged against the real context of the dispute—the relationship of Polish Communism to Soviet Russia; instead, the question was obscured and confused by reference to past quarrels and ideological definitions.

The original Polish Communist Party was founded in December 1918 by two socialist groups: the Social Democratic Party of Poland and Lithuania and the left wing of the Socialist Party of

Poland.[3] The original fusion was in itself a promise of the future
ambivalence of Polish Communism. The Social Democratic Party,[4]
at one time the party of Rosa Luxemburg, had been pervaded by
intellectual Marxism and was usually hostile to the notions of
"bourgeois nationalism." The doctrinaire Marxism of the Social
Democrats led them to reject the principle of national self-determination, which together with some other of Rosa Luxemburg's
theoretical postulates brought about her alienation from Lenin and
a temporary separation of the party from the Social Democratic
Party of Russia.[5] Lenin, a revolutionary pragmatist, may well have
disagreed with Rosa Luxemburg not because of any ideological
convictions but simply because her theory, and purely intellectual
doctrinaire Marxism in general, would have weakened the revolutionary appeal of socialism for the masses. He was later to quarrel
with Rosa Luxemburg about her theory of imperialism, which was
different in some details from the one Lenin propounded (his theory
was largely borrowed from a British writer, J. A. Hobson). The
Social Democratic Party was thus to pass into the annals of Communism as a bona fide Marxist Party, but tainted with "Luxemburgism." A vague scent of heresy has clung to the memory of that
otherwise exemplary precursor of Polish Communism, though very
few Polish Communists who nowadays mention "Luxemburgism"
would be actually capable of explaining its full meaning.

The old Polish Socialist Party, on the other hand, had been
blessed or cursed, depending on one's point of view, with the exact
reverse of the ailment of the Social Democrats. It had been a strongly
nationalist party whose Marxism was, at times, overcome by purely
nationalist postulates and whose activity in Russian-occupied Poland
included "direct action" against the Russian authorities, especially
in the years 1904 and 1905. Though its left wing was professedly
less nationalistic, it still brought to the merger of 1918–19 a tradi-

[3] See M. K. Dziewanowski, "Social Democrats versus Social Patriots: The
Origins of the Split of the Marxist Movement in Poland," *American Slavic and
East European Review*, February 1951.
[4] Its full name was "The Socialist Party of the Kingdom of Poland and of
Lithuania," thus decrying any pretense to an all-Polish character.
[5] N. N. Popov, *Ocherk Istorii Vsesoyuznoy Komunisticheskoy Partii* (*Out-
line of the History of the All-Russian Communist Party*), Moscow, 1927, p. 70.

tion quite different from the internationalism of the Social Democrats.

In interwar Poland, the Polish Communist Party did not play a very prominent role. Its political influence was strictly localized in a few regions. It could not compete with the Polish Peasant Party for political influence among peasants, nor with the Polish Socialist Party among the workers. The Party soon become illegal,[6] but a harder blow than persecution by the Polish regime was rendered to Polish Communism by the purge of 1937–38, which paralleled the great Russian purge. In Moscow perished the top leaders of the Polish Communist Party, such people as Warski, Leszczynski, Walecki, and others. The hereditary ailment of "Luxemburgism" seemed to facilitate in the body of Polish Communism the growth of the much more virulent and fashionable disease of the thirties— "Trotskyism." In Poland the Party was shot through with real and reputed Trotskyites, but also with agents of the police. And so in 1937 and 1938, at the orders of the Comintern, the Polish Communist Party went out of existence. The same fate very nearly overcame at that time another clandestine body of Communism, the Communist Party of Yugoslavia, but there the Comintern was lucky enough to find a superb organizer and a proved disciple of Stalinism, who not only purged the Yugoslav Communist Party of "Trotskyism" and fractionalism but also managed to put it in a working and fighting condition. For Poland the Comintern could not yet find a Polish Tito. The Polish Communist Party was, of course, to be recreated and reorganized, but immediately after the purge the war intervened and the cause of Polish Communism received an unexpected twist.

Today one of the revered heroes of Polish Communism is Marian Buczek, who was released from jail in September 1939, went on to fight the invader, and met his death from a German bullet. Marian Buczek is safe because he is dead, but there is no doubt that after 1948 his Party career, and indeed his freedom, would have been seriously handicapped by the circumstances under which he was raised to the Communist pantheon. Some day a full account may be published of the reaction of the Polish Communists to the Russo-

[6] Yet, cover-up organizations for the Communist Party were allowed to exist and to compete in elections until the thirties.

German treaty of 1939 and the subsequent division of their country between the two powers. When, following the German attack upon Russia, Polish Communism again began its organized existence in Poland, it did so under the name of the Polish Workers' Party. It was not an enemy of Polish Communism but one of its top leaders who, in describing the reaction of various ultra-left groups in the Polish underground to the Communist proposals for collaboration, quoted their reply: "But you [the Polish Workers' Party] are Moscow's agents, while we were born and have grown on Polish soil." [7] The Polish Communists had to struggle not only against the Germans but also against the official Polish underground connected with the London government and against the hostility and distrust of a vast majority of their countrymen. They never attained a position of importance approximating that of the other groups fighting the Germans. Their armed force, at first called the People's Guard and later, more grandiosely, the People's Army, appeared insignificant compared to the "official" underground army—the National Army.[8]

The underground history of the Polish Communist Party is extremely obscure. Even in the new Communist Poland there has been a paucity of memoirs and stories of the exploits of the People's Army during the war, partly, one suspects, because its achievements were not particularly effective, but mostly because the story involves too many people who have since fallen into disgrace and because it would not be a safe venture to describe wartime Communism in any detail. The impression conveyed by the rather sketchy accounts which come out in various Party debates and accounts of today is that the command of the Polish Workers' Party was deeply conscious of its numerical and moral weakness, and that it spared no effort to recruit allies among various radical socialist and peasant groups in the underground. The Polish government-in-exile, and hence its "official" underground, were not too popular among the latter, since the London government—a coalition of all the major Polish political parties—still smacked too much in its at-

[7] Franciszek Jozwiak-Witold, during the September 1948 meeting of the Central Committee of the Polish Workers' Party (*Nowe Drogi*, September–October 1948, p. 65).

[8] Actually, in Polish, *Armia Krajowa*, which translates awkwardly into the Country, or Homeland, Army.

mosphere and personnel of the prewar semi-dictatorial regime of Poland. However, even the radical socialists and peasants could not quite bring themselves to collaborate with "Moscow's agents." At a crucial moment in its development the Party changed its leadership. Its first Secretary-General, Marceli Nowotko, was killed, and his successor, Paul Finder, soon was caught and executed by the Germans. The choice of the Central Committee—to give this appellation to a handful of conspirators—fell upon "Comrade Wieslaw." The name concealed the identity of Wladyslaw Gomulka, before the war a member of the Communist Party of Poland and a functionary of the Chemical Workers' Union. Gomulka's accession to "power" over the bodies of his two predecessors was made, later on, the subject of a sinister comment. It was also to be alleged that his election coincided with the period when the system of communication between the Central Committee and the "comrades in Russia" broke down for a few months, since the imprisoned Party functionaries were the only ones in possession of the code.[9] Yet among the group which elected Gomulka were his future tormentors, such docile followers of "international Communism" as the future President of Poland and Gomulka's successor as the head of Polish Communism, Boleslaw Bierut, and a leader of the Communist "army," Franciszek Jozwiak-Witold. It did not occur to them until five years afterward that they had elected a "nationalist Communist," and it did not occur to them until six years afterward that they had elected a man who in some mysterious and unexplained fashion had, perhaps, had something to do with the deaths of his predecessors.

Thus an obscure labor-union functionary was, by the choice of a few fellow conspirators, designated as the head of Polish Communism. That the choice fell upon Gomulka is a testimony to his value and importance in the underground Communist movement. By becoming head of the Polish Workers' Party in November 1943, Gomulka secured for himself the position of one of the most important political leaders in postwar Poland. For there was no doubt that at the end of the war the Soviet government, which had with-

---

[9] Zenon Kliszko, in his speech before the November 1949 plenum of the Central Committee of the United Workers' Party of Poland (*Nowe Drogi*, November 1949, pp. 86ff.).

drawn its recognition of the Polish regime in London in the spring of 1943, would insist on having at least a pro-Soviet government in Poland and that the Polish Communists would play an important part in liberated Poland. It was not yet clear that the Western Allies would voluntarily give a free hand to the Russians, or that they would be forced to do so; nor was it apparent that the Secretary-General's position would be even more elevated and that he would become in effect the leader of the postwar Polish state, approaching the status of a dictator. Such visions of grandeur were probably quite distant at the time, and the future apportionment of ministerial portfolios was probably a matter of less consequence to the members of the Central Committee than were the ways and means of avoiding the fate of their comrades who had fallen into the hands of the German police.

As is often the case with a group of men whose ideological motivation is very strong, even the presence of extreme danger did not remove all squabbling and quarreling within the Central Committee. Later it was made to appear that the issue dividing the Polish Communists during the war had been that of "nationalism" versus "internationalism," that is, a certain distrust of the Soviet Union and of the resources of Polish Communism, on one hand, against an unbounded faith in the eventual victory of Communism in Poland and the help of Soviet Russia, on the other. It is much more likely that the real issue dividing the high command of Polish Communism during the war was one of pure strategy. Were the Polish Communists to wait until the Red Army had overrun all of Poland and then create a purely Communist government, or were they to attempt to construct a broader front and an underground government in which the Communists would play the leading part, but which would have the appearance, at least for the benefit of the West, of a union of progressive and democratic forces in Poland? Needless to say, all the factions of Polish Communism awaited eagerly the arrival of the Red Army, so that could not be an issue. By the end of 1943 it was clear that the Soviet Union would demand, and probably get, the eastern provinces of prewar Poland, that is, those Russia had obtained in its 1939 deal with Germany. But again, much as the Polish Communists may have resented the prospect of parting with an ancient section of Poland, those provinces had always been conceded by Polish Communism to Soviet Russia, and before 1939 the Communist bodies operating there were known significantly as the Communist Parties of Western Ukraine and Western Byelorussia. So the only issue that could have divided the Central Committee was the problem of strategy mentioned before; and, though an element of nationalism may have been injected into the picture, it was not in the form that was stressed four years afterward, when it was magnified and changed beyond recognition.

Shortly after Gomulka's accession to the leadership, the Polish Workers' Party organized its own underground government—the National Council of the Country (*Krajowa Rada Narodowa*). The mere fact of its organization seems to testify that the Polish Communists determined at first to go ahead by themselves and organize their own government, which would take over once the Red Army had pushed the Germans out of Poland. The purely Communist character of the National Council, though it did put up a pretense of having a wide national character, could not be concealed, and the failure of the Communists to attract anybody of note into its membership is attested by the fact that the president of the Council became Boleslaw Bierut, a colleague of Gomulka on the Central Committee and an obscure Communist agent of long standing. Thus at first the concept of trusting in "one's own forces," that is, in the imminence of the Soviet occupation of Poland, seems to have prevailed among the Polish Communists. It should be noted that in setting up their own government in Yugoslavia, almost at the same time, the Yugoslav Communists succeeded both in giving it, ostensibly, a broad national character and in selecting as its figurehead a well-known prewar Yugoslav politician, Ivan Ribar. The Polish Communists could contemplate their handiwork, the National Council, with anything but complete satisfaction. Not even the ultra-left elements in Poland, fed up as they were with the Polish government-in-exile and with its local representation, the Council of National Unity, could be persuaded that the National Council was anything but what it really was—a Communist agency. It is likely that the problem of further strategy—whether to stick with the original, purely Communist "government," or whether to attempt at all costs to expand the basis of the future Communist government of Poland—agitated Polish Communist leaders during the first months of 1944. The whole story needs to be stressed, since it played an extremely important part in the crisis of 1948.

In the spring of 1944 the fortunes of Polish Communism underwent a shift. The Red Army was approaching what are now the frontiers of Poland. Soviet diplomacy was working ceaselessly to discredit the Polish government in London and to gain the concurrence of some of its elements to a deal with Russia which would restore the Curzon Line as the frontier between postwar Russia and Poland and reward Poland with the eastern German provinces of Silesia and Pomerania and a part of East Prussia. In March a delegation of the National Council, that is, of the Polish Communists in Poland, went to Russia, and on May 22 it was received by Stalin.[10] It is unreasonable to suppose that the activities of the delegation in Russia were confined to having tea at the Kremlin. Before May 1944 the Polish Communists in the occupied territory were, despite their communications with the "comrades in Russia," largely on their own. In May they had an opportunity to discuss their strategy not only with their Polish Communist colleagues in Russia but also with the competent Russian circles. It could thus be no accident that one month afterward, on July 1, 1944, an article in the Communist underground journal, *Trybuna Wolnosci* (*Tribune of Freedom*), called upon the progressive elements within the old parties in Poland, especially within the Peasant Party, to break with the London government and to collaborate with the Polish Workers' Party. The article went on to say:

We hold the view that the main task of the day is to unify and to consolidate all the forces of the democratic camp. Not because we want to eliminate any [political] group. We consider that, in the condition of Poland today, a broad national front has to arise, embracing everybody who is fighting for the liberation of Poland.[11]

The appeal was not surprising. It paralleled what the Polish committee in Moscow (the so-called Union of Polish Patriots) was saying at the time, and it paralleled the efforts of the Soviet diplomacy which was then wooing all sorts of Polish elements abroad. This was the period, after all, when Stalin was receiving people

[10] *Nowe Drogi*, September–October 1948, p. 47.
[11] *Ibid.*, p. 21. My translation.

like Professor Oscar Lange, then from the University of Chicago, and Father Orlemanski. The Polish Workers' Party and its National Council were obviously considered too weak a foundation upon which to build postwar and pro-Soviet Poland. The article in the *Tribune of Freedom*, written by Wladyslaw Bienkowski, a factotum of Gomulka's, corresponded to the policy of the U.S.S.R., even if it did not respond directly to a specific set of instructions. But four years afterward this article was to be interpreted as a classical manifestation of Gomulka's "nationalist deviation" and of his distrust of the Soviet Union.[12] Bienkowski's article did not represent anything new even insofar as the Polish Workers' Party was concerned, for the Party had before attempted to seduce some elements of the Polish Socialist Party and the Peasant Party, and its attempts had been crowned with a very limited degree of success.[13]

In July 1944, after the Soviet offensive had liberated much of Poland and after the Russians had set up the Lublin government, which in its personnel was a combination of the National Council of the Polish Workers' Party and the parallel body in Russia, the Union of the Polish Patriots, the Premier of the Polish government in London, Stanislaw Mikolajczyk, set out on his bitter trip to Moscow. There he saw not only Stalin but also members of the Lublin government. The tactics prescribed in Bienkowski's article of July 1, 1944, were followed by the Communists. The Polish government-in-exile was undermined and the way was prepared to set up in liberated Poland a coalition government which would mask Communist preponderance and possession of the essence of power. This government would enable the Party headed by Gomulka to consolidate its position without provoking a civil war and without impeding the economic recovery of the country and alarming the Western allies, who were ready to soothe their con-

[12] My interpretation here represents a reasoned reconsideration of the view expressed in my article, "The Crisis in the Polish Communist Party," *Review of Politics*, January 1950, where I wrote that Bienkowski's article may have expressed a degree of diffidence in the Soviet Union on the part of the Polish Communists. In the light of further evidence, that interpretation seems no longer tenable.

[13] Thus Edward Osobka-Morawski, a prewar Socialist but not of any standing in his party, and a few others were gained in August 1943. See Jan Krzysztof Kwiatkowski, *Komunisci w Polsce (Communists in Poland)*, Brussels, 1946, p. 43.

science by seeing a few non-Communists in a Polish government. Gomulka's role as an underground leader ended in the summer of 1944. On January 5, 1945, the U.S.S.R. recognized the Lublin Committee as the Provisional Government of Poland. Following Yalta, a renewed effort by the Allies established Mikolajczyk and some men of his former government, together with the Lublin group, as the Provisional Government of National Unity. Out of twenty-one ministers in the new government, fourteen were members of the Lublin Committee. Gomulka was chosen First Deputy Prime Minister. Soon he was to add to his responsibilities the Ministry of the Recovered Territories (that is, the western territories acquired from Germany). The period of armed struggle was over, and now the Polish Workers' Party was to begin the long process of transformation which by 1948 was to make Poland in reality, if not officially, a totalitarian one-party state.

In his book, *Roosevelt and the Russians*, Edward R. Stettinius, Jr., was to count as a qualified success of Anglo-American policy the fact that the Polish government as it actually emerged in June 1945 included Mikolajczyk and other non-Communist leaders.[14] It is very easy to see now that the inclusion of certain non-Communist leaders in the Polish government had been, as a matter of fact, an avowed aim of Soviet policy before Yalta and that the Polish Communists, whether willingly or not, were also made to pursue the same aim. And it is easy to understand why. In 1945 the Polish Communists had neither the personnel nor the ability to run the state by themselves. They needed technicians, administrators, and economists, many of whom were to be found only abroad and among those Poles who would not return to work for a purely Communist government, but who would be reassured by the presence in the government of people like Mikolajczyk. The specter of a civil war was not absent in Poland in 1945, and the arrival of "democratic leaders" and their inclusion in the government served to shift the arena of the struggle to the political level, where, the Communists were confident they would be eventually victorious. The same strategy was pursued in every satellite country, and

[14] "The agreement on Poland was, under the circumstances, a concession by Marshal Stalin to the Prime Minister and the President" (*Roosevelt and the Russians: The Yalta Conference* [New York, 1949], p. 303).

Poland in 1945 was the country in which Communism was weak and the task of imposing the structure of a "People's Democracy" appeared to be the hardest of all the satellites. The policies of the united front and the coalition government, rather than being concessions to the West or, as alleged afterward, signs of the "nationalist deviation" and "rotten liberalism" on Gomulka's part, were in fact necessary steps in the transformation of Poland into a satellite state of the U.S.S.R.

As an instrument of that transformation, the Polish Workers' Party and its leadership between 1945 and 1948 deserved well of the Soviet Union and world Communism. The Party had by far the most difficult task of all the Communist Parties of the satellite countries. The Polish Communists in 1945 did not have at their disposal a large military force, as did their comrades in Yugoslavia, nor did they have a large degree of genuine popular support such as the Czech Communists enjoyed. The Poles had to operate in a traditionally anti-Russian and anti-Communist society where, unlike the situation in Bulgaria, Rumania, or Hungary, none of the older and more popular parties had been compromised by collaboration with the Germans. They had behind them the bayonets of the Red Army, but bayonets by themselves cannot dig coal, rebuild cities, or collect grain. Much of their success can be explained by the bloodletting and exhaustion caused by the war and by the apparent disinterest or inability of the West to change the growing pattern of the totalitarian state. But an important part of the explanation lies in the character and skill of the leaders of Polish Communism.

Accompanying the Russian army to Poland were those Polish Communists who had been either domiciled in Russia or who had served in the Polish detachments with the Red Army. Many of them were immediately coöpted into the highest Party organs, the Central Committee and its subdivisions, and assumed correspondingly high state positions. It was at the same time natural and unavoidable that the very top positions both in the state and in the Party should be retained by those Communists who, during the war, had worked in the underground: Boleslaw Bierut became President of the National Council, that is, head of the state; Gomulka was retained as the Secretary-General of the Workers' Party; the Minister of War and commander in chief of the Polish army was Marshal Rola-

Zymierski. Zymierski was technically not a member of the Polish Workers' Party, but he had been wartime commander in chief of its People's Army. Immediately below these men were often other Communists—those who had come from Russia. In the Politburo of the Polish Workers' Party as it was reconstituted after the war the two elements were nicely balanced. There was no room among the Polish Communists, therefore, for the feeling of cohesion and fraternity which pervaded the Communist Party in Yugoslavia. In a sense its leaders were strangers to each other. Likewise, the position of Poland vis-à-vis Russia did not permit, or so it seemed in 1945, the combination of national pride and Communist fervor which was so characteristic of the leadership of the C.P.Y.

And finally, to point out one last great distinction between the situations in Yugoslavia and Poland, Polish Communism was weak from the point of view both of numbers and of popular esteem. It had not led a great armed movement of resistance and liberation. Though by October 1945 its membership had risen from the thirty thousand of the preceding January to two hundred and ten thousand, the increase could hardly indicate an accession of devoted and reliable members.[15] It was the strategy of the Communist leaders which enabled them during the next three years to build up the power of their Party to the point, ironically enough, where the Party itself could be purged and some of them liquidated politically without lessening the Communist grip upon Poland. They managed to do it while guiding the country along the road of economic reconstruction and expansion which was taking place despite Russia's economic exactions. Though it is extremely doubtful that, as Miss Warriner says, "by 1948 the government had made a brilliant synthesis of revolutionary policy and national feeling," [16] by 1948, the government did in fact succeed in applying a veneer of nationalism and economic success to its policy of dictatorship and subservience to Russia. But the events of 1948 were to rub off some of this coating.

The official voice of Polish Communism was fond of repeating, before the summer of 1948, that there was no need for Poland to repeat the experience of the U.S.S.R., and that in Poland socialism

---

[15] The figures are in Kwiatkowski, *Communists in Poland*, pp. 79–80.
[16] Warriner, *Revolution in Eastern Europe*, p. 27.

could and would be achieved through different means and without the violence and disruption of the Russian experiment. The official voice was most often that of the highest functionary of Polish Communism, Gomulka-Wieslaw. Thus, in January 1947, the Secretary-General in a speech dwelt upon the significant differences between the development of socialism in Poland and in the U.S.S.R., stressing such seemingly startling points (for a Communist, at least) as the absence and the lack of need for the dictatorship of the proletariat in Poland, and the fact that in Poland socialism could be achieved through evolutionary means and could evolve into a pattern quite different from that of the Fatherland of Socialism.[17] To be sure, Gomulka was then wooing the Socialist Party, which, stripped of its "rightist elements," was to be amalgamated with the Polish Workers' Party, and the essence of his speech differed but little from similar pronouncements in the same period made by the Communist notables in Hungary and Czechoslovakia. But the Secretary-General made such pronouncements almost too frequently. He was fond of disparaging the record of the old Polish Communist Party with its accursed legacy of "Luxemburgism," and of drawing a favorable picture of the development of the Polish Socialist Party, which despite its many faults had correctly embraced the principle of national independence.

Not that Gomulka could ever be accused of un-Communist softness or liberalism. When it came to the question of political power there could be no compromise. The Polish Peasant Party of Mikolajczyk attempted to compete with the Communists, so it had to be broken through legal chicanery and terrorism, and its leader had to flee the country. But the prevailing tone of Polish Communism was one of moderation, and it had a soothing effect on the country. The peasants were assured again and again that following the land reform there would be no collectivization for a long time to come, if at all. The Catholic Church was not attacked directly, nor were its economic privileges as yet curtailed. The Socialist Party was pressed hard at times to get rid of its "rightist" elements and to prepare for its merger with the Communists, but on the surface a certain atmosphere of comradely equality was observed, and Gomulka himself used to speak in warm tones about its traditions and

[17] Wladyslaw Gomulka, "Strong through Unity," *Nowe Drogi*, January 1947.

its leadership. In the intellectual sphere a degree of freedom was allowed which, while not satisfactory from the Western point of view, compared favorably with the conditions in the other satellites, not to speak of the U.S.S.R. Was the whole period of moderation a purely tactical maneuver or was it a reflection of the genuinely moderate views of Gomulka and his entourage? The 'answer probably lies somewhere in between. Gomulka was between 1945 and 1947 an effective and, even from the point of view of Russia, a desirable leader of Polish Communism. His personality and behavior were such that he could arouse among the rank and file of the Polish Workers' Party (most of whom were not, as yet, indoctrinated Communists), and even among some Socialists, a degree of confidence in and enthusiasm for him as a Polish Communist who had a mind and personality of his own. It is at the same time very likely, and indeed in view of Gomulka's future behavior quite probable, that the man who had been before the war a minor Communist functionary, uninitiated in matters of high policy, now had his head turned by the extent of his power; perhaps, forgetful of the origins of his authority, Gomulka was beginning to have a policy of his own.

Gomulka's position within his Party was, even at the moment of his greatest influence, not entirely free of ambiguity. It was rumored long before his fall that he was by no means the top Communist in Poland. On the other hand, many such reports came from sources eager to impart an ultra-conspiratorial flavor to a situation which from that point of view required no embellishment. Many people having the most direct connection with the political situation in Poland before 1947 could still be misinformed about the organizational structure of Polish Communism. Thus, former Premier Mikolajczyk, who had to flee Poland in 1947, could still give a list of the Politburo of the Polish Workers' Party which was largely incorrect.[18] Admittedly, a Communist Party never loses entirely its conspiratorial atmosphere. It is still possible to reconstruct Gomulka's position with a fair degree of accuracy. It is

---

[18] In the *Pattern of Soviet Domination* (London, 1948; printed in this country under the title *The Rape of Poland*), p. 258, Mr. Mikolajczyk lists as members of that body in 1948, among others, Ochab, Modzelewski, Kliszko, and Jedrychowski, none of whom were members at the time.

quite clear that he never had anything approaching the power of Tito or even the prestige of Dimitrov. In Yugoslavia, the Zhujoviches and Hebrangs were in the nature of an exception. In Poland they sat right in the Politburo and controlled important sectors of the Party and the state. Gomulka was not a military figure. The army was under the nominal leadership of Marshal Rola-Zymierski, a former professional soldier who during the war cast his fate with the Communists and served as the commander in chief of the People's Army. Actual control of the army was in the hands of two old Communists, Marian Spychalski, First Deputy Minister of War, who had served in the underground during the war, and Karol Swierczewski, a veteran of the Spanish Civil War, who had served as commander of the Polish troops attached to the Red Army. Swierczewski met his death under rather obscure circumstances, supposedly from a terrorist's bullet, in 1947. The army, staffed to some extent with Russians officers, was outside Gomulka's realm of control. Within the state administration the Secretary-General's influence was probably potent though often exercised indirectly. The secret police was directed by Stanislaw Radkiewicz, a post-liberation arrival from Russia and a member of the Politburo. The economic sphere was in the hands of another Communist notable and "Moscow Pole," Hilary Minc, whose economic policies paralleled Gomulka's utterances and who has gained, even among the opponents of Communism, a good reputation as a capable and realistic administrator. The Polish Communists, insofar as they were allowed to, pursued before 1948 a policy of reconstruction and moderate socialism in dealing with the national economy. The policy was self-professedly a temporary one.[19] But underlining Gomulka's assurances was the fact that large-scale collectivization was not even a subject of public discussions by the Party until the summer of 1948.

Within his Party the Secretary-General's position was one of great power but not of omnipotence. There were real and concrete circumstances precluding the latter. Gomulka had not built and reorganized Polish Communism as Tito had done with Yugoslav Communism. Half the members of the Politburo as it was recon-

---

[19] A statement to that effect is contained, for example, in an article in *Nowe Drogi* for July 1947 entitled, "About the meaning of certain differences in evaluating the current economic policy."

stituted after the war were strangers to Gomulka. Even within the Communist underground Gomulka's leadership had lasted but a few months and under circumstances not favorable to the building up of personal power. Ambassador Lane was sure that the top leader of Polish Communism even before 1947 was not Gomulka but Jakob Berman.[20] Berman's role during the purge of 1948 and 1949 was to suggest very strongly that he was the manager of the proceedings against Gomulka and his group. He may have been the official mentor and observer within the Workers' Party even before that. But it is unlikely that before 1948 he could have actively had a more prominent role in Party matters than Gomulka. The latter, after all, had to perform a day-to-day role as the leader of the Party. To the mass of membership of the Party, unaware of the intricate balance of power within the high command, Gomulka was allowed to assume a heroic stature. Decisions on personnel, on Party tactics, and so forth had to be cleared through him, and there is enough evidence to suggest that "Comrade Wieslaw" was not free of the dictatorial temper appropriate to his position. Limited as his opportunity to secure patronage was, it still, of course, remained quite considerable. Some of the most strategic Party posts were filled by the people who had been closest to Gomulka in his underground days. Thus Kliszko and Bienkowski, who were to share his disgrace, were in charge, respectively, of the personnel and the education apparatus of the Party. Certainly, the manner in which the 1948–49 crisis was handled suggests that Gomulka was an incomparably more influential leader and potential enemy than were his fellow sufferers for Titoism in Bulgaria and Hungary.

The Polish Communist Party, to call it thus rather than by its official name, had undoubtedly the most difficult task of all the Communist Parties in the satellite countries. It must have been, also, following the war, the object of the special solicitude and watchfulness on the part of the Soviet Union. Yet before Gomulka's disgrace in September 1948 no major purge had occurred within the Party. If the definition of a puppet includes its easy maneuverability and removal by the hand of its master, then perhaps the situation in the Polish Communist Party before 1948 makes the designation of this Party as a puppet of the U.S.S.R. something of

[20] Arthur Bliss Lane, *I Saw Poland Betrayed* (New York, 1948).

an oversimplification. And when the purge did come, it occurred not in a puppet-like fashion but as a crisis which almost split the Communist structure in Poland.

Now, it is almost axiomatic that control over policies is not a satisfactory substitute for controlling the personnel of a government. Titoism was a natural excrescence upon the body of organized Communism in Eastern Europe before the Yugoslav crisis. Imperceptibly, as the Russians could not fail to notice, their Communist colleagues in the satellite states were already growing fond of their power and were beginning to view the social and economic problems of their countries from the inside, from the point of view of men who had to handle those problems, rather than from the viewpoint of faithful servants of international Communism. In Poland by 1948 some of the prerequisites of Yugoslav Titoism were not as yet established. The Polish Communists probably could not run the country on their own without the power of the Soviet Union behind them. Moreover, the Polish Communist Party was not united, and it did not possess an omnipotent clique like the "Tito clique" in Yugoslavia. But passage of time could effect a change in both of those factors. By the end of 1947 the Polish Peasant Party, the only legal competitor for power, had been effectively destroyed by Polish Communism. The Polish Workers' Party was due by the end of 1948 to absorb the Polish Socialist Party which, though purged of its rightist and anti-Soviet elements, still possessed a wealth of organizational and administrative talent that would strengthen the grip of Polish Communists upon their country. Gomulka had been making speeches in which he lauded the traditions of the Polish Socialists (and urged them to cast off the unhealthy elements among them); he used to say further, at times, that the new united workers' party would express a synthesis of old Polish Communism and old Polish Socialism with its patriotic traditions. Was that a type of Communist "campaign oratory" or a hint that in the new united party Gomulka, who in the ordinary course of events would become its leader, would attempt to strengthen his personal position with the help of former Socialists who were still susceptible to a nationalist appeal, that he would, in fact, become a veritable dictator of the Party and the state?

The creation of the Cominform in the summer of 1947 was taken by Gomulka to mean that the hand of the U.S.S.R. would lie more heavily than before upon the domestic policies of the People's Democracies. With a fine example of Communist euphemism, he was later to refer to it as a turn of history which almost made him lose his balance.[21] Gomulka played the host at the conference which set up the Information Bureau of the nine Communist Parties. But he is supposed to have expressed his misgivings to his colleagues in the Politburo.

At the first Cominform conference Gomulka mentioned a matter which figured in the background of the tense situation within the Polish Communist Party. He referred to the work his Party was performing in eradicating the anti-Soviet sentiment in Poland and then went on to say, "The principal lever in this question is the problem of our Western territories and the knowledge that the Soviet Union helped Poland settle its frontiers on the Oder and Neisse."[22] That statement implied the fear in certain Communist circles in Poland that the Soviet Union might at one time or another reverse its 1945 position on Poland's western frontiers and again seek an alliance with German nationalists at the expense of the Polish Recovered Territories. Quite likely, Gomulka was simply thinking aloud. The recovered territories constituted the strongest card of Polish Communism in attempting to win some popularity among the Polish people. The speech of Secretary of State James F. Byrnes at Stuttgart in September 1946, when he affirmed the reservations of the United States on the subject of the Polish frontier as constituted at Potsdam, had been eagerly seized upon by the Communists in Poland and had, even in Ambassador Lane's opinion, done an irreparable damage to the standing of the Western Powers in the country.[23] Conversely, the Oder-Neisse frontier became an argument which the Polish Communists have used ever since as indicating that Communism and Soviet Russia are the only defenders of Poland against a recurrence of German militarism and territorial ambitions. But the Secretary-General of the Polish Communists was not likely to trust the German Communists, who were,

[21] *Nowe Drogi*, September–October 1948, p. 138.
[22] *For a Lasting Peace*, November 10, 1947.
[23] Lane, *I Saw Poland Betrayed*, p. 265. Mr. Byrnes stated that the frontiers were accepted by the United States only provisionally at Potsdam, and thus implied that Poland might have to return its western provinces to Germany.

under Soviet supervision, organizing Eastern Germany. Gomulka's utterance at the Cominform conference was probably another indication that the "internationalist" view was not yet firmly implanted in his Party.

On June 3, 1948, just as the Russo-Yugoslav dispute was reaching its climax, but three weeks before the meeting of the Cominform which issued the detailed condemnation of the Yugoslav Party, there took place a plenum of the Central Committee of the Polish Workers' Party. What transpired at the June plenum is not known to us directly; the only sources are the many accounts of various incidents of the plenum given during a meeting of the Central Committee held from August 31 to September 3, 1948, and reported in the Communist organ, *Nowe Drogi*. The main event at the June plenum was a speech by Gomulka containing yet another "historical analysis" of the sources of Polish Communism. Once again the Secretary-General attacked the traditions of the Social Democratic Party and praised the record of the Polish Socialist Party, particularly its attachment to Polish independence. Several members of the Central Committee took up the point of Gomulka's speech. Then the Committee adjourned, and the majority of its members returned to their everyday tasks probably unaware that they had just witnessed the beginning of a violent crisis in the Party and heard the exponent of "Polish Titoism." Three months later Bierut appraised the effect of Gomulka's speech as follows:

> The June report of Comrade Wieslaw was undoubtedly a conscious and premeditated revision of the Leninist analysis of the history of our movement. The resolution of the Political Bureau voted immediately after the June plenum contained a complete critique of the errors revealed in Comrade Wieslaw's report at the June 3d plenum of the Central Committee.[24]

Since the speech itself is not available, it is difficult to appraise its content from secondhand reports. But the question remains: Was Gomulka's a conscious deviation in the sense that it was an attempt to steer the Polish Workers' Party toward a more independent course of action, or was something read into it which was not in the speech itself? In other words, did Gomulka attempt to increase his personal control over the Party by an appeal to na-

[24] *Nowe Drogi*, September–October 1948, p. 13.

tionalist sentiment, or was his speech really innocuous but seized upon by the Communists as a pretense for getting rid of him? Here the circumstantial evidence points clearly to the first alternative. At the time of the speech the Yugoslav crisis was reaching its most critical stage. The Central Committee of the Polish Workers' Party was not supposed to know about the quarrel between Moscow and Belgrade, but those of its members who sat in the Politburo were kept informed by the Russians of the development of the quarrel and were undoubtedly given copies of the Russian letters to the Central Committee of the Communist Party of Yugoslavia. All during April and May the Politburo of the Polish Workers' Party must have been receiving the Russian letters with their fulminations against nationalism in a Communist Party, the neglect of the agrarian question, and so forth. It is inconceivable that Gomulka should not have realized before his speech that the Kremlin was about to change its line toward the satellites and that this was not the moment, if he wished to remain on the safe side, to go on trumpeting about the wicked internationalist nihilism of the Social Democratic tradition and a similar error of the old Polish Communist Party and to contrast them with the attachment to Polish independence of the Socialist tradition. Yet he chose to make his speech, and he likewise supported a conciliatory attitude toward the Yugoslavs. The speech itself was made without a prior consultation with the Politburo, a fact which, according to Bierut, constituted "a precedent-breaking violation of the organizational principles of a Marxist party." [25] Gomulka thus took the initiative in the crisis and threw his great prestige into the fight.

But very likely his fate had been decided some time before. Polish Communism no longer needed as its leader a man who could speak so easily about the nationalist tradition of the Polish Workers' Party, and who was said to be developing dictatorial tendencies. The events in Yugoslavia were demonstrating that a man who had led a Communist Party in his country during the war was apt to suffer from some aberrations which made undesirable his continuance as a leader of a People's Democracy. A secretary-general of a Communist Party is not usually a naïve man. But Gomulka's dazzling progress from a small official of Polish Communism, with

[25] *Ibid.*, p. 14.

no experience in the higher offices and problems, to the leader of his Party and state must have turned his head. His behavior was to show that he, a ruthless and impetuous fighter when it came to dealing with the enemies of Communism, tended to be rather soft and overly idealistic when it came to an intra-Party struggle. Previously his comrades, many of whom lived in considerable fear of him, had always been ready to applaud his speeches and chant his name at Party rallies, and he may have thought that a speech was the only thing needed to keep Polish Communism in its destined course and to preserve its rather limited internal autonomy. In three months he was to see the erstwhile friends and subordinates indulge in masterful analyses of the sources of Comrade Wieslaw's deviation and errors.

In the summer of 1948 the Polish Communist Party was thrown into an acutely critical situation. The Yugoslav Communists had undergone a crisis, but there Tito's faction had been strong enough to eliminate the few "Cominformists" and the Party had preserved its cohesion. But in Poland the highest functionary of the Party found himself in opposition to the majority in the Politburo. When confronted with criticisms of his speech, Gomulka refused to retract his views. The few men composing the highest council of Polish Communism held almost continuous meetings throughout June. At one point Gomulka proposed to resign without withdrawing his opinions.[26] But the Politburo could not openly acknowledge a major split in the Party, nor could it permit its leader to resign before and instead of recanting. Finally, according to the official version of the crisis, Gomulka asked for and was granted a sick leave. "During my leave," he said later, "I wanted to do something which would prevent the spread of rumors about me—namely, I wanted to open the Exhibition of the Recovered Territories. I wanted to open it with a formal, say ten-minute, speech. However, as it is known, that did not happen." [27] Gomulka's own description of what took place during his sick leave suggests strongly that during July 1948 he was in effect under house arrest.[28]

In July another plenum of the Central Committee took place;

[26] According to Bierut (*ibid.*, p. 13).
[27] *Ibid.*, p. 49.
[28] *Ibid.*

this meeting ratified the Cominform's resolution of June 28 attacking Tito and calling upon the People's Democracies to begin in earnest the collectivization of agriculture. Here was an unprecedented situation: the Central Committee was discussing the determination of matters of policy of the highest importance, but its leader, the acknowledged head of Communism in Poland, was not present. Even in the carefully edited official account of the dispute, some of the tension of those summer months is allowed to be revealed. In his first recantation Gomulka was to mention the rumor which was obviously spread in certain Party circles "that Comrade Wieslaw is defending Poland, while the others are selling out Poland."²⁹ Also, the Party was in danger of being split between the Communists who had fought in the underground and the "Muscovites," that is, those who had come from Russia at the end of the war.³⁰ It must have become clear to the leaders of the Politburo that the crisis could not be solved by an arrest of Gomulka or by a timely "accident." There were still too many people in the Party who idolized the fallen leader, and the question "what are they doing to Comrade Wieslaw," which must have agitated the rank and file of Party membership, could lead to very unpleasant consequences. Curiously, the Politburo opened negotiations in July with its Secretary-General; and, most curious of all, its emissaries were two other "deviationists," men who were friends and protégés of Gomulka—Kliszko and Bienkowski. There were, it seems, some arguments which could be made only privately, which could be suggested to Gomulka only by his personal friends.

Gomulka's own position in the crisis still presents many points of ambiguity. Though officially silenced, he was a man with tremendous prestige and considerable power. Nothing is so indicative of this as the frantic effort of his enemies to make him repudiate his views publicly and the considerable caution with which he was treated for a year and a half after his public disgrace. In his speech at the September plenum, Berman was to refer to Gomulka's "Hamlet-like" indecision, and there was evidently something in the Secretary-General's character which prevented him from fighting to the end for his power—which, he probably realized, could mean

²⁹ *Ibid.*, p. 145.
³⁰ Speech by Jozwiak-Witold, *ibid.*, p. 69.

in the long run his life. It may have been that he could not bring himself to ruin his Party by an open struggle for power or that his friends brought him a plain warning of how the Soviets were regarding his position. In his retirement during the summer of 1948 he limited himself to criticizing the resolution of the Cominform on the Yugoslav question and its implied appeal, or order, to the Communist Parties of the satellites to speed up collectivization.

On August 16, he rejoined the Politburo, and again there began a quarrel about the content of the "self-criticism" which the Politburo was pressing upon him. At times Gomulka would agree, at other times he would fight back. At one point he announced that he was withdrawing his resignation as Secretary-General.[31] But he had failed to strike when the moment was most propitious, and the struggle was largely lost. The Politburo finally suspended him and designated as his successor Boleslaw Bierut, President of the Republic. Bierut was a Communist of long standing and had participated in the Communist underground. He was, in addition, a man with considerable Moscow experience. It was primarily his work in the underground, however, that made him more desirable as Gomulka's successor than Berman or Zawadzki, both of whom were persons of greater standing and power in the Party. In view of his position as President, Bierut was supposed not to have been active in Party affairs. It is a bit remarkable, therefore, that having on August 28 announced solemnly his decision to reënter the arena of Party activities, Bierut was able to deliver on August 31 a detailed analysis of the crisis in the Party. In this as in many other respects the plenum of the Central Committee called for August 31 to "settle" the crisis was in reality a theatrical affair designed to reeducate the Party in the new policy and the new character which the Cominform was imposing upon it.

The battle over the leadership had been fought and decided before the Central Committee convened on August 31. Now the Party was to receive a lesson in Stalinist self-criticism and in its new course. The plenum was an enlarged one: in addition to the Central Committee, the provincial secretaries were also present to participate in the deliberations. The agenda had been drawn by the Politburo, which now presented a solid front against Gomulka. In

[31] According to Bierut (*ibid.*, p. 15).

addition to Gomulka, who was still formally a member, and Bierut, the Politburo was composed at the moment of the meeting of the following: Jakob Berman (also secretary of state in the Presidium of the Council of Ministers); Alexander Zawadzki, the leading organizer and emergency man of the Party; Roman Zambrowski, mainly in charge of the propaganda activities of the Party; Hilary Minc, Minister of Industry and the economic boss of Poland; Marian Spychalski, Deputy Minister of War and in charge of the ideological and political education of the army; and Stanislaw Radkiewicz, Minister of Public Security. The plenum was to coöpt into the Politburo Franciszek Jozwiak-Witold, the former chief of staff of the People's Army, largely, one suspects, as a measure of demonstration that there were good and internationally-minded Communists among members of the wartime underground. Those eight men had already determined the fate of Gomulka, and they were the only ones to know the full story behind his precipitous fall. The rest of the Central Committee was to listen, to follow, and to accept unanimously what the Politburo proposed.

That there was a third and decisive party to the dispute was carefully ignored in the debate. It appears as an axiom of Communist etiquette that no mention should be made of the position and desires of Soviet Russia. But once in a while, through usual Communist euphemism, the truth is allowed to penetrate. A turn of phrase, an intentionally ambivalent reference, fortifies occasionally the suspicion that even the Politburo of the Polish Workers' Party was not an entirely free agent in the crisis. At a subsequent plenum Roman Zambrowski referred scathingly to one of the deviators, Bienkowski, who in searching for a proper definition of his recantation refused to use the term "self-criticism," because it has Russian connotations, and substituted the word "autocriticism." Bienkowski's linguistic pedantry was thought to be in extremely bad taste.[32] He among all the accused received the severest penalty at the September plenum. Otherwise, the only reference to Soviet Russia was the continual charge of distrust of the Soviet Union flung at Gomulka and his supposed unwillingness to learn from the experience of the "first Socialist state."

The main point on the agenda of the Central Committee was

[32] *Nowe Drogi*, November 1949, p. 104.

"the resolution about the rightist and nationalist deviation in Party leadership, its sources, and the ways to overcome it." The resolution summarized in some detail the charges already suggested here: Gomulka's "chauvinism"; his and his aides' attack at the internationalist tradition of the old proletarian parties in Poland—the Social Democratic and the Communist Parties; and his hesitations about the Yugoslav crisis and about collectivization. But Gomulka could not be presented merely as a nationalist and an opponent of premature collectivization. According to a well-known pattern, his deviation had to follow logically from a long-standing and basic opposition to the principles of Leninism and Stalinism and from his unworthy weakness and willingness to capitulate in the face of the class enemies. Thus by his own admission Gomulka was to sign away his past and destroy the legend of an intrepid leader who had brought the Party from insignificance to victory. Hence Point Five of the resolution centered around the now famous article of July 1, 1944, written by Gomulka's friend Bienkowski, which urged the progressive element in the underground to abandon the London government and to establish an alliance with the Communists. That article, a typical example of the Communists' wartime propaganda and written probably at the urging of Moscow, was now made to appear a heinous crime of Gomulka, who, disregarding the growing strength of the Polish Communists and the approach of the Red Army, was willing to capitulate to the reactionaries.

Nothing in the whole debate approaches so closely the realm of Orwellian fantasy as this desperate effort to force a man to confess that a standard piece of Communist propaganda, written according to and probably at direct instructions from Moscow, was in fact a diabolically clever plot to turn the Polish Workers' Party against Russia. The amount of insistence put into the effort to force Gomulka to agree to Point Five, the pressure exerted by the very men who had been with him in the underground, who had read and approved the article, and who now after four years suddenly found its treacherous meaning, borders on self-induced insanity. Gomulka, to his credit, refused at first to vote for Point Five, though he agreed more or less to the rest of the resolution.

The three days of the debate were spent in an attempt to force Gomulka to accept the resolution without any reservations. From various isolated incidents and utterances was woven a composite picture: The Secretary-General and his associates are not to plead guilty to an error or an indiscretion, but they are to plead guilty to a frame of mind and temperament which unavoidably disposed them toward activity harmful to the Party. They are to probe into their own mentalities and expose those minor doubts and hesitations which, by even being entertained, dispose a Communist toward deviation and treason. "We have characterized the errors of Comrade Wieslaw, which, as it is attested by the resolution submitted by the Politburo, are neither isolated nor accidental but constitute, despite internal contradictions, a definite and systematic viewpoint which is rightist and nationalist in its character." [33] Gomulka, it is interesting to note, was called upon to do the same thing the Russians had wanted Tito to do. There is as yet no question of treason or of punishment. Confess that you have erred, the Politburo commanded, that you have not behaved as a Communist should, and subscribe to our analysis of the sources of your behavior! But Gomulka could not shift the discussion to a national level and say, as Tito and his partners had said, "Much as we love the Soviet Union, we cannot love our country less." For Gomulka's accusers were his colleagues, not the Russians. At times the appeal to Gomulka to recant takes on the aspect of almost pleading: "Recant before it is too late, before irreparable damage is done to the Party and to the nation."

The carefully edited account of the debate presented in the Communist organ, *Nowe Drogi*, cannot conceal, however, a variety of attitudes toward the deviators. There were many members of the Central Committee who expressed their personal sympathy for and strong emotional attachment to Comrade Wieslaw. Such supporters were found, in particular, among the former underground Communists, for whom Gomulka undoubtedly symbolized that period of danger and struggle. Their sentiment makes doubly clear why Gomulka's "deviation" had to have a long history. Even at the period of his supposed heroic leadership, he was to be shown to have entertained false liquidationist sentiments.

There were also those members for whom the debate was obviously a long-awaited opportunity to settle their accounts with the

[33] *Nowe Drogi*, September–October 1948, p. 25.

man who was their superior and whose hand, one can surmise, lay heavily on some of the comrades. Edward Ochab's speech is a classic example of the attitude of this group:

> In your present position, Comrade Wieslaw, you will become the symbol for the bourgeoisie, for the rich peasants, for reaction . . . I have been informed by our comrades from Silesia—the area where Comrade Wieslaw was so popular, where we worked so hard for his prestige —that at numerous mass meetings not a voice was raised in his honor; people somehow felt that something was "fishy." [34]

The unfortunate article of Bienkowski was for Ochab not a mistake but a "document of shame." It is not to be wondered that Ochab's career following the plenum was dazzlingly successful. Within a year he became a member of the Politburo and Deputy Minister of War. Another up-and-coming Party member, Franciszek Mazur, invoked as a crime of Gomulka his silence during the period from June to August, which, Mazur unwittingly revealed, threw some Party organizations into confusion. "The Comrades would ask: 'Why is he silent? Why don't you cut short the whole thing? The enemy is getting more insolent and the weaker circles of our Party are disintegrating. One must resolve the whole business.' " [35]

But the prevailing tone was more cautious and more pleading: Let Comrade Wieslaw recant fully and all will be well. It was suggested that true nationalism does, in fact, call for a full and unconditional recantation. Comrade Wieslaw and his friends, it was held, were afraid that "a full realization of Socialism in Poland" might interfere with Poland's independence and sovereignty. Quite the contrary, said Minister of Foreign Affairs, Modzelewski. By realizing socialism in Poland we are strengthening our frontier on the Oder and Neisse.[36] The reference and the hint are unmistakable: If anyone thinks that the issue can be settled completely right here in Poland, let him think again.

Berman's speech was almost cordial in its reference to Gomulka and contained an oblique warning that the Secretary-General was not to be attacked too fiercely: Let Comrade Wieslaw recant, let him repudiate his pretended followers, and all will be forgotten and

[34] *Ibid.*, p. 63.
[35] *Ibid.*, p. 102.
[36] *Ibid.*, p. 118.

forgiven.[37] Let him repudiate his "mystical notions" that he is defending some supposedly threatened national sovereignty, and let him march together with the Party.

It is impossible to visualize the effect on Gomulka of his ordeal at the September plenum. Virtually disarmed beforehand, abandoned by his closest colleagues and friends, he had to sit for three days and listen to about forty people plead, abuse, cajole, and attack him in turn. In his first speech he admitted most of the charges: his "rightist-nationalist" deviation, his original belief that collectivization would be premature, and his doubts about the correctness of the Cominform's resolution regarding Yugoslavia. Finally, at the end of the debate, he was willing to plead guilty to Point Five: his wartime distrust of the U.S.S.R., and his willingness then to compromise with reaction. His final speech, even when it is borne in mind that the speaker was at times a ruthless and unscrupulous fighter who liquidated opposition by terrorist means and who had not hesitated at first to subordinate his country to Soviet Russia, is a rather moving, if strange, testimony to that unusual idealism of the vanishing type of Communist leaders.

> I have come to the plenum, not because I hoped or desired to be defended by you, Comrades, or to remain as Secretary-General . . . I have come with the idea that you Comrades will free me from my responsibilities and will allow me to work in a small Party position . . . Nobody can flee the responsibility. There are two ways: one may break with the Party and flee the responsibility, or one may stay with the Party and face his duty.[38]

And here Gomulka revealed his fatal weakness in the struggle for power: the idealism and sentimentality of a "home-grown" Communist, which prompted him to deliver himself and the Party into the hands of those whose Communist fanaticism was combined with a more cynical notion of power and its meaning. It may have amused the managers of the proceedings, who were fully aware that what was happening was but the first step, to hear Gomulka declare that "for me it is difficult not to say what I think." And in the same vein, while recanting, he still returned to his main sin: his insistence on a Polish road to socialism. The historical circum-

[37] *Ibid.*, pp. 112–116.
[38] *Ibid.*, p. 137.

stances during the establishment of socialism in the U.S.S.R. were different from those now in Poland. "Therefore, there must be some elements of a Polish road to socialism." [39] And his attitude toward the U.S.S.R.? He wanted good, neighborly relations between Poland and Russia, but he did not seem to realize that there should be a straightforward connection between the Communist Parties of the two countries. There is an element of conscious or unconscious irony in his admission of Point Five:

> It may have been harder for the comrades who were not in the country during the [German] occupation to take a correct attitude toward Point Five of the resolution. Yet without having been in the country they evaluated the problem correctly on the basis of the discussion and guided by the compass of Marxist analysis, while I, who had had a direct contact with the situation, evaluated it incorrectly. [40]

It was a strange recantation, but the Politburo must have realized that nothing more could be dragged out of Gomulka, so his third and final speech was generously adjudged to be a satisfactory form of self-criticism. His resignation was accepted by the Central Committee. He was not formally removed from the Politburo, but it is clear that in fact he ceased to be its member. Four of his followers were demoted from full to alternate members of the Central Committee. The unfortunate Bienkowski was thrown out altogether. Another deviationist, Moczar, a man with an enviable reputation as a partisan fighter and political terrorist, was let off with a reprimand. [41]

Having disposed of the main business of the plenum, the Central Committee turned its attention to the problem of collective agriculture. The connection between the two items of the agenda was not incidental. Before their recantation Gomulka and his group had not believed that it was timely to begin collectivizing Polish agriculture. Being Communists, they could have no reservations about collectivization in the long run. Yet in Poland the problem was beset with particular difficulties. The mass of peasants in Poland, as elsewhere, is both radical and conservative—radical, insofar as

[39] *Ibid.*, p. 143.
[40] *Ibid.*, p. 139.
[41] His excuse was that as a head of the secret police he had been too busy exterminating various enemies of the Party to realize the Secretary-General's deviation (*ibid.*, pp. 107–108).

they detest privilege, the rich peasant, and political authority; conservative, insofar as they wish to retain their old customs, way of
life, and religion. The process of agricultural reforms was initiated by the Communists as soon as the Red Army reached Poland.[42] The western territories, from which the Germans were being expelled, gave
a particular scope for the redistribution of land. So did the landed
estates. On September 6, 1944, all estates over fifty hectares in
central Poland and over one hundred hectares in western Poland
were ordered by the Lublin government to be parceled out (ex-
cepting the property of the Church).[43] Though the plots were
small (it was claimed by some that they were intentionally so to
make them unworkable), the majority of the peasants could not
but be content with the reform which had been promised, but not
far advanced, by the prewar Polish state. To the believers in the
"Polish way to socialism," collectivization appeared in 1945 as a
long-range and distant project, conditioned by the need, first, for re-
educating the peasants, and secondly, for stabilizing and strengthening the Communist rule. While the radicalism of the Polish
peasant had been satisfied, his conservativism had to be appeased.
Instinctively, he distrusted the Communists, and he had always held
on to his land with incredible tenacity. Between 1945 and 1948
talk about collectivization was hushed. It was not Gomulka but
Ochab who during that period wrote: "One should conduct a
policy which would not scare the peasants."[44] The June 1948
resolution of the Cominform, with its directive to the People's
Democracies to start collectivization and the fight against the class
enemy among the peasants, must have been a particular shock to
the Polish Communists. On purely practical grounds, they were
scared of the whole issue.

The agricultural policy formulated at the plenum by Hilary
Minc shows all the signs of this trepidation. The Polish Communists
still felt themselves to be in a beleaguered fortress, yet they were
prompted to start upon a task which the Communist Party of the
U.S.S.R. had tackled in earnest only after ten years in power, and

[42] Kwiatkowski, *Communists in Poland*, p. 69.
[43] Sanders, "Changing Status of the Peasant in Eastern Europe," pp. 80–81.
[44] Cited in Kwiatkowski, *Communists in Poland*, p. 121.

which almost wrecked the regime. Hence Minc's obvious hemming and hawing on the issue. Who, for instance, was to be considered the class enemy in the village? Not necessarily a peasant who owned a great deal of land. Then, a man might hire laborers and still not be a *kulak*. The criterion had to be a flexible one, and Minc warned forcibly that every prosperous farmer, every *serednyak*, was not to be taken for a class enemy.[45]

As for collectivization, the Party proposed to go slowly and cautiously. For 1949 it was planned, at most, to collectivize only 1 per cent of privately owned farm land, and from then on the pace was envisaged at 1 per cent, at most, for each of the next three or four years. Those Party members who attempted to use violent means to persuade peasants to join in a coöperative were to be severely punished.[46] The form of the coöperative undertakings was shrouded in vagueness equal to that of the identity of the class enemy. The peasant was not to lose title to his land when he joined a coöperative. Several forms of the *kolkhoz* were sketched, all of them permissible, ranging from a simple producer's coöperative for rationalizing soil cultivation and for common use of machinery, but fully preserving the principle of private property and individual reward (analogous to the Russian *toz*), to a more advanced coöperative where the peasants still would own individually their cattle as well as a modicum of land. The latter, called by Minc the most advanced type of coöperative, was still not as socialistic as the *artel*, the prevailing type of the Russian *kolkhoz*.[47] It was stipulated that the Party would not tolerate an excessively Communist collective which would attempt to socialize everything, including the peasant's cattle, fowl, his house or garden.

Minc's position on the problem of collectivization betrays two very interesting phenomena. On one hand, the Party spoke with complete authority. There was not even a pretense that the Polish Workers' Party was legally but one of several parties in the country in 1948, or that officially it did not even possess a majority in the Diet. The Communists were not talking about what they would like to see happen, but what would happen, and what their supposed

[45] *Nowe Drogi*, September–October 1948, p. 160.
[46] *Ibid.*, p. 176.
[47] *Ibid.*, pp. 177–178.

colleagues in power, the Socialists and the Peasant Party, would have to accept. Poland was already a one-party dictatorship in fact though not in name. It is equally obvious that the agricultural policy had been thought through and devised by the Politburo. The rest of the Central Committee was informed about the decision and asked to discuss it, but no one would dare to oppose it or attempt to change an important feature. And the discussion ironically illustrates the hypocrisy of the proceedings against Gomulka. Where is the principle of collegiate responsibility, supposedly slighted by Gomulka, if this extremely important new policy is imposed upon the nation as the result of a decision arrived at by eight people? Gomulka had been attacked because of his implication that some Party members might resort to violence in carrying out collectivization. Nobody, it was alleged, was even thinking in terms of compulsion in connection with the peasants, and only an ideologically sick mind could envisage Communists doing such things. But the possibility was concrete enough to evoke a stern warning from Minc. The Party and the Politburo will do this or that, but it is not up to an individual member to ask why.

But the degree of assurance exhibited in connection with what the Party would or could do politically was not matched by an assurance of what the result of the policy would be. The effect of Minc's words was almost: "Here is something dangerous, something extremely sensitive, something we would prefer not to do right away if we could get away with it. We are going to do it slowly and cautiously." The policy was announced without the euphoria which almost always characterizes the launching of a major social policy by a Communist Party. Even in the matter of phraseology, the Party felt impelled to conform to the Russian pattern. At the July plenum the "experience" of the U.S.S.R. with collectivization was omitted from the preliminary announcement of the policy, but now, Minc said, "We have understood that we were wrong not to speak about the experience of the U.S.S.R. in refashioning agricultural life when we set up the program of changing the life in villages in Poland at the July plenum." [48] The problem of collectivization was tackled carefully, and it reflected not

[48] Minc, quoted in *Nowe Drogi*, September–October 1948, p. 203.

only the tenacity of the Polish peasant, the realism of Minc and of others charged with the national economy, but also the external pressure applied under the guise of the Cominform resolution. The new course had been charted, and the Party would follow it, but as cautiously and slowly as the Russians would permit.

The carefully edited columns of the Party organ are but an imperfect substitute for actual knowledge of the situation as it developed within the Polish Workers' Party after the September plenum. Gomulka and his group were defeated. The Party was launched on a new course. The example of the U.S.S.R. previously kept carefully in the background and alluded to but cautiously became the model and reference for everything in Poland. The Party press since 1948 has kept the Soviet Union in the foreground of every pertinent news item, and no Party official has been able to get through a speech without several references to Marshal Stalin and the Red Army. It is as if the new masters of the Party felt themselves on trial for their reliability; as if Titoism, far from being a disease entirely curable by surgery, was, in fact, an organic degeneration striking every Communist Party once it achieved power —a malignant condition which has to be watched and periodically checked.

On December 15, 1948, the purged Polish Workers' Party absorbed the Polish Socialist Party. The latter, in its name at any rate, perpetuated until the merger the tradition of a great socialist party which, in addition to its distinguished progressive record, had been the political movement that sustained Polish independence as its chief postulate. Now, purged of its "rightist" leaders, its main figures abroad, the Socialist Party still brought into the Communist fold a multitude of experienced administrators, trade unionists, and organizers. The Unity Congress was carefully staged. Out of 1539 delegates, 1013 came from the Workers' Party and 526 from the Polish Socialist Party. The latter, which only a year before had made a show of independence and whose leaders had talked about the need in Poland for an independent socialist party, had lost in the intervening year its *esprit de corps* and its courage.[49] The merger was in effect a surrender. The new United Workers' Party selected

[49] See "The Fate of Polish Socialism" by "R" in *Foreign Affairs*, October 1949.

a Politburo of eleven members. Eight of them came from the old Politburo of the Workers' Party, and three from the Socialists.[50] Bierut became chairman of the United Party, thus offsetting the fact that the post of Secretary-General went to a former Socialist, Jozef Cyrankiewicz, Prime Minister of Poland and the man who more than any other leader had been responsible for the emasculation of Polish Socialism and its easy absorption by Communism. Moreover Cyrankiewicz's position was carefully limited in the secretariat by the appointment of two co-secretaries, Roman Zambrowski and Alexander Zawadzki, who had both come from Moscow rather than the underground.

The proceedings of the Unity Congress were not without dramatic interest. The assembled, including the delegates of the fraternal party of the U.S.S.R., Ponomarenko and Pospelov, could watch and listen to the one-time leader but now horrible example of deviationism, Wladyslaw Gomulka. After his public disgrace, Gomulka lingered on as Deputy Prime Minister and even nominally as a member of the Politburo. His importance at the time of the Congress still warranted his inclusion in the Central Committee of the United Party. Hilary Minc asserted later that the delegates had to be persuaded to vote for Gomulka, and the statement is quite credible.[51] Gomulka was included by the Politburo in the list of candidates to show the Party's unity, but it would have been suicidal for any Communist to come out for him with enthusiasm. As a matter of fact, a "spontaneous" demonstration was arranged against Gomulka after his speech, which, though in no way different from his recantation, was considered "vile."

After the September plenum Gomulka could not make a single speech or move without being denounced. Like a ghost, he moved through the Party meetings and chronicles, wondering aloud if there might not be after all an element of a "Polish road to Socialism" and protesting his loyalty to the Soviet Union and Communism. In January 1949 he was discharged as Deputy Prime Minister and Minister of the Recovered Lands. Almost as a gesture of

---

[50] *For a Lasting Peace,* January 1, 1949.

[51] Hamilton Fish Armstrong's assertion that in the elections Gomulka "received more votes than any other candidate except Bierut" (*Tito and Goliath,* p. 149) is mistaken. All such elections are, of course, by acclamation.

derision he was given the post of Second Vice-President of the Supreme Control Commission. He had proved himself, after all, to be a "romantic," and there is a degree of deliberation in the publicity given to his speeches, full as they are of hesitation and expressions of inner doubt and divided loyalty. They cannot fail to evoke a degree of sympathy in a man brought up in the liberal tradition, but to a hardened Communist, even if he be a potential Titoist, such expressions exhibit a nauseating sentimentality and softness that can only disqualify a man for the task of leadership of a Communist Party.

But Gomulka's loss of prestige did not make the Communist Party in Poland, now officially known as the United Workers' Party, safe from Titoism. It is worth while to observe the variety of measures applied in this most important of the satellites to minimize and eradicate potential Titoism. In the first place, no single leader has been allowed to inherit the mantle of leadership torn away from Gomulka. His titular successor, Bierut, has been built up as the nation's leader, but the day-to-day activity of the Party appears to be supervised by the triumvirate of Alexander Zawadzki, Jakob Berman, and Roman Zambrowski. The machinery of the state is in the direct charge of yet another set of Communist leaders. There is, of course, a considerable amount of overlapping between the two sets of leaders, but no single person is allowed too great an accumution of offices. When Zawadzki, who has been performing a variety of specific organizational tasks for the Party, assumed the position of Chairman of the Trade Unions, he resigned simultaneously as Deputy Prime Minister. It may be too much to see a definite pattern toward a careful apportionment of power, yet aside perhaps from President Bierut no Communist is given an amount of publicity approaching that previously expended on Gomulka.

The Polish army has always been a particular concern of the Communist regime. The prewar Polish regime of 1926–1939 was in fact based on a military group, and the propensity of the army for a political role has always been strong in Poland. The Polish army, as it was reconstituted after the war, was based heavily upon the officer material provided by the Polish units that had fought with the Red Army during the war. There was some influx of Russian officers, though the exact extent is hard to ascertain. Theoretically, until the fall of 1949, the army remained under Marshal Rola-Zymierski, its commander in chief and the Minister of War.

Zymierski was a man with a shady past. A regular army officer under the old regime, he had been convicted of taking bribes and was discharged from the army. At the beginning of the war he offered his services to the regular Polish underground army, but, rejected, turned to the Communists.[52] Whether it was his skill as an underground leader or the fact that he had been a regular army officer, Michal Zymierski became "General Rola"—the commander in chief of the People's Army. His usefulness continued beyond the war: a man with his past was not likely to become a national hero, and the fact that he was not a "real" Communist guaranteed his political insignificance. Politically, the army remained in the charge of General Marian Spychalski, an old-line Communist and member of the Politburo, who thus continued his wartime role as the chief of the intelligence section of the People's Army. Spychalski had been even during the war a man of considerable political importance. It was he who in the spring of 1944 led the delegation of the Communist underground and of the Communist-sponsored National Council to Moscow.[53] It was his past, and probably the very measure of importance and confidence he had enjoyed in Polish Communism during the war, that was to doom Spychalski in the new phase upon which the Party entered following the crisis of 1948.

The whole tone of the Party press and the nature of its work had to change following the September plenum and the Unity Congress of December 1948. The Party bowed before and followed the Cominform. The "Polish road to socialism" now joined the list of deviations. But the process of eradicating Titoism could not be accomplished merely by the removal of Gomulka or by the purge of the Party following the "unification." The Polish Communists who presented the most fertile ground for Titoism had to be again purged and reconstructed more fundamentally than by just changing a few leaders. A more determined effort had to be made to secure some real basis for the allegiance of the Polish Communists. Thus throughout 1949 one hears continually about the inviolability of the Polish-German frontier on the Oder and Neisse. To the defeated op-

---

[52] This is the version asserted in Kwiatkowski, *Communists in Poland*, p. 104.
[53] *Ibid.*, p. 47.

position within the Party was attributed the devilish plot of maligning the intentions of the U.S.S.R. in connection with the frontier. Various statements by East German Communist leaders were paraded to show a change of heart among the German Communists and their acquiescence in the Potsdam decision. It is not likely that such frequent protestations by the German Communists about the permanence of the Oder-Neisse frontier would have been made without strong Russian pressure. And, in turn, the Russian attitude on the subject becomes understandable only if we assume that the ruling circles in Russia reached the decision that the loyalty of the Polish Communists, at least for the time being, could not be assured by repression alone.

But the Polish Party had to undergo yet another public purge. The remnants of Gomulka's popularity had to be destroyed, and the status of near-traitor had to be established for him and for those closest to him. Unexpectedly, a new issue and a new personality were to be injected into the last or next to the last chapter of Gomulka's story.

Early in the fall of 1949, Marian Spychalski was dismissed from his post, and Edward Ochab was given the position of Deputy Minister of War. Ochab, like Spychalski, was a Communist with a long record of work for the Party. Unlike his predecessor he had not been in the underground, but in Moscow and with the Polish units of the Red Army during the war. His appointment was but the first step in the reconstruction of the Polish army, for in November of the same year Marshal Konstantin Rokossovsky of the Red Army was hastily converted into a Polish citizen and, supposedly at the request of the Polish government, was given the command of the Polish army and the Ministry of War.

Rokossovsky's appointment stirred up a mass of speculations and rumors. On the surface, it was the farthest public extension yet of Soviet interference in the affairs of Russian satellites. That the Soviet government should not be satisfied with its indirect influence over Poland's army, with its military mission, and even with a number of former Russian officers within that army, that it should send openly one of its officers to take command over a satellite's army, appeared to the world as an unabashed confession of the relationship existing between the two countries. It is, however, almost certainly incorrect to assume, as the press in the West has done, that Rokossovsky was sent to Poland in a political as well as a military capacity. Though he was almost immediately coöpted into the Central Committee of the United Polish Workers' Party and then (May 1950) into its Politburo, it is unlikely that he plays directly a major political role. The Kremlin has not shown in the past a tendency to entrust its high military officers with the top political functions, the major exceptions having been such military figures with long Communist backgrounds as Voroshilov and Bulganin. Rokossovsky's appointment probably does have a political significance, but in a different sense. The time came in 1949 to integrate the Polish army more fully into the Communist system. Marshal Rola-Zymierski, having completed his task, was allowed to retire, since he was not a "real" Communist. At the same time, the army was too important as a segment of power to entrust it to a prominent Communist leader. A Titoist in the position of commander in chief, and with friends in the Party, could turn out to be a far more powerful enemy than a secretary-general. Thus the appointment of a Russian marshal, even though he was of Polish origin, could not but neutralize political potentiality inherent in the post, for how conceivable is it that a Russian marshal should lead a nationalist deviation in Poland? In addition, there were undoubtedly military reasons for the appointment.

Rokossovsky's appointment preceded the last phase of the Titoist crisis in the Polish Communist Party. When and if the Polish Communists stray away again from the path prescribed for them by the Cominform, it will be done by different people and under different circumstances from those which prevailed in the crisis of 1948–49. The last appearance of Gomulka as a Party functionary took place at the plenum of the Central Committee which met on November 11, 1949. This time, in addition to Gomulka and Kliszko, another deviationist, Marian Spychalski, took the floor.

Spychalski's role as a deviationist was completely unexpected. In September 1948 he delivered one of the most severe diatribes against Gomulka. His whole background had been that of a devoted Communist; he was one of the founders of the Polish Workers' Party. What then were his sins? Again the accusers reached into the past and came up with a fantastic accumulation of errors and betrayals. In his role as the intelligence chief of the People's Army, Spychalski allegedly allowed several enemies of the Party to penetrate into its ranks. Was it carelessness or treason? A whole army of ghosts was evoked by Spychalski's accusers, led by Bierut. The names mentioned were little known; they were the names of minor officials uncovered as spies and liquidated. Somehow, through Spychalski's machinations, they all had penetrated the Party, the army, or the state apparatus. The irrationality of the charges was so striking that, like the famous article of July 1, 1944, used against Gomulka, they certainly concealed something else. If the Communist underground had been penetrated by spies and class enemies during the war, how could the fault lie only upon Spychalski, or upon Spychalski and Gomulka? Certainly some of the accusers were more intimately concerned with the People's Army and its personnel than were the accused.

Was Spychalski's real fault contained in the charge, which was phrased rather delicately and given no undue emphasis, that he allowed "valuable Soviet specialists to depart prematurely"? Was that a euphemism concealing his possible opposition to the increasing penetration of the Polish army by the Russians? The vision of a Communist minister chasing out a group of Russian generals, who, eager to go home, entrain for their country and thus deprive the Polish army of their invaluable experience, is not very convincing. Spychalski's real sin may have been his knowledge and incautious revelation of the Party's secrets during the war. His position during the war gave him an access to the real story of the Polish Communists' contacts with Moscow. He was with the delegation which went to Russia on behalf of the underground in the spring of 1944. Did he by any chance let slip that Gomulka was being punished for the very things which in wartime had been suggested and ordered by the "comrades in Russia"? The same session of the Central Committee which witnessed Spychalski's abject and panic-stricken recantation heard Stanislaw Radkiewicz, head of the Ministry of Internal Security, warn against a betrayal of the Party's secrets.[54] Whatever the real reason for Spychalski's disgrace, he had been in a position to know a great many Party secrets, among them the greatest of all—the real story, from its inception, of the

[54] *Nowe Drogi*, November 1949, p. 168.

relationship of the Polish Workers' Party with the leaders of Soviet Communism.

The plenum was held in an atmosphere quite different from that of its predecessor of 1948. This was a period of purges and hysteria, and many members of the Central Committee obviously did not know where they stood or whether an incident of the past would return to haunt them and reduce them to the ranks of "deviators." Spychalski himself is a classic example of the Communist self-accuser. In his speeches he achieved a considerable degree of self-abasement and cringing: "Despite my great mistakes, I dare to beg you to leave me in the Party." [55] And the answers he received were equally characteristic: "As for the so-called self-criticism of Comrade Spychalski, that self-criticism was limited to things already known to Party leadership and did not advance the whole matter one step further." [56]

The plenum was oriented toward a new version of Titoism. The year before Titoism had been a matter of ideological deviation. In 1949, following the fantasies of the trial of Rajk and the new line toward Yugoslavia, it had become a vast panorama of treasons and plots and espionage activities. The deviationists were encouraged to go beyond the accusations against them and to spare their comrades some work by confessing to even greater crimes. Thus, a member concentrating on the Gomulka group could say: "What Comrade Kliszko said is only a small part of what he could reveal." [57] The time had come for the transition from deviation to treason.

Gomulka was still the central figure. Spychalski and Kliszko were easily broken and were treated with a certain contempt by the rest of the Central Committee. But Gomulka was treated differently. One year before he had been urged in cordial tones to return and to "march with the Party." Now the accusation took on a more somber character. Hadn't his two predecessors during the war fallen into the hands of the Germans? The official charge against Gomulka was still his "lack of vigilance." But beneath this charge was a more terrible layer of insinuation. Many an accusing speech achieved the effect of saying: Was it merely a lack of vigilance which led such people as Gomulka to tolerate as their closest subordinates spies and provocateurs? Minc reminded Gomulka that he had achieved

[55] *Ibid.*, p. 78.   [56] *Ibid.*, p. 78.   [57] *Ibid.*, p. 162.

his position during the war because the previous Secretary-General had been betrayed to the Germans. Wasn't that one accident too many; wasn't it suspicious that those experienced and loyal Communists had been betrayed and succeeded by a "nationalist," a man who was to show himself partial to his colleagues from the underground and unfriendly toward Polish Communists who had spent the war in the Soviet Union?[58] Wasn't Gomulka distrustful of the German Communists? His previous recantation had had to be torn from him. Hadn't he attempted to summon other People's Democracies to support his idea that each of them had to follow its own separate path to socialism? [59] Minc's speech was so hysterical that its very violence lends substance to the rumor that he himself had come close to sharing the fate of his leader and now had to cover him with vituperation.

The "one accident too many" version of Gomulka's and his group's activity was taken up by the other participants in the debate. This time no holds were barred in the attack upon the former Secretary-General. It is curious to find a complete inversion of normal values so startlingly exhibited. Gomulka was criticized for allegedly having used as a criterion for selection to a state or Party post whether the man in question was a "good Polish patriot." He had readmitted into the Party those Communists who had been thrown out for Trotskyism but who during the war had rendered distinguished service. Still more criminal, when a Party member was accused of anti-Russian sentiments, Gomulka had asked for the proofs before punishing the wretch.[60] It would be pleasant to believe fully in such reports and to accept Gomulka as a Bayard of the Communist movement. Yet nothing worse could be said in 1949 about a Communist leader than that he was a liberal and a patriot; hence, we should not be too ready to accept Gomulka as a noble spirit, without fear and above reproach.

Still he was, for a fallen Communist, a man of considerable moral courage. His speech, which, barring an unusual course of events, was to have been his last free public pronouncement, was quite different from the cowardly and groveling utterances of

[58] *Ibid.*, p. 117.
[59] *Ibid.*, p. 118.
[60] *Ibid.*, pp. 174–175.

Spychalski and Kliszko. Why, asked the fallen leader, was he being blamed for everything that had gone wrong in the Party? There were others who shared the responsibility with him, and they were now his accusers.[61] Why was he being dragged in the dirt and humiliated repeatedly, when his whole life had been devoted to the Party, to the cause of Communism? He indignantly refused any share in the responsibility for the deaths of his predecessors, Marceli Nowotko and Paul Finder. As for his political sins, he turned upon his main enemy in the Party and asked, "Don't you think, Comrade Ochab, that my definition [of the nature of the People's Democracy] was applicable not only to Poland, and that the leaders of other People's Democracies took [prior to 1948] a position analogous to mine?"[62] Why was he then singled out as a deviationist?

But the time had passed for a counterattack. His first recantation had accomplished its purpose. He now stood as a broken man, a self-discredited leader, whom it was quite safe to ridicule and attack. And even his plea and query met a derisive and threatening answer. "Doesn't Comrade Gomulka know how the Party talks to an enemy?" asked Alexander Zawadzki; "I think Comrade Gomulka does know . . . And he knows how the Party would talk to him were the Party to treat him as an enemy."[63] And the words, with Rajk's trial in the background, had an unmistakable meaning and warning.

The plenum was full of tension and even hysteria, but it was not without a tragicomic relief. The relief was provided by those former Socialists now members of the Central Committee (and even allowed to speak in it); they were, not unnaturally, awed and bewildered by this quarrel among the real Communists. More than one former Socialist begged the comrades not to forget that there were some traces of deviationism among the old Socialist group. Even Cyrankiewicz did not dare to talk about the main issue of the plenum, but devoted his time to a defamation of the tradition of his old party.[64] Other former Socialists, some of them a year or two before courageous defenders of the independence of the Socialist

[61] Ibid., p. 113.
[62] Ibid., p. 116.
[63] Ibid., p. 157.
[64] Ibid., p. 100.

Party, were now trotted out to vilify their own background and former associates and to relate, incredulously, that they had been allowed to retain a state post or had even been given a small job in the Party. Oscar Lange, in execrating the Socialist tradition, found as its most disgusting trait "a snobbish regard for so-called public opinion." [65] He, also, had traveled a long road very fast.

But the record of the plenum, intentionally misleading as it often is, is particularly valuable in giving an insight into the minds of the genuine Communists. Here is heard the accusing yet discordant chorus: the cold and merciless voices of the real leaders of the Party, who turn without hesitation and with real sadism upon their former friend and leader; the voice of an obtuse Party hack who as an editor of a journal has received a great many anonymous letters praising Gomulka, and who notwithstanding their anonymity is quite certain that they were written by bandits and reactionary priests; and the voice of true fanaticism crying "No one has a right to be angry with the Party; the Party has to be loved." [66] The plenum was in fact a fantastic and startling spectacle, a preview of what human minds and personalities have to undergo in order to become genuinely regimented.

Polish Titoism was destroyed by the November plenum. Gomulka, Kliszko, and Spychalski were removed from the Central Committee and were forbidden to participate in any form of Party work. In his final summing up, Bierut put the official stamp of approval upon the "one accident too many" version of the wartime deaths of Gomulka's predecessors. Thus the dignitaries who had entered the plenum as mere deviationists emerged from it as veritable murderers and *agents provocateurs*.

In Poland the crisis of 1948–49 brought out the true nature of Titoism as an organic disease of Communist Parties when in power. Titoism in Poland, for the reasons specified above, was not successful. Gomulka and his group were chastised and subdued. But it was merely one demonstration and one outbreak of the disease and not its sources that were destroyed.

[65] *Ibid.*, p. 170.
[66] Jozwiak-Witold, *ibid.*, p. 142.

III. THE COMINFORM AND THE PEOPLE'S DEMOCRACIES

Titoism did not appear in the rest of the satellites with the same intensity that it exhibited in Yugoslavia and Poland. Superficially, this statement seems to be contradicted by a whole series of names of purged deviationists within the satellites. Patrascanu, Kostov, Rajk, Novy, and more recently Klementis and Kochi Xoxe seem to attest the universality of the phenomenon of Titoism. Side by side with the removal of the notables have been continuous purges of the rank and file of the Communist Parties of the satellites and other devices which have resulted in a considerable number of members being dropped or expelled from the Party.[67]

As explained before, neither the disappearance and liquidation of some of the top leaders nor the pruning process among the mass of followers needs Titoism as an explanation. The Parties were swollen by the accession of opportunists and even of former members of the Fascist and pro-German parties. At first the newcomers were welcome. Later they became a useless ballast. Once firmly in power, or lined up for armed struggle, a Communist Party needs a solid and devoted body of followers and not a heterogeneous mass.

Within the leadership the transition from struggle to administration always requires a change in the personnel. Especially when the process of consolidating political power is largely finished and the phase of social and economic transformation is begun, a new and different type of leadership is required. This happened in the twenties in Russia and it has been happening since 1948 in the satellites. The new phase called for different skills, and those Communists who could not adjust had to go. And by a peculiar psychological twist, the failure to meet the new tasks became more often than not a decisive bit of evidence that the official in question lacked the "Marxist grace" which assures every bona fide Communist measure complete success. An unfulfilled production schedule or a policy that arouses too much popular resentment becomes a testimony not to human fallibility but to the lack of socialist zeal and, perhaps, to malice and treason.

However, and this again should be continually kept in mind, there has been no more convenient way to remove a competitor for power

[67] See Seton-Watson, *The East European Revolution*, pp. 311–312.

or a person obnoxious to the rulers of a satellite state than by accusing him of being a Titoist. His removal would then accomplish two ends: it would eliminate a dangerous rival, and it would become a dramatic occasion for a display of the danger of and the penalties for nationalism and anti-Russian feelings, though the accusations might be completely fabricated. Here again the parallel to Trotskyism and the use to which it was put in Russia during the great purge are very telling.

So far the general prevalence of purges has been explained from a purely rational point of view. There would be very little use in discussing why Leader X was liquidated by Leader Y if all that a purge signifies were explained by personal animosities and accidental occurrences. The purges offer a valuable testimony of the structure and spirit of political power within organized Communism. Our insight is limited, except in the two cases discussed, by the paucity of evidence, yet it is possible to penetrate at least some of the atmosphere surrounding the high command of Communism.

Viewed in a different way, the campaign against Titoism transcends a purely rational and calculating decision of the ruling elite of world Communism. To the rulers of Russia and to their deputies in the satellites, Tito's break with the Cominform was a profound shock. It is not that they reacted frantically to Tito's apostasy, for deviations and apostasies are an old story in Communism. It was the sight of a Communist Party following almost unanimously an upstart leader against the acknowledged master of world Communism that distressed and even panicked the Kremlin and its agencies. Hence the search for and the campaign to destroy any similarities between Tito's regime and that of the other satellites. The bill of accusations against Tito issued by the Cominform became, in fact, like a set of examinations which every loyal Communist Party had to pass.

Thus, all during the summer and fall of 1948 the governments in Eastern Europe were reëxamining and speeding up their collectivization programs, the drive achieving full intensity in 1949.[68] Only

---

[68] "Although the agricultural co-operatives were growing rather rapidly during 1949 in Hungary, the small-scale production by individual peasants remains the dominant type . . . During 1949 the first Rumanian collectives were started . . . In Czechoslovakia during 1949 the government began to put strong

in Bulgaria had collectivization begun in earnest prior to the Cominform's resolution. Elsewhere, its new timing was a direct outcome of
Tito's heresy.

The same inescapable change took place in regard to the whole
complex of social and economic policies and the tone of cultural
life. Until 1948 visitors to Poland or Czechoslovakia found considerable freedom of expression and thought, and, if they did not
probe too deeply, they did not discover too many traces of the
police state. Beginning with 1948, the screws were tightened, and
a vigorous campaign hit every actual or potential center of independent thought in the satellites. The intellectual, who before 1948
could congratulate himself on the state's patronage of the arts and
sciences, now could see more clearly the other side of the coin; the
Soviet pattern of control over thought and expression now began
to take shape. The fight against "cosmopolitanism," meaningful perhaps in Russia but hardly applicable to the satellites (since it could
not be accompanied by a campaign for cultural nationalism), was
still an order of the day in every satellite state. Careful obeisance
began to be paid by the scientists to the Michurin-Lysenko school of
biology. Most disconcerting must have been the experience of the
linguists who, prodded to include Soviet theories in their investigations, began to bone up on the Soviet linguistic school only to find
its creator, N. Y. Marr, topple from the Soviet pantheon following
a dictum of Stalin. Thus, because Tito had quarreled with Stalin,
even the intelligentsia in Eastern Europe discovered, prematurely,
the price a totalitarian regime exacts for its interest in and patronage
of the arts and sciences.

The most substantial beneficiary of the earlier period of the
People's Democracies was the worker. Extolled by the press and
wooed by the government, he was placed on the pedestal as the
ruling class of the new state. Now his freshly won social benefits
and all the flattery were followed by a drastically tightened labor
discipline and sharply increased working norms. Both the worker
and the manager found themselves, as in the Soviet Union, the front
fighters in the battle for increased production, and they met with

---

pressures on all farmers owning as much as 15 hectares to combine their holdings into collective farms" (Sanders, "Changing Status of the Peasant in Eastern
Europe," p. 87).

correspondingly high casualties. The line separating inefficiency, including every physical inability to meet a plan, and treason became suddenly obscured. Eugeniusz Szyr, deputy chairman of the State Planning Commission in Poland, indicated the beginning of the application of Soviet methods in economic matters when he wrote:

> There is a belief among some of our honest but backward and opinionated technical intelligentsia that every collision of ships, every fire or railroad disaster, can be traced to someone's sloppiness, insufficient training, or carelessness . . . From such an attitude there is but one small step to a premeditated destruction of evidence, which is equivalent to collaboration with the criminal. Therefore, all the trials concerned with economic sabotage should be fully publicized.[69]

And he went on to cite several cases of supposed sabotage and the death penalties meted out for them. There is but "one small step" from Szyr's attitude to seeing in every economic inefficiency, in every prolonged labor absenteeism, a deliberate effort at economic sabotage. The right to strike withers away.

Workers, peasants, intellectuals—all face new duties and hardships as the result of Titoism. The main change is evident not so much in new measures and policies as in the character of their execution. Gone is the talk of the specifically Polish, Hungarian, or Rumanian circumstances regulating the progress toward socialism in those countries. Now the emphasis is directly on following in every step the Russian precedent and of advertising the fact as strenuously as possible. Gone is even the fiction of equality which characterized the establishment of the Cominform. Titoism has led the leaders of the satellites to such slavish professions of dependence upon the U.S.S.R. that it is now difficult to recall that at one period their public pronouncements were different and their references to Soviet Russia more dignified.

The effect of Titoism upon the ruling circles of the Communist Parties in the satellites has already been alluded to and more fully described in Poland in the case of Gomulka. In general, the situation following the Cominform's excommunication of Tito led to a vicious circle. The increased pressure to conform, to bow toward the Soviet Union, and to regulate every satellite's policies in the spirit of the Cominform's resolution had to result in a number of

[69] *Nowe Drogi*, September–October 1949, p. 41.

disharmonies within the Communist ranks and a number of administrative and economic difficulties, all of which were conveniently grouped under the name of Titoism. The discovery or invention, as the case might be, of Titoism, and the punishment of the culprits, of necessity brought about an accentuation of the repressive measures and of Soviet control. The drive against the traitors, the public trials of Kostov and Rajk, and the denunciations of the once famous and powerful Party leaders have all served as dramatic advertisements of the new policy. How could it be better displayed and emphasized than by a living drama in which the chief propagators of the previous policy were discovered and brought to confess, voluntarily, of course, that they had been traitors, agents of Tito, and, through him, servants first of the German secret police and then of the Western imperialists?

The purged notables share several common characteristics in their backgrounds. It has been noted more than once that many of them had during the war fought in the Communist resistance movement. They have been classified as "native" Communists, in distinction to their compatriots who spent the war years in Moscow. Another distinguishing mark of the purged dignitaries is their record of jail sentences under the old regimes. Both Rajk and Kostov were imprisoned during the war and, despite their reputation as prominent Communists, released or sentenced only to jail, while some of their comrades were less fortunate. The Communist movement has always feared the *agent provocateur*. In the hysteria attending a purge, the fact that a prominent Communist is a survivor of a fascist jail tends to make him open to suspicion.

The story presented in the trials of Rajk and Kostov has managed to connect the divergent strains of Titoism, the Communist underground during the war, and finally the life stories of the two men into a vast and systematic plot. Kostov, Rajk, the leaders of contemporary Yugoslavia, all appear in the story as *agents provocateurs* of long standing, servants of the Germans and of the Anglo-Americans, yet all the while masquerading as good Communists. It follows that all the major gatherings of Communists in Europe in the thirties—in Spain during the Spanish Civil War, in the internment camps for escaped loyalists in France, and so forth—must now be officially declared to have been polluted by the presence of spies and police agents, must now be recognized as reunions of the future Titoists.[70] It also follows that participation in the Spanish Civil War and a prison sentence under a fascist regime, both of which used to mark the *curriculum vitae* of a really distinguished Communist, should now become marks of distinction which their possessors would like to erase from their past. The fact that an adventurous and militant Communist past is by itself an embarrassment rather than a help in making a career in the Communist Parties of the satellites reflects, of course, not only current hysteria about Titoism but also something else. As in Russia in the late twenties and in the thirties, the ascendant type of the Communist leader in Eastern Europe tends to be the cautious bureaucrat, usually trained in Moscow, rather than the militant leader of the wartime underground. Titoism has shown the unreliability of the latter type, and it is only natural that, once the conquest of power was completed, Moscow has tended to favor the less romantic but also the more reliable type of Party leadership.

Yet it is a mistake to see the purges of 1948 as simply the victory of the Muscovite element over the resistance movement and to assume that every wartime resistance leader is in disgrace.[71] There are several veterans of the Communist resistance movement who not only remain in Moscow's good graces but who have been most instrumental in purging their deviationist colleagues. To this group belong such well-known leaders as Bierut and Jozwiak in Poland, Vladimir Poptomov in Bulgaria, and Vilem Siroky in Czechoslovakia. Likewise, there are few Communist leaders in Eastern Europe who at one time or another did not serve a prison sentence for their political activities. There would be very few Communist leaders

---

[70] Thus Rajk, according to the story at his trial: "Before the defeat of the Spanish war of liberation he escaped to France, where in the internment camps of St. Cyprien, Gurs, and Vernet he made the acquaintance of the Yugoslav agents of foreign espionage services. These, such as Bebler, Kosta Nadj, Goshnjak, Maslarich, Mrazovich, etc. had either been in Spain, like Rajk, or carried on their provocative activities later in the internment camps. The French and American espionage services and the Gestapo all established themselves in these camps" (*László Rajk and His Accomplices before the People's Court* [Budapest, 1949], p. 8).

[71] "These purges corresponded to the victory within the party leadership of the Muscovites over the wartime Resistance leaders" (Seton-Watson, *The East European Revolution*, p. 314).

left in the satellites if all the criteria for suspicion were systematically applied.

Clearly, much as the phenomenon of Titoism in a special sense and the accompanying phenomenon of political purge are almost universal throughout the satellite area, there is no single formula or set of formulas that would enable us to generalize about them. It must be kept in mind that a political trial in a totalitarian regime is not an attempt to ascertain the truth or to mete out justice; it is not even primarily a way of dealing with political opponents of the regime. Its first and foremost purpose is to serve as a means of political propaganda and education, to dramatize and illuminate policies of the regime as they never could be by speeches and written exhortations. Following Rajk's trial a series of public meetings were held throughout the People's Democracies, at which the "lessons" of the trial were discussed. It is easy to see what the lessons were supposed to be: Tito's treachery of long standing; the presence of his accomplices in every People's Democracy; connections between Tito, the Gestapo, and the Anglo-American imperialists. The immediate lesson to be applied was the necessity for increased production as an answer to the warmongers; also, that the slightest criticism of the U.S.S.R. denotes a probable saboteur and foreign agent. One may ridicule such techniques and see in them a crude imposition of methods which could perhaps work in Russia after twenty years of Communism but which will probably be ineffective in less indoctrinated societies. But the cumulative effect of the trials and of the propaganda is not negligible.

In general, it is possible to penetrate the veil of propaganda and distortion only if we have two clashing viewpoints and arguments. That was the case in Yugoslavia and, to a slighter extent, in Poland. What can be the story, however, behind the disgrace of Laszlo Rajk in Hungary? He was one of the most prominent Communists in Hungary. As the leader of the Communist underground, he was the only one among the ruling group who had spent the war years in Hungary, though he was interned under the Horthy regime between October 1941 and October 1944. After the war Rajk emerged from yet another internment to become one of the most powerful men in the Hungarian Communist Party. He became the secretary of the Party for Budapest, and in 1946 Minister of Home Affairs. His post traditionally carried with it the supervision of the security police and the delicate task of consolidating the grip of Communism in Hungary. It was not an office to be entrusted to a "soft" Communist or to a man whose loyalty to the Soviet Union was questionable. In Hungary, it is worth adding, the U.S.S.R. could and did interfere more directly than in the other satellites, since Hungary was technically a defeated and occupied country. It is unlikely that Rajk's appointment was not directly approved by the Soviet authorities. He was a key man in transforming Hungary into a satellite country. Within the ruling elite of his Party, Rajk, it is said, enjoyed some popularity, based again on the fact that he, unlike his colleagues Matyas Rakosi, Ernö Gero, and Mihaly Farkas, had an active record in the resistance movement.

Rajk could not aspire to the very top leadership, which was enjoyed by Matyas Rakosi, one of the veterans of the Communist movement. Rakosi, having spent most of the fifteen years preceding World War II in Hungarian jails, escaped the great purge of the thirties which felled so many Communist notables. In 1940 he went to Moscow, whence he returned to become Deputy Prime Minister and the real boss of Hungary. Rajk, ever since he joined the Communist Party of Hungary in 1931, had led the typical career of a Communist agent. In contrast to Rakosi, he was a young man, one whose whole life was a long record of service to Communism, notwithstanding the fact that his immediate family had been connected with the pre-1945 regime in Hungary. It is just possible that Rajk had even greater ambitions than his post warranted. It is not entirely improbable that he "discovered" some evidence linking his chief with a Titoist plot and that he engaged in an intrigue against Rakosi. But all this must remain a matter of conjecture.

Following his visit to Moscow in the summer of 1948, Rajk was transferred from the Ministry of Home Affairs to that of Foreign Affairs. The shift was a well-known Communist maneuver and an unmistakable sign that his downfall had started. In June 1949, Rajk was transferred again, this time to a jail. On September 16, 1949, Rajk and his supposed accomplices faced the People's Court. Together with him were Gyorgy Palffy, who, upon the Communists' accession to power in Hungary, had advanced from a discharged first lieutenant to lieutenant general and chief of military intelligence;

Tibor Szönyi, former chief of the Party's personnel section; Andras Szalai, Szönyi's deputy; and Pal Justus, deputy president of the Hungarian radio. There had to be a Yugoslav official thrown in, so Lazar Brankov, who had denounced the Yugoslav regime at the time of the split, was brought in to testify about his spying activities. The main group—Rajk, Szönyi, Palffy, and Szalai—were men prominent in Hungarian politics between 1945 and 1948. Conceivably, they were engaged at some time or other in a plot against Rakosi and some other leaders of the Communist Party in Hungary. But the evidence offered at the trial is completely worthless.

All the accused duly confessed, and their story presented a picture of a fantastic plot engineered and guided by such diverse personages as Tito, Allen Dulles (Szönyi spent the war years in Switzerland, which made him a natural choice for the Dulles angle), and Noel H. Field. All of them went to great lengths to trace the genesis of their treachery to their *kulak* and bourgeois backgrounds, their work for the police under the prewar Horthy regime, and their contacts with Tito. The villain of the piece appeared to be, in addition to Rajk, General Alexander Rankovich, the efficient Yugoslav Minister of Interior, who for reasons not difficult to divine has been, next to Tito, the particular object of hatred for the Cominform press and publicity. The main points of the story are so nonsensical that they hardly appear to require any refutation. Yet in a recent book written by a non-Communist, the trial of Rajk and his associates is given a great deal of credence: "Most terrible was the manner of its telling, for Rajk drove home every point against himself with merciless logic. It is internally consistent; it cannot be dismissed as lies." [72] This "internal consistency" can be best shown by comparing two points of Rajk's testimony as recorded in the official account. On page 38 Rajk states, "I was expelled from the Party [for his Trotskyist activities in Spain in 1938]"; but seven pages later he has to explain his prominence after the war in the Hungarian Communist Party: "My activities were not known to the leadership of the Communist Party. They knew me as the best member of the Communist Party." [73]

The trial was, as a matter of fact, ineptly staged. Several of the

[72] Warriner, *Revolution in Eastern Europe*, p. 60.
[73] *László Rajk and His Accomplices before the People's Court*, pp. 38 and 45.

accused received permission to consult their notes while confessing to their enormous crimes. The presiding judge, Dr. Peter Janko, exhibited an intimate knowledge of all the details of the confessions, his role being that of a prompter rather than a questioner. The four People's judges—four typical workingmen chosen to serve with one expert, if this be a proper description—wisely kept their mouths shut. As mentioned before, there are several gross and provable inaccuracies in the indictment and the testimony.

Still, the trial is interesting as an example of the peculiar propaganda technique indulged in by the regime. The scope of the testimony was very wide, enclosing in its circle of villainy not only the major enemies of the regime—the United States and Yugoslavia—but also those persons and movements whom the regime wanted to publicize as the enemies of the people. Thus, after hearing Pal Justus' confessions about his connections with Rankovich and through him with American agents, the presiding judge, in what was probably intended to be a dramatic and revealing gesture, asked two of the accused whether they had ever belonged to a Zionist organization.[74] Szalai, in baring the details of his spying work for Yugoslavia, confessed to having furnished the Yugoslav attaché with information about the strength of the Hungarian Communist Party, the fulfillment of the economic plans, the preparations for the general elections in Hungary, and its results.[75] Since the Hungarian government publishes its own statistics on all those points, the only conclusion can be that a high Party official has access to different and more accurate data than those published by his government.

Whom is the trial with its fantasies designed to convince? Its managers could not have expected that there would be many people in the West or among their unindoctrinated countrymen willing to accept the story as being "internally consistent" or possessing "merciless logic." It must have been addressed to men already trained in blind and unquestioning obedience, to the rank and file of the Communist Party members in Hungary, elsewhere in the satellite area, and in the U.S.S.R. And what kind of people can be made to believe that Tito, as alleged in the trial, was counting on Cardinal

---

[74] *Ibid.*, p. 202. Both the Soviet Union and the satellites have condemned Zionism, as a part of their drive against "cosmopolitanism."
[75] *Ibid.*, p. 168.

Mindszenty to assist him in his conquest of Hungary? It is rather frightening to contemplate the mentality of these people, who were capable of releasing the record of Rajk's trial in several languages, confident that Communists everywhere would take every word of it as true. Unwittingly, they presented the world with a true picture, not of facts, but of their own minds. The Communist Party of Hungary was revealed as a body of docile followers ready to absorb any story provided it comes from high enough quarters. It is also pointed out how easy it is for a group of conspirators holding strategic positions in the Party, the state, and the army to carry on their nefarious activity and almost to succeed with the help of a foreign power. What does this picture represent? It represents, ironically, the essence of the strategy employed by the Communists in taking over one state after another in Eastern Europe.

Rajk himself and his most important associates were executed. Their real guilt still remains an enigma. It is possible for an ordinary Communist official to get enmeshed in a minor intrigue or to be liquidated, as in any totalitarian regime, because of an error. In the case of Rajk and Szönyi, there must have been a more serious encounter with the Party command. It is unlikely that a leader of Rajk's stature could be liquidated without Moscow's permission. His story is not one of national Communism, and it is doubtful that it had anything to do either with Tito's rebellion or with anything transcending the boundaries of Hungary. Rajk and his fellow-accused, having offended the leadership of their Party in some unknown way, died as an offering to "international" Communism and to the new line required of all the satellites as a consequence of Titoism. In their deaths, as in their lives, they were made to serve the Party and its masters.

Rajk's case was a spectacular example of a powerful leader suddenly brought down, the master of life and death of his fellow countrymen suddenly appearing himself to plead guilty and to forfeit his life at the altar of the Party. Yet, aside from the drama of his deposition and death, reminiscent more of that of a medieval oriental vizier than a twentieth-century bureaucrat, Rajk's case offers little to illuminate the causes and methods of Communist rule in Eastern Europe. It is in another satellite country—Bulgaria—that one can see and analyze a typical case of a Party purge caused by the confluence of three factors, all of which required a living sacrifice: Russian pressures, inter-Party intrigues, and considerable administrative failures of ruling Communism. The three factors coincided neatly and led to the most extensive purge any East European Communist Party has yet undergone in the postwar era.

Bulgarian Communists have always been in a peculiar position vis-à-vis their Russian colleagues. Just as their own country has always felt close to the great Slavic power to which it owed the achievement of its own independence and to which it has always looked in reconstructing its national culture after centuries of foreign occupation, so have the Bulgarian Communists always been particularly close to the greatest Communist Party. It was a symbolic coincidence that an early split of the Bulgarian Socialist Party into "broad" and "narrow" factions, the latter to transform itself later into the Communist Party of Bulgaria, took place in 1903, the same year that the Social Democratic Party of Russia was undergoing its epoch-making divisions into the Bolsheviks and Mensheviks.

In the early days of the Comintern, Bulgarian Communists played a leading role in the machinery of that organization. The Communists of that small Balkan country, one of the poorest and most primitive in Europe, occupied at times the leading positions in the Third International. One of the earliest notables of international Communism was a Bulgarian, Vasil Kolarov. In the middle thirties, as revealed during the purge in Bulgaria, the personnel director of the Balkan section of the Third International was Traicho Kostov. Among its sections in the Balkans, the Comintern until 1941 always appeared to favor the Bulgarian Communist Party over the more unruly Yugoslav and Greek Communists. But the most significant achievement of the Bulgarian Communist Party before the war came not in Bulgaria, where the Party was banned under a semi-fascist royal regime, but in Germany. In the early days of Hitler's rule, a Bulgarian Communist leader was the central figure at the trial following the Reichstag fire. The behavior of Georgi Dimitrov before the court, his defiance of Marshal Goering and other leading Nazis, brought him an international reputation. Released from the Nazi jail, Dimitrov came back to Moscow, hailed as a national hero. He was chosen Secretary-General of the Comintern, and his figure became almost synonymous with the policy of united fronts against Fascism and Nazism, symbolical of what seemed to be the new and genuine desire of the Communists to stand together with socialist and progressive forces everywhere against the threat of totalitarianism.

Sixteen years after Dimitrov had faced the Nazi court in Leipzig, another prominent Bulgarian Communist faced totalitarian justice, this time of his own Communist government. But when Traicho Kostov attempted to defend himself against charges more preposterous than the ones leveled at Dimitrov, he was booed and derided by the audience. When he referred to his bad health endured during the war in a fascist prison, gales of laughter swept the courtroom, according to the official account of the trial. When he repudiated his forced written confession, he was cut short by the court, and instead of his oral testimony, his forced confession was read.

Between the two trials lies the peculiar history of Bulgaria and the Bulgarian Communists. The Bulgarian government once again made a bad gamble in World War II. It joined the Axis in 1941, but this time, unlike its accession to the Central Powers in World War I, Bulgaria had no choice. When Hitler intervened in the Balkans in the spring of 1941, German troops entered the country. Bulgaria, as an ally, was given the objects of its long ambitions, Yugoslav Macedonia and Greek Thrace. Until 1941 Bulgaria had held only a part of "greater" Macedonia, and after 1945 her holdings were again reduced.

Like other Balkan countries, Bulgaria, for all the paraphernalia of democratic institutions, has seldom known a period of genuine representative government. Her government at the time of the war was held personally by King Boris. In 1943, upon his return from Germany, Boris died under rather obscure circumstances, but under the regency the government remained fascist and at war with the Western Allies. One thing the Bulgarian government could not bring itself to do: declare war upon Russia. Though it was now Soviet Russia, it was still the state and nation for which many Bulgarians who had nothing to do with Communism felt genuine affection.[76] Toward the end of the war in the Balkans, the government made some efforts to contact the Allies, but a peace in 1944 would have prevented the Red Army from occupying Bulgaria, and so suddenly on September 5, 1944, without informing their allies, the

[76] See Seton-Watson, *The East European Revolution*, pp. 90–98.

Russians declared war, and two days later Marshal Tolbukhin's army "liberated" Bulgaria.[77]

Bulgaria was perhaps the one country in Eastern Europe in 1944 to which the Russians did not need to send a single soldier in order to secure a friendly and even submissive government, had they been interested only in that. Even before their entrance, a wide coalition of parties had banded together to overthrow the pro-Axis government. The Fatherland Front for once, though inspired by the Communists, was not a Communist Party plus a few gullible or corrupt non-Communists masquerading under a different name. It was until 1945 a genuine coalition consisting of the Communists, the Agrarian group of Nikola Petkov and Dr. G. M. Dimitrov, the Socialists, and the "Zveno" Party, led by two officers with rather mixed political antecedents: Kimon Georgiev and Damian Velchev. The Communists during the war had organized some partisan and terrorist activity. Their most important leaders, including Dimitrov and Kolarov, stayed in Moscow. Inside Bulgaria the Party was led by another veteran, Traicho Kostov. Though imprisoned for a time, Kostov was able to get out, and he emerged from his underground activity as a Communist hero, renowned for his "hardness" and ability. His two chief coadjutors were Anton Yugov and Dobri Terpeshev, chief of the Communist "Army" during the war.

The early days of the war witnessed a clash between the Yugoslav and Bulgarian Communists about Macedonia, which was decided by the Comintern in favor of the Yugoslavs.[78] In the eyes of the Comintern, as early as 1941, the Communist Parties of the Balkans were assuming a different order of importance (based, of course, on their changing relative usefulness to the U.S.S.R.) from that which they had had during the twenties and thirties. But the loyalty of the Bulgarian Communists was not shaken. Inspired by messages from their Moscow-residing leaders, they played a leading part in constructing the illegal Fatherland Front. With the entrance of the Soviet army in September 1944, the front became the government of Bulgaria.

The usual Communist-Soviet tactics employed elsewhere in Eastern Europe were turned on in Bulgaria: first, repression of the

[77] *Ibid.*, p. 97.
[78] See Chapter 3, above.

enemies of the U.S.S.R.; then, a purge of the ruling front until it became a thin veneer hiding the Communists themselves. In Bulgaria the variation on the standard pattern was the extreme violence applied at every stage of the process. The first liberated government was headed by Kimon Georgiev, a man with a shady political past. Georgiev became an obedient tool of the Communists; when the moment came to replace him with a Communist, he was still retained in an inferior position, and he has hung on since then in a variety of official jobs of decreasing importance. The Fatherland Front initiated its rule in an orgy of bloodshed, the non-Communists in it little reflecting that the severe measures applied against the wartime officials would soon be vented upon them by their Communist colleagues. According to official statistics, more than two thousand former officials had been sentenced and executed by March 1945.[79] Thousands of others were imprisoned for long terms. The first purge was efficiently supervised by the Minister of the Interior, Communist Anton Yugov.

The next wave of purges was directed against the non-Communist participants in the Fatherland Front, which had to be turned from a genuine coalition into a typical Communist front. In Bulgaria, as everywhere else, the Communists made special efforts to find friends within each non-Communist party and to assist them in the task of taking over their party, with its funds and newspapers and party machinery. Thus both the Agrarians and the Social Democrats split, with the Communist puppets on one side, and intransigent sections which demanded a genuine coalition on the other. The latter were led respectively by Nicola Petkov and Kosta Lulchev, who withdrew from the "coalition" and formed opposition parties. The process of communization had to be speeded up. In 1945 the almost legendary figures of Bulgarian Communism, Vasil Kolarov and Georgi Dimitrov, returned to their country. The latter's arrival was made to coincide with the anniversary of the Russian Revolution.[80] Dimitrov was obviously typed to become the Lenin of the Bulgarian Communist Party. On his arrival he assumed formally the leadership of his Party from Kostov, just as his great predecessor also relieved the Bolshevik leaders on the spot in Russia in 1917. One

[79] Seton-Watson, *The East European Revolution*, p. 212.
[80] Elisabeth Barker, *Truce in the Balkans* (London, 1948), p. 60.

year afterward Dimitrov was Prime Minister, and the subservient Georgiev had been reduced to Vice-Premier. From then on the veteran Communist presided over the political liquidation and judicial assassination of the Communists' erstwhile allies. Petkov went to his death, his fate determined, among other things, by the Western Allies' intervention on his behalf. Other opposition leaders followed, and the remaining non-Communist parties became mere shadows or peripheral agencies of the Communists. Bulgaria had found its Lenin, but who was going to be the Stalin of Bulgarian Communism?

After the end of 1944 real political power in Bulgaria belonged to the Communists. Theoretically, the United States and Great Britain shared in controlling Bulgaria as a defeated country. Theoretically, there were as late as 1948 genuine opposition parties. But from the beginning it was the Russians and the Bulgarian Communists who settled Bulgaria's foreign and domestic policies. The violence with which the opposition was dealt presaged a similarly violent purge within the Communist Party. Nothing is more disturbing than the blithe attempt to dismiss as something typically Bulgarian the judicial murder of Petkov and the similar fortunes of many other genuine Bulgarian democrats.[81] These acts were typical of Bulgarian Communist methods, and the perpetrators of the trials soon had an opportunity to sympathize with the fate of Petkov and Lulchev.

The hierarchical picture within the Bulgarian Communist Party was confused. Its leader Dimitrov, though only in his sixties, was rumored to be ailing. His companion Kolarov was even older and in recent years had held a succession of honorific posts, such as that of Foreign Minister and President of the National Assembly. The actual job of running the government was in the hands of the wartime trio of Kostov, Yugov, and Terpeshev. Yugov, as Minister of the Interior, held one of the most important positions in a totalitarian country; Terpeshev, wartime partisan leader, became head of the Planning Commission. Traicho Kostov was Deputy Prime Minis-

[81] "In the past, it must be remembered, Petkov and the opposition *en masse* would have been assassinated. The treason trial is an advance in that it is a rationalization, an attempt to make punishment the expression of the community's denunciation of the crime" (Warriner, *Revolution in Eastern Europe*, p. 23).

ter in over-all control of the national economy and was reputed until the beginning of 1949 to have been the real moving spirit of the Bulgarian Communist Party and the government. It was he who threw his energies into the task of rapid collectivization of Bulgarian agriculture. Kostov's Communist enthusiasm, like that of his Yugoslav counterparts, may have been greater than his economic knowledge. He certainly had grandiose industrial plans for backward Bulgaria. He pushed the Russians to provide the machinery for the electrification plan which was the first prerequisite of even a modest progress toward Bulgaria's industrialization.[82] It was also Kostov who, according to Yugoslav Communist sources, had viewed with suspicion the plan for the South Slav union under which Bulgaria would be amalgamated with Yugoslavia—a plan which until late 1947 enjoyed the support of the U.S.S.R. So it is likely that in Moscow Traicho Kostov became classified as an unreliable man, a fanatical Communist, to be sure, but so much absorbed in the affairs of his country that he was developing a "nationalist" viewpoint which might clash with his loyalty to the Soviet Union.

In January 1948 the project of the Balkan Communist Union was shelved.[83] Dimitrov recanted his previous public espousal of it, and the cession of Bulgarian Macedonia to Yugoslavia, to which the Bulgarian Communists had become reconciled, or had been forced to reconcile themselves, was now abandoned. And in the spring of 1948 the Tito affair exploded, and every satellite Communist Party had to search among its own leadership for real and potential deviationists.

Superficially, Kostov was safe. He had been an enemy of Tito. He was the leading proponent of rapid collectivization which now became the leading measure of loyalty required by the U.S.S.R. of its satellites. He was at the meeting of the Cominform which in June 1948 condemned Tito. In December 1948, at the Fifth Congress of the Bulgarian Workers' Party, which now openly called itself Communist, Kostov played a leading role and was confirmed as a secretary of the Party and a member of its Politburo.[84] On January 28, writing in the official organ of the Party, Kostov extolled Soviet-

[82] Barker, *Truce in the Balkans*, p. 120.
[83] See Chapter 3, above.
[84] *For a Lasting Peace*, January 1, 1949.

Bulgarian friendship. Ironically, in view of his impending fate, his article mentioned that the alliance of the two brotherly nations enabled the Bulgarians to extend and deepen their collaborations with the U.S.S.R. and to learn all the time new and fruitful lessons from the Soviets.[85] The Bulgarian Communist Party now recovered its position as the favorite of Soviet Russia among the Communists in the Balkans, and it was Bulgaria that was now envisioned as the possessor of Greater Macedonia once Tito's clique had been eliminated in Yugoslavia and once the Greek Communists were free to rule over and partition their own country. In January 1949 Traicho Kostov still appeared as the logical successor to the top leadership of his Party and country after his ailing superiors, Dimitrov and Kolarov, had been gathered to their reward.

On March 26, 1948, a plenum of the Central Committee of the Communist Party of Bulgaria met and the picture was totally changed. On the motion of Kolarov, Kostov was ejected from the Politburo and was castigated for his anti-Russian attitude. His anti-Russian activities consisted in his refusal to provide a Russian trade mission with Bulgaria's economic data.[86] Behind the curt language of the communiqué was hidden an intricate and still puzzling drama of Russian and intra-Party intrigue. The meeting took place on March 26, yet it was announced only on April 5. Such was the precipitous speed of Kostov's disgrace that the Communists forgot or overlooked the official etiquette to which they usually conform. For in addition to dismissing Kostov from his Party positions, the Central Committee of the Bulgarian Communist Party also fired him as Deputy Prime Minister and chairman of the Committee for the National Economy, which, of course, it had no legal right to do. An added element of mystery is provided by the fact that Georgi Dimitrov, the Secretary-General of the Bulgarian Communist Party, does not seem to have participated in the proceedings against Kostov. He was still in Bulgaria, though reputedly ill; but he is not mentioned in the report, which states that the main speeches at the plenum were delivered by Kolarov and by another member of the Politburo, Vladimir Poptomov.

What were Kostov's official sins? The first case presented by

[85] *Rabotnichesko Delo*, January 28, 1949.
[86] *Ibid.*, April 5, 1949.

the Bulgarians was a restrained one. Writing in the Cominform journal, Kolarov accused Kostov of being a "nationalist" and anti-Russian. His anti-Russian sentiments had been expressed simply in an attempt to protect Bulgaria's economic interests from the exploitation which this already incredibly poor country was enduring at the hands of its protector. Kolarov ineptly admitted that much when he wrote, after criticizing Kostov for withholding Bulgaria's production costs from the U.S.S.R., "but it is an obvious fact that were we to base our trade relations with the Soviet Union on the same principles as those governing our trade with the capitalist countries we would be faced with insurmountable difficulties and would be finally confronted with economic disaster." [87] Kostov was also reputed to have assailed some of his colleagues for violating the principle of collective leadership, and he had quarreled with Dimitrov. But Kolarov did not even hint that Kostov was a traitor or a "Titoist."

Elsewhere, Kostov's disgrace was already being differently interpreted. To the Yugoslav Communists, Kostov was an enemy, and any trouble in Bulgaria was an occasion for exultation. Previously, when there had been the discussion of the Balkan union, Tito must have been preparing a dossier on the Bulgarian Communists. The occasion to take a dig at a fallen enemy, though he was obviously being liquidated for the same sin as Tito's—standing up for his country—was too much to overlook. Thus it was that Marshal Tito gleefully related and interpreted Kostov's fall in his speech to the People's Front:

There [in Bulgaria] the last few days have seen the arrest and apprehension of many leaders of the Communist Party of Bulgaria, who stand accused of having been in the service of foreign espionage agencies. Some of those people have been the most fervent calumniators of our country and of its leaders following—and even before—the resolution of the Cominform. I shall say something only about the case of Traicho Kostov, a member of the Bulgarian Politburo. He was arrested during the war under the regime of King Boris and was kept in prison together with a group of Communists. Though known as one of the main leaders, he alone had his life spared, while the others were killed. Why? . . . We have today proofs in our hands that among the functionaries of certain Communist Parties can be found agents of certain capitalist states.

[87] *For a Lasting Peace,* May 15, 1949.

Those people had been recruited while in the hands of the Gestapo, like Hebrang and some others in our own country.[88]

The Yugoslavs thus showed themselves to be still suffering from the Communist psychosis that a man who survives a fascist jail is probably an *agent provocateur*, if it is politically convenient that he should be so designed, and by the violence of their hatred toward Kostov they rendered absurd the future charge that he was an accomplice of Tito's.[89] Before Tito's speech, nobody in Bulgaria had suggested that Kostov had been an *agent provocateur*.

Aside from his clash with the Russians, a clash which probably consisted of some incautious remarks by a man exasperated with the Russians' refusal of economic help and with their exploitation, which prevented the accomplishment of his pet economic schemes, Kostov was obviously the victim of an intra-Party intrigue.

Among the Bulgarian Communists who returned to Bulgaria toward the end of the war was Vulko Chervenkov, whose main claim to fame at that time consisted in being Dimitrov's brother-in-law. Chervenkov soon achieved a leading position in the Bulgarian Communist Party. A member of the Politburo, he participated in the original meeting of the Cominform, and with Kostov he was at the June 1948 meeting which condemned Tito. Whether he achieved his Party position through nepotism or because of his special ties with the Russians is not entirely clear. Within the Communist government Chervenkov was, at first, given the not too important position of minister in charge of the Commission for the Arts, Sciences, and Culture. In the early days of the Communist regime his Party standing was clearly inferior not only to that of Kolarov and Kostov but also to that of such veterans as Terpeshev and Yugov. But something seemed to push Chervenkov up. Early in 1949 he appears to have replaced his ailing brother-in-law at most state and Party functions, his picture appearing almost daily in the official press.

Following Kostov's disgrace, Chervenkov's star began to rise rapidly. Dimitrov seems to have been absent from the Party and state affairs. Though his prestige was freely used in denouncing Kostov,

---

[88] *Borba*, April 10, 1949.
[89] An overclever interpretation would hold Tito's speech as a Machiavellian attempt to dissociate himself from Kostov, but that would be clearly absurd.

Dimitrov's name dropped out of the press in March 1949. During the state visit of the Czechoslovak ministers Zapotocky and Klementis early in April, Dimitrov was conspicuously absent. Finally, on April 15, it was announced in *Rabotnichesko Delo* that Dimitrov had been granted a sick leave and was undergoing a cure in the U.S.S.R. Chervenkov took over the leadership of the Party, and the aged Kolarov became acting Prime Minister. There followed a period of rapid and involved maneuvers designed at purging the government and the Party of Kostov's adherents and at weakening the position of the other two possible contenders for the leadership, Terpeshev and Yugov. On April 23 a special committee was set up to reorganize the Council of Ministers. The fiction that Dimitrov was only temporarily absent was maintained by making him chairman of the committee, in which capacity he "presented," through Kolarov, a plan for the reorganization. Increasingly Chervenkov was set forth as the real deputy of Dimitrov. The latter's death on July 3, 1949, was followed within a few days by a wholesale shake-up of the government. Kolarov became Prime Minister, but Chervenkov became his first deputy. Yugov and Terpeshev were outmaneuvered in a rather remarkable manner. Appointed on July 20 as deputies of the Prime Minister,[90] they were a few days later relieved of their positions of actual importance—Yugov's job as Minister of the Interior and Terpeshev's as chief of the Planning Commission—on the pretense that their functions as deputies of the Prime Minister precluded them from holding other ministerial posts.[91] That there may have been an actual clash involved in the shift is suggested by the fact that the reorganization of the government on July 20 had been voted by the National Assembly, but the relieving of Yugov and Terpeshev, which came only a few days later, was approved only by the Presidium of the Assembly. Also relieved on August 7 was Minister of Finance Ivan Stefanov, who was later a codefendant at Kostov's trial.

As rapid as the disgrace of the old guard was the ascent of those who could be identified as Chervenkov's men. Two of his subordinates in the Commission for the Arts and Sciences found themselves quickly advanced up the Party ladder. Karlo Lukanov became

[90] *Rabotnichesko Delo*, July 21, 1949.
[91] *Ibid.*, August 7, 1949.

a minister on August 7 and a few months later the head of the Planning Commission; Ruben Levi, formerly an inferior official, became head of the Propaganda Division of the Bulgarian Communist Party.

The real story of Dimitrov's attitude in the last months of his life toward his eventual successor is as ambiguous as was that of Lenin toward Stalin. The Yugoslavs, whose word on the matter is to be taken with a grain of salt, have always maintained that Dimitrov had been a special friend of Tito's, that he had urged the Yugoslavs to stand firm against the Cominform, and so forth.[92] Dimitrov's death, the Yugoslavs add, cannot be entirely explained by his disease. He was taken to Russia in April of 1949 with all his belongings, as if he were never coming back to his country.[93] It is difficult to determine what truth there is in the Yugoslav assertions. They hurt the sensitivity—or should it be called the guilty conscience?—of the Bulgarian Communist leaders enough to provoke a vehement official statement, signed by Kolarov and Chervenkov, denying Djilas' assertion that Dimitrov had urged Tito to stand firm against the Cominform and Moscow.[94] One thing is certain. There is no authenticated statement by Dimitrov, while he was still alive, which would indicate his preference for Chervenkov and his abhorrence of Kostov. Once he was dead, various supposed letters of Dimitrov were published. In one to Chervenkov he praised fervently his brother-in-law, who out of modesty published the letter on the front page of the Bulgarian press only some months after Dimitrov's death.[95] Another letter of Dimitrov's was found just before Kostov's trial. Strangely enough, it warned the Bulgarian Communists against Traicho Kostov. Dimitrov during his lifetime enjoyed tremendous prestige in the Communist world, yet his power was not great enough to prevent the liquidation of many of his closest colleagues in purges both in Russia and in Bulgaria. He never gave a sign of anything but docile Stalinism. Reproved by *Pravda* in January 1948 for his talk about the Balkan federation, the hero of world Communism recanted like any inferior Communist official. Did he toward the end of his life manage to make a gesture of independence

[92] See, for example, *Borba* for December 12, 1949.
[93] *Ibid.*
[94] Printed in *Rabotnichesko Delo*, November 10, 1949.
[95] *Ibid.*, August 20, 1949.

or of defiance which repudiated his whole record of devoted and uncritical obedience to the Kremlin? No one can answer with assurance. After his death he was practically deified in Bulgaria. His funeral became one of those Communist festive occasions which, like Stalin's birthdays, bring the Communists from all over the world to render homage to the dead and even more to exalt their successors. His body, like Lenin's, was preserved in a mausoleum. The Bulgarian Party is now referred to as "Dimitrov's Party." But the story of Dimitrov's last few months still remains a puzzle.

The inner-Party intrigues were heightened and in some measure caused by the socio-economic crisis which Bulgaria underwent in 1948 and 1949. In Bulgaria the psychology of the Communist leaders at the end of the war was quite similar to that of the Yugoslav group in this respect: though their country was poor and backward, the mere fact that socialism was taking over would magically change the situation. Bulgarian agriculture was going to be collectivized, and Bulgaria was to become an industrial country. While their more cautious and realistic colleagues in Poland, Czechoslovakia, and Hungary, who had so much more to work with, went ahead slowly, first reconstructing their economies and then thinking about socialism, the Bulgarian Communists plunged into collectivization at full speed long before the Cominform policy of collectivization was laid down in 1948. By 1947 5 per cent of the land was already collectivized.[96] It was not the extent of collectivization, however, but the methods used which proved dangerous. Though Miss Warriner insists in her book that membership in the collective farms was largely voluntary, the testimony of the Bulgarian Communists themselves is quite different. The plenum of the Central Committee of the Bulgarian Communist Party held in June 1949 issued a detailed condemnation of the methods used to propagate collectivization. The plenum spoke quite openly about the compulsion applied to force the peasants into collective farms and about collective farms confiscating the land belonging to the remaining independent peasants, or forcing them to exchange their lots for those of inferior quality.[97] The speaker castigating these sins and violations was none other than Vulko Chervenkov.

[96] Warriner, *Revolution in Eastern Europe*, p. 153.
[97] *Rabotnichesko Delo*, June 21, 1949.

Reading between the lines of his report, one receives the impression of widespread resistance of the peasants to forced collectivization and of the Party's attempt to eschew the blame for its own policy. Characteristically, Chervenkov coupled his remarks about agriculture with an attack on those Communists who "underestimate" the Fatherland Front. The distrust of the Bulgarian peasant toward the Communists had to be overcome partly by hiding the Party's collectivization policy behind the "broad" national front. Since 1949 Bulgaria has been in fact undergoing a violent agricultural crisis, not unconnected with the peasants' unwillingness to deliver grain at the price fixed by the government. And who was guilty for the excesses, for the ultra-left measures which scared the Bulgarian peasant from the idea of collectivization? Traicho Kostov himself. In an article in *For a Lasting Peace*, Bulgaria's Minister of Agriculture, Titko Chernokolev, pictured the accursed and ruinous activity of Kostov. His sabotage and his collectivization by compulsion almost wrecked the whole collectivization program. The Party was compelled in June 1949 to suspend further collectivization for some time in order to remove the abuses and to reassure the peasant.[98]

But the Bulgarian Communists could not extricate themselves from the morass of their economic ineptitude and doctrinaire policies, even though the evil influence of Kostov had been removed. An article in December 1949 testified to the decrease in grain deliveries by the peasants, though the harvest had been normal. Likewise, it was revealed that 100,000 bread rations were being stolen daily and that the government was unable to establish any effective control of incoming and outgoing stocks of grain foods.[99] And on May 6, 1950, the Minister of Agriculture, Chernokolev, was reprimanded by the Central Committee and the Council of Ministers for exactly the same transgressions which he had attributed to the baneful influence of Traicho Kostov. His ministry has also been guilty of violating the "voluntary principle" in recruiting membership for the collective farms. It has also made plans without a previous authorization of the government and has consequently

[98] *For a Lasting Peace*, November 18, 1949.
[99] *Rabotnichesko Delo*, December 7, 1949.

damaged Bulgaria's economy.[100] Enforced collectivization has remained the official policy, however, and it is only when it brings economic disasters that reprimands are issued and scapegoats are to be found.

Bulgaria's economy provided a somber background to the Party crisis. It might have seemed that in Bulgaria collectivization would encounter less resistance than elsewhere. The country had the tradition of voluntary labor-farm coöperatives dating back to the reforms of the Agrarian Party in the 1920's. There were few *kulaks*, in the proper sense of the word, in Bulgaria. Yet, whether it was a mixture of the regime's brutality, inefficiency, and exploitation by the U.S.S.R. or simply of the peasants' distrust, the effort to collectivize private holdings in Bulgaria has proved, by the Communist leaders' own admission, more damaging to the country's economy in Bulgaria than elsewhere in Eastern Europe (with the possible exception of Yugoslavia). And the Party crisis undoubtedly deepened the disorganization of the economic machine. Within the few months of the crisis between April 1949 and February 1950, Bulgaria had three different finance ministers; the presidency of the Planning Commission was held by three men in succession; and about equally frequent personnel changes affected the Ministries of Transport and Agriculture. Each personnel change was accompanied by changed directives and often by the imprisonment or political disgrace of the dismissed dignitary. It is no wonder that a state of chaos seized the already pitifully poor economy of Bulgaria and that the country which had been potentially the most faithful of Soviet Russia's satellites has become an added danger spot for the Soviet empire in the Balkans.

Within the Party the purge was in its turn heightened by the economic crisis. In June 1949 Kostov's disgrace was completed by his expulsion from the Central Committee and from the Party. Old Kolarov once again delivered the report before the Central Committee, analyzing in detail the traitorous career of the man who was once the hero of Bulgarian Communism.[101] This time Kostov was

---

[100] *Ibid.*, May 6, 1950. In June 1951 Chernokolev was dismissed as minister and, apparently, relieved of his membership in the Politburo.

[101] *Ibid.*, June 24, 1949.

accused of a liaison with Tito. Kolarov's remarks would imply that Kostov attempted to fight back after the March plenum and that he, in fact, managed to smuggle into the official Party organ a treacherous analysis of the economic situation of Bulgaria. The old Comintern official warned obliquely those Bulgarian Communists who still remained unconvinced of Kostov's guilt by saying that if Kostov's anti-Soviet activity did not have bad results for the Bulgarian Communists, it would only be because of resolute steps taken against the traitor. The hand of the Cominform and of Moscow appears, not too subtly, in the picture.

Ever since his first disgrace, Kostov had held, as a cruel jest, the post of the librarian of the National Library in Sofia. He was now arrested. His imprisonment was followed by the arrest of many other Bulgarian Communist notables. Ivan Stefanov, former Minister of Finance; Nikola Pavlov, formerly administrative secretary of the Politburo; and Nikola Nachev, formerly deputy chairman of the State Economic Council, were only the most prominent among those who followed Kostov in his imprisonment and disgrace. In December 1949 the whole group was arraigned before a special court.

The essence of the indictment could have been predicted from Rajk's trial. Once again the charges had the familiar content: the anti-Soviet plot; connivance with Tito; collaboration with the spies of the Western Powers; economic sabotage; and so forth. Without acknowledging its debt to Tito, who mentioned it as early as April, the indictment charged Kostov with espionage and *agent provocateur* work for the old Bulgarian regime.

The charge of Titoism was perhaps the most absurd of all. Among the Bulgarian hierarchy which was dispatching Kostov to his death was a man who had been most closely connected during the war with the Yugoslav Communist Party. Vladimir Poptomov, Minister of Foreign Affairs and member of the Bulgarian Politburo, had been a member of Tito's government and his Party as late as 1944. Poptomov, a Macedonian, switched sides at the end of the war. Yet it was Kostov, the Bulgarian Communist reputed to be an enemy of Tito, who was accused of being a puppet of the Yugoslav dictator.

All the accused, with one exception, pleaded guilty in the typical fashion of a purge trial. But it was Kostov alone who created a scandal by repudiating his written confession. After acknowledging his previous ideological quarrels with Dimitrov, Kostov denied ever having been a foreign agent, an accomplice of Tito's, or having plotted Dimitrov's and Kolarov's deaths. He had been tortured before, one police questioning under the old regime leaving him with a broken back, and now the old Communist fighter, in a gesture of incredible hardness, refused to plead guilty in open court. His oral examination was interrupted, and the court had read his written confession. The official report contained in *Rabotnichesko Delo* gives Kostov's oral answers only on one point which does look mysterious in his record: his reprieve by the fascist government of Bulgaria during the war. Everything else is passed over.

Otherwise, the trial had the usual paraphernalia: several former high Bulgarian officials (mostly connected with economic matters), the usual Yugoslav agent, and written confessions of spying for the British and Americans. Some officials not actually at the trial were also mentioned as traitors. Thus Petko Kunin, who only in August succeeded Stefanov as finance minister, is mentioned as a member of Kostov's clique;[102] but he, presumably, was not yet ready for a trial. The South Slav federation also made its appearance at the trial as a diabolical concoction of Tito and Kostov, vigorously resisted by Dimitrov.

Kostov went to his death. His codefendants received long prison sentences. And the final morbid touch: on December 17 *Rabotnichesko Delo* carried the text of Kostov's reputed letter in which he pleaded fully guilty as charged and begged for a commutation of his sentence to life imprisonment. The text was accompanied by a photostatic copy of the letter. No one accused can go to his grave without having recanted. The sentence was executed.

Kostov's liquidation appears to have merely whetted the appetite for power of Vulko Chervenkov. At the Central Committee meeting held on January 6, 1950, Chervenkov lashed out at two other notables of Bulgarian Communism, Dobri Terpeshev and Anton Yugov. Once again Kostov's treachery was discussed and condemned, but the real object of Chervenkov's speech was to dis-

[102] *Ibid.*, November 30, 1949. Kunin was tried and convicted several months later.

credit and destroy the two leaders who may have stood in his way. Terpeshev was assailed for having known, while head of the Planning Commission, of Kostov's anti-Soviet moves and yet of not having done anything about it.[103] And how was it that Anton Yugov, for four years Minister of the Interior, did not learn about Kostov's treachery? [104] These two members of the Politburo, Chervenkov asserted, were almost associated in Kostov's guilt. Again, as in the case of Gomulka, the "one accident too many" motif was intruded as a prelude to the charge of treason.

The vehemence of the attack upon Yugov and Terpeshev may well have indicated their coming ejection from the Party and another purge trial. Both of them were persons of the highest standing in the Party. Terpeshev's sixty-fifth birthday a few months before had been celebrated with messages of congratulations from Party organizations all over Bulgaria and from Dimitrov. Yugov had held a crucial position in the Communist state for a long time. One year before, either of them would have been a more logical successor than Chervenkov to the mantle of leadership in Bulgaria. The charge was probably made up: there was no more reason for Terpeshev or Yugov to know of Kostov's "activities," whatever they were, than there was for any other member of the Bulgarian Politburo, including Chervenkov. The latter had obviously read about Stalin's tactics in seizing power in Russia between 1924 and 1928. After Bulgaria's Lenin had died and her Trotsky had been eliminated, the time was ripe for pushing out the Bukharins and Rykovs.

But, somewhat mysteriously, Chervenkov's hand was stayed. Whether it was the opposition of his colleagues or, what is more probable, the restraining hand of the U.S.S.R. that checked him, the complete elimination of Yugov and Terpeshev was denied, at least for a time, to Chervenkov. Terpeshev was removed as a member of the Politburo. On January 20 Yugov and Terpeshev were retained as ministers in Kolarov's new government. Both of them forfeited their positions, already nominal, as deputies of the Prime Minister, but Yugov became Minister of Industry and Terpeshev of Labor. Yugov was retained in the Politburo, and though both he

[103] *Novo Vremye,* January 1950, p. 15.
[104] *Ibid.,* p. 19.

and Terpeshev were several times publicly criticized during 1950 and had to perform self-criticism, something appeared to protect them, and especially Yugov, from the fate of Traicho Kostov.[105] It is not inconceivable that after its Yugoslav experience the Cominform and its Russian masters did not relish the idea of an entirely unified and dictatorially dominated Party. Some personal enemies of Chervenkov may have been thought to be useful lying around, just in case. And the shock of a too violent purge could have proved fatal to the already severely damaged Bulgarian Communist Party. It is significant that though Dimitrov had died in July 1949, and though Chervenkov became Prime Minister after Kolarov's death on January 24, 1950, he did not become officially the Secretary-General of the Bulgarian Party until November 1950. The final appointment was delayed for reasons which remain obscure.

Chervenkov's personal ascendancy over his Party is now probably greater than that of any other satellite Communist leader. He is certainly publicized and featured as the successor to Georgi Dimitrov, and the parallel of the apostolic succession from Lenin to Stalin is openly and repeatedly drawn. Chervenkov's speeches imitate Stalin's style and mannerisms more determinedly than those of any other East European leader. Bulgaria under his guidance has become, of all the People's Democracies, the closest to being a Russian province. But the extent of his domination over the unfortunate country and over his continually purged Party is probably more apparent than real. There must not be another Tito, even a pre-1948 Tito, in a satellite of Russia.

The Kostov affair, like that of Gomulka, illustrates the extreme of the transformation of Communism following the Yugoslav crisis. The East European Parties have been purged. Their most energetic leaders have been removed. The emphasis is now on docility, on complete obedience, and on following to the letter every instruction of the Cominform. Some Parties have escaped a major purge. In Czechoslovakia and Rumania the only leaders sacrificed up to now would have been unable to lead their Parties astray. Their removal was a gesture of compliance rather than a sign of a deep crisis such as those which shook the Poles and the Bulgarians.

[105] In the spring of 1951 Terpeshev was to all practical purposes exiled by being appointed Bulgarian minister to Rumania.

The survival of leaders like Gottwald in Czechoslovakia and Gheorgiu-Dej in Rumania, neither of whom is entirely trusted in Moscow, is due to a combination of their skill in opportunism and their entrenchment as national figures in their countries. Last, but not least, neither of them is a Tito in terms of the control of their Parties.

What is the balance sheet of Titoism in the countries of People's Democracy? It is easy to scoff at the crudity and sometimes psychopathic flavor of the Russian methods of rooting out their actual and potential opponents. It must be admitted that the Russian control over the Communist Parties of their satellites is today immeasurably greater than it was in 1948. If there is no major upheaval, it is unlikely that we shall again see in Eastern Europe another Communist leader ready to defy Moscow and capable of carrying his Party with him. Today, a fiat of the Cominform can remove, though not without serious dislocations, the most influential leader of a satellite country. But the price paid for this achievement has been great. The combative and energetic Communist leadership of the earlier days is gone, and it has been replaced by a dull uniformity and mechanical execution of orders. Until and unless a new generation of Communist fanatics is brought up in the satellites, their Parties will lack the genuine revolutionary spirit. Today they lean more and more on the strength of their great protector. Should a major crisis or emergency confront the U.S.S.R., the Communist Parties of the satellites may well prove to be sources of weakness rather than strength to their master.

CHAPTER 6

Conclusion

With the passage of time, Tito's Yugoslavia has become a part, though a strange part, of European politics. It has no longer the flair of novelty. The spectacle of a Communist state set up in opposition to the Kremlin has ceased to amaze people, but it has not ceased to intrigue them. Is Yugoslavia still a totalitarian and Communist state? Is Tito's revolt an isolated incident or a forerunner of a major trend? What lessons and comforts can the embattled West draw from the curious incident of the Yugoslav affair?

It is notoriously dangerous to generalize about the future without understanding the present. And the present, in the case of Yugoslavia, is not static, it is dynamic. Seldom has a group of people undergone within a short period of time a psychological change comparable to that of the rulers of Yugoslavia within the past three years. Three years ago they were fanatical believers in Communism and devout followers of the U.S.S.R. The fact that they had to fight for their lives against the Cominform could not, at first, disturb their allegiance, since it was based on something deeper and more far-reaching than an intellectual belief and preference. Then, as the campaign of the Cominform mounted, as the Russians accused Tito and his group of things which transcend human imagination both in hideousness and in sheer nonsense, the

Yugoslavs professed to see the naked imperialism of the Kremlin hiding behind the apparel of Marxism and Leninism. Yet they continued to work and to write, not only as Communists, but as Moscow-trained Communists. Everything that *Pravda* and the rest of the Russian and Cominform press had taught the Communist world since the end of the war about the West remained true for the Yugoslavs. Their own struggle within Yugoslavia against what remained of the old order and old attitudes has not relented.

Gradually, and painfully, the Yugoslav Communists replaced one dream by another: Soviet Communist was crumbling under the weight of its own devices. All over the world the Communists were straining at the leash, and, eager to follow in Tito's steps, they were ready to challenge Soviet imperialism. Those British and American writers and politicians who assumed so glibly that the Chinese Communists would readily, and as a matter of course, shake off their Russian connections can take comfort in the fact that those reputed experts in Titoism, Marshal Tito and his group, until late in 1950 were fervent propagators of the belief.

Ex Oriente lux: Looking at Asia, the Yugoslav Communists saw the continuation of their own movement: the Communists of China and Indo-China, paralleling their own experiences, would surely soon learn what the Russians are really like. The early childlike belief in the Soviet Union was followed by a similarly naïve revulsion. How can any Communist who sees the methods employed by the Kremlin still adhere to and obey the U.S.S.R.? Communism would spread, and its very expansion would sound the knell of the falsifiers of Marxism and Leninism.

In the September 15, 1950, issue of the Croat paper *Vjesnik* there is a cartoon illustrating the transition of the Yugoslavs to the next stage in their journey to political realism. Under the heading "There Is No Pity" are represented two gladiators in a Roman circus, one representing South and the other North Korea. They are locked in a deadly struggle, and neither of their equally unsympathetically portrayed sponsors, the United States and the Soviet Union, is willing to give them a sign to relent. For a few days after the attack upon South Korea the Yugoslav government hesitated about its attitude in the United Nations and elsewhere. The attack called for the reassertion of the principle of collective security.

Yugoslavia could be next on the list. But it was the North Korean People's Government which was fighting the reactionaries. The recently beloved Asiatic Communists were fighting their local Drazha Mihailoviches. How could a good Communist favor a reactionary government?

By August the struggle had become, for the Yugoslavs, one between two rival imperialisms both equally unconcerned with the interests of the Korean people. And when in November 1950 the Chinese Communists joined in the fight, another illusion of the Yugoslav Communists was well-nigh destroyed. For two years they had been glorifying the Chinese leaders. Biographies and endearing stories about Mao Tse-tung, Chu Teh, and the others had filled the columns of the Yugoslav press. Chinese Communists had been widely applauded. They had presaged a new era of Communism when it would expand all over the world and would destroy the excrescence upon it: the curse of Stalinism. Now, for the time being, the hope disappeared, and the fact of the collaboration between Peiping and Moscow once again forced the Yugoslav Communists to imbibe political realism.

With 1950 the Yugoslav Communists approached a new stage in their relations with the West. For some time they had relied upon economic help from the West to save them from the results of their economic incompetence which aggravated the disorganization of their country.[1] As late as January 1949 the Yugoslav government applied for admission to the Council for Mutual Economic Assistance set up by Russia and the satellites. The application was a gesture of ideological preference, since the Yugoslav government must have known very well that it would be rejected with indignation by the People's Democracies. In their isolation, the Yugoslavs found themselves compelled, step by step, to accept economic aid from countries they still regard as capitalist, for their own situation was growing steadily more desperate. The fervor of the earlier period, when they believed that the words "Socialism" and "Communism" could by themselves work miracles and transform a backward and devastated country into an advanced industrial power,

[1] Most authorities agree that between 1945 and 1949 the Yugoslavs attempted a vastly overambitious scheme of internal investment and likewise went too far in their collectivization.

cooled off. Since 1950 collectivization has been arrested. Grandiose industrialization plans have been pared down. Economic realism has been much slower in coming than its political counterpart, but it is finally penetrating the minds of the rulers.

Is Yugoslavia today still a Communist, or even a Stalinist, country insofar as her internal policies and the mentality of her leaders are concerned? To this question one must give a barely qualified *yes*. Much has been written in American newspapers about the efforts of the Yugoslav Communists to democratize their country. In many cases the interpretation has been based upon a misunderstanding of a totalitarian regime. When one reads, as in a June 8, 1951, dispatch from Belgrade quoted in the *New York Times,* that the Central Committee has decreed that no individual pronouncements of the Communist leaders but only decisions duly assented to by a majority of the Central Committee, the Politburo, or the Party Congress are to be binding upon Party members, one should remember that this is nothing new or startling. It happens to be a rule of the Communist Party of the U.S.S.R. as well. It is still difficult to imagine a Yugoslav Communist standing up and criticizing Tito or Rankovich. To a considerable extent the Yugoslav Communists have been able to relax their totalitarian discipline insofar as the non-Communists are concerned. There is no doubt that much as the regime is feared or even hated by a considerable proportion of the population, it enjoys a wide measure of support in its defiance of the U.S.S.R. It is easy to capitalize on patriotism; it is easy to go through a series of ostentatious moves—trials with some appearance of impartial proceedings permitted, a degree of criticism of inferior officials, greater leniency toward former enemies of Communism—all designed to accentuate the differences between Yugoslavia and the U.S.S.R. The essence of dictatorship is hardly affected. Nor could any sane man demand that the Yugoslav government relax the slightest bit when confronted by an enemy who knows very well how to take advantage of the slightest appearance of chaos and political strife. The Yugoslav Communists have no need to reproduce in full the terror prevalent in Bulgaria. They are naturally friendlier to the West than they were in the days before 1948. But one should not attempt to discern democracy or liberalism in Tito's Yugoslavia, for such an attempt will not help in the evaluation of the country's strength and weaknesses.

But what has been happening to the minds of those people trained from their adolescence in the love of the Soviet Union? The cry "Stalin—Tito—Party" is no longer heard in Yugoslavia. Here, the evolution has been complete. The rulers of Russia are now the destroyers of Marxism and enslavers of the proletariat. Milovan Djilas, in a series of remarkable articles written for *Borba* in the fall of 1950, subjected the contemporary scene in the U.S.S.R. to the most biting criticism that has come recently from a Communist pen. Again, there is an unconscious and terrible irony in the writings of Djilas, for the criticism of the U.S.S.R. is quite uncorrelated to the still similar reality of Yugoslavia. Soviet Communism has become bureaucratized, writes Djilas. Espionage and the police penetrate every aspect of life; dull uniformity has settled over the life of the nation. Socialism has been abandoned in the Soviet Union and replaced by a new and obnoxious imperialism and state capitalism. For the first time a Yugoslav reviews Russia's behavior during the period from 1939 to 1941, and Djilas finds it the acme of hypocrisy.[2] All the slight grievances of the war, then neglected in the overwhelming loyalty to the U.S.S.R., are now recalled, magnified, and thrown passionately against the former idol. The Russians minimized the importance of Tito's movement. They urged an ignoble caution upon the Partisans. They bargained for spheres of influence in Yugoslavia, and when the Yugoslav Communists began to win, they started to "poison the mind and alertness of the people and the Party by means of 'brotherhood,' banquets, 'Slavism,' 'internationalism,' and with forged 'Marxism-Leninism.' " [3] Where is the former picture, the reality, of the Partisans singing of Stalin and being exalted beyond belief by the news of Soviet victories? The Djilas of 1941–1944 would not recognize himself in 1950 lambasting the very same people whom he had deified only a few years before.

The leaders of Yugoslavia have retained their Communism and in fact consider themselves the true guardians of the creed prostituted by the masters of the Kremlin. People can retain courage and

[2] *Borba*, November 19, 1950.
[3] *Ibid.*

cohesion when confronted with overwhelming odds only if they are supported by a strong belief. Had the ruling elite of Yugoslavia been composed in 1948 of political cynics, it is unlikely that they could have preserved their cohesion and the sense of solidarity which alone has kept them from disintegration. Can the group around Tito preserve its ideology and sense of mission, or is it, barring an external intervention, slated to transform itself into a group of political opportunists clutching power for power's sake? There is every indication that the men around Tito are still inspired by their creed but that the danger has now, at last, forced them to supplement Marxism with genuine nationalism. The Yugoslav Communists will never become liberals. They will never abandon the essence of the police state. But, given time, their regime may lose some of the totalitarian features of the Communist state. It may become a state in which people who are not connected with politics, while not free, may breathe more freely. It is foolish to expect more even under the most favorable circumstances.

And in a sense, it is overly optimistic to expect that Tito's Yugoslavia will be given a chance at a long and peaceful development. To the Cominform Titoism, even when confined to one country, is a psychological danger which it cannot tolerate for long. Nothing is more irritating to a totalitarian movement than a living monument to its own errors. In the satellites Titoism is now, at best, a distant danger. Yugoslavia has been isolated as a source of growing infection. But the achievement of Tito and his group must be present in the minds of Communist leaders everywhere in the satellites, at each step they take in subordinating their countries to the U.S.S.R. To the people of those countries, the continued existence of a state which has broken away from Moscow is a reminder that the U.S.S.R. is perhaps not omnipotent, that their own fortunes are perhaps not irreversible. It is a reminder which the free world can ill afford to see replaced by that other lesson: that whoever challenges the absolute sway of the Soviet Union is doomed to destruction.

The Cominform has amplified its original propaganda line that the Communist Party of Yugoslavia is dominated by four or five men who seduced it from its allegiance to the Communist camp. The "honorable task" imposed by the Cominform in June 1948 upon the working class of Yugoslavia—the removal of Tito, Ranko-vich, Djilas, and Kardelj—has remained unfulfilled. In November 1949 the task became larger. This time the Cominform listed several additional leaders of Yugoslavia among the provacateurs whom the working classes of the country had to get rid of before being readmitted to the club.[4]

The fight against Tito has become the most important ostensible purpose of the Cominform. Gone is the pretense of the equality of the members of that body. Gone is the studied attempt at a dignified "exchange of information" among the Communist Parties. The main exchange consists in the circulation of fantastic stories about Yugoslavia and the genesis of Tito's desertion.

It is a matter of some surprise that the Russians have not attempted, as yet, to deal more resolutely with Yugoslavia. For a year or so after the break it was judged inadvisable to set up a "Free Yugoslav Government" in Rumania or Bulgaria or to stir up guerrilla warfare within Yugoslavia itself. There was, obviously, still some hope that the "healthy elements" within the Yugoslav Party would be capable of some action without direct intervention by the U.S.S.R. Many angles were tried to arouse the unexpectedly sluggish "healthy elements." In the spring of 1949 the Greek Communists, already suffering from serious reverses, were made to declare publicly for a "free and greater" Macedonia, thus revealing a degree of subjugation they always had been suspected of—the willingness to see their country partitioned at the bidding of the Cominform. But this crude attempt to stir up irredentism in Yugoslav Macedonia seems to have had less effect upon the cohesion of the Yugoslav Party than upon the already declining fortunes of the "Free Greek Government." Sometime in 1949 Tito stopped supporting the Greek Communists, and after that their military activities dwindled almost into insignificance, while their Party itself was being purged.

Within Yugoslavia only a few minor purges have followed the great decision of 1948. Just as in the satellites "Titoism" is a term which now covers a wide variety of sins or, depending on one's point of view, the absence of them, so in Yugoslavia the charge of "Cominformism" is preferred as a matter of course against some

[4] *For a Lasting Peace*, November 29, 1949.

Communists whose only visible trespass has consisted in an administrative failure or in an unkind word about the Marshal or his entourage. It is not to be wondered that occasional purges in the C.P.Y. have struck hardest at officials connected with the economic machinery of the state. Yugoslavia's economy was for three years in the hands of two people who in the crisis of 1948 turned out to be enemies of the Tito group: Andrija Hebrang and Sreten Zhujovich. Independently of any infiltration of the economic machinery of the state by the Cominformists, the most likely place where a Party official will fall down on his job is in a ministry of agriculture or industry. And such a failure must almost inevitably lead to a charge of "sabotage" and hostility to the regime.

Tito's Yugoslavia is not free from the curse of the prewar state —strife among its nationalities. Formally, new Yugoslavia is a federation of six states. National aspirations of the Macedonians and the Montenegrins, as well as of the Slovenes and the Croats, are now recognized by their separate states. National equality, always with the limitations peculiar to a totalitarian state, now exists in Yugoslavia. In Tito's official entourage are to be found Croats, Slovenes, Moslems from Bosnia, Montenegrins, and Macedonians, as well as Serbs. A written Macedonian language has been constructed and is in use in the Federal Republic of Macedonia, thus confounding the skeptics, who still see in Macedonian but a dialect of the Bulgarian language.

But the dilemma of conflicting nationalisms within one state has never been susceptible of an easy solution. The tradition of Croat grievances and the memory of the massacres of Serbs by the Ustashis in wartime Croatia still hang over Yugoslavia. There are indications that many Serbs, including some Serbian Communists, have not reconciled themselves to the new Yugoslavia, where their privileged position is gone. The tradition of separatism is not entirely dead among the Croats. The specter of national conflicts has not been entirely banished by the principle of legal equality and federalism, nor has it been assuaged by common subjection to the dictatorial regime. Hence the government's extreme sensitiveness to any incident or development which, in any sense, might exacerbate the national problem. To the Cominform Yugoslavia's national troubles are a weapon of great potential effectiveness. It would be awkward for the Russians or for their satellite agencies to proclaim openly for independent Croatia or to persuade the Serbs that they should resume an undisguised hegemony in Yugoslavia. The only appeal which the Cominform can use must be addressed to the Yugoslav Communists. But they cannot be openly called upon to resume their national squabbles, since the Cominform in its propaganda still adheres to the fiction of the appeal to the "healthy elements" of the Yugoslav Party, whether they be Croat, Serb, or Macedonian. But clandestinely much can be made of the local grievances of individuals and of national groups throughout Yugoslavia. The new policy is in a sense a return to the strategy of the Comintern in 1928, when, in order to undermine the Yugoslav state, it was ready and willing to promise quite incompatible things to the various nationalities inhabiting Yugoslavia. But this time the Cominform is faced by a group of rulers who understand only too well the strategy of Moscow, and who are alert to the danger.

September 1950 witnessed one of the most significant purges within the C.P.Y. since 1948. The purged notables were three Serb ministers of the government of the Federal Republic of Croatia. These gentlemen, bearing the euphonious names of Zhigich, Opachich, and Brkich, represented the Serb minority within the goverement of Croatia. They were, significantly enough, connected with the economic side of the government: Dushko Brkich as Deputy Prime Minister, Rade Zhigich as Minister of Industry, and Stanko-Chanica Opachich as Minister in charge of Housing, the Lumber Industry, and Forestry. Their sins as enumerated by Tito's deputy for Croatia, Vladimir Bakarich, consisted of a veritable accumulation of all possible types of treason against Yugoslavia. Zhigich, Brkich, and Opachich spread Serbian chauvinism and anti-Croat sentiments. They circulated the Cominform's slanders about Tito's Yugoslavia. And, it is almost needless to add, they sabotaged the economic program of the government.[5]

The three accused (who, of course, were not given a chance to answer the charges) displayed violent Serbian chauvinism. Zhigich, especially, spread rumors that the Croatian government was discontinuing the building of Orthodox churches and that former

[5] Bakarich's speech before the Assembly of the National Republic of Croatia, reported in *Vjesnik*, September 14, 1950.

Ustashis were being left unpunished and even in positions of influence and power within the government.[6] The latter charge is not very far from the truth. During the war, as we have seen, the Partisans did not hesitate to accept into their ranks the former Ustashis, and some of them still hold positions of importance in the provincial government in Croatia.

The unfortunate trio was expelled from the Party, and from their official positions, and imprisoned. The government was anxious to handle the national angle of the dispute with utmost care. A special meeting of the Council of Serbs in Croatia condemned the attempt to divide the two brotherly nations, and the replacements for the fallen ministers were chosen from among the Serbian community in Croatia.

An interesting aspect of the crisis is the way the Yugoslav Communists handled it. In essence, it was a "normal" purge of the type encountered in the satellites. The accused were burdened with an accumulation of all conceivable treacheries: economic sabotage, activity on the behalf of the Cominform, and so forth. But the government was clever enough to avoid some of the external characteristics of a Communist purge. Bakarich's speech to the Croatian Assembly referred to the purged more in sorrow than in anger. The Croat Prime Minister, a man of intelligence and of some knowledge of Western parliamentary usages, recounted repeated attempts on his part to bring the deviationists back into the fold, and exhibited, as if by accident, the patience and tolerance of the Yugoslav Communists in dealing with such matters. Whether truthfully or not, the accused were presented as spreading defeatist rumors to the effect that the U.S.S.R. could crush Yugoslavia in eight days. Zhigich in particular was presented as a man who could not get Pan-Slavism and the love of Stalin out of his system. The seed of chauvinism, the moral of the story is, carries with it the potentialities of treason and of economic sabotage. Actually, Brkich, Zhigich, and Opachich appear to have been guilty of nothing more than an inability to keep up with the anti-Stalinist evolution of the C.P.Y. and of some incautious remarks about their Croat colleagues. But a political purge has many uses.

The Yugoslav leaders, much as they have failed in other respects,

[6] *Ibid.*

deserve credit for two achievements. They have shown themselves masters at holding on to power under the most adverse set of circumstances that could confront a totalitarian regime. Connected with their skill is the undeniable fact of their courage. In the beginning it was the courage of desperation. Now it has become the courage of national pride. No one knows what the future has in store for Tito's Yugoslavia. Conceivably, the state may break down because of its inherent contradictions, or it could go down before a really determined military effort of the U.S.S.R. and its satellites. But there will not be capitulation or an easy victory for aggressor.

II

Titoism, as a historical phenomenon, deserves attention quite aside from its current political importance. To a student of government, the story of Tito is a sample of the meaning of political power. It illuminates the nature of political allegiance and the influence on it of ideology, of economic considerations, and of nationalism. The revolt of Tito and the halfhearted attempts in the same direction by Gomulka and Kostov illustrate, to a historian, the eternal dilemma and contradictions of imperialism. Anyone who tries to understand our civilization and its social and religious restlessness may well be absorbed by the story of a small group of people—the Yugoslav Communists of the forties—who, having embraced with religious intensity the cult of the Soviet Union, bear today even in their disillusionment the ineradicable imprint of their original faith.

The events in Yugoslavia and the reaction to them in the satellites bring out very well the nature of contemporary Communism. Quite apart from its theoretical development, Communism has today become a system and ideology of power. During the war it was fashionable in the West to analyze the Soviet Union and the practice of Communism there in terms of "positive" and "negative" elements of the system. The latter were often considered as mere excrescences upon the body of organized Communism, due to disappear as soon as contact with the West would remove the Soviet Union's misunderstanding and fears of the Western democracies. It may be pertinent to observe, without quarreling with any classification, that the developments in Eastern Europe since the end of the war cannot be understood if we divide the motives and policies of the Soviet Union into their "good" and "bad" components. Communism in action is today a very intricate religion of power. The ideology of Communism has been neither abandoned nor pushed aside in the expansionist drive of Soviet Russia. It has become an integral part of the interpretation of political power by the masters of world Communism. Collectivization, political terror, industrial planning, and mass education and indoctrination are not separate items of a political program, either as relics of earlier idealism or as results of today's corruption, but they all fit together into the composite picture of the Communist understanding of political power.

Collectivization, for example, is not only construed as the means of increasing agricultural output and of removing the curse of private ownership, but also, and primarily, as the way of destruction of social individualism, which is always a danger to the Communist state. Mass education and the removal of illiteracy are not only worth-while social objectives, but they also destroy the remnants of particularisms and nonconformity in society, and they make the people more susceptible to the all-permeating voice of the state. The thirst for political power of a totalitarian regime is not satisfied by mere political obedience on the part of the people; it requires, as an ideal, constant and undisturbed activity by every citizen and his allegiance to the state.

It follows, therefore, that Communism as a social and economic reform movement has become an illusion. It has no social or economic postulates save as they are considered the means of achieving and perpetuating political power. The history of the Communist Party *in Russia* is not that of a party devoted solely to political power. It was in its early days a history of clashing ideologies and viewpoints. But in the ruling regimes in the satellites, and in Yugoslavia, is seen the reflection of the new character of Communism. Nearly every social and economic reform initiated by the Communists in Eastern Europe would have been done, and in some cases done faster and more drastically, by a combination of the Socialist and Peasant Parties. This in a country like Bulgaria holds true even of collectivization. It is those Communists who tended to think about their ideology in terms separate from the power interests of the Soviet Union, or who even gave an appearance of thinking so, who have been eliminated and branded as Titoists. Communism, as interpreted for the satellite states, no longer means a specific body of doctrines, and it does not necessarily mean even anything analogous to the Communism of the U.S.S.R. It means following and anticipating every wish and directive of the Soviet Union.

It is here that the significance of Tito's Yugoslavia is fully brought out. An ideology, which in its essence is nothing but a worship of power, by its very victories must endanger the power system which propagates it. Because Tito and his group were devout Stalinists, they could not part voluntarily with their rule, even when threatened with the hostility of the very people they had worshipped. And in their rebellion they demonstrated that, for the rulers of Russia, the Communist fanaticism of their foreign colleagues is a poor substitute for a purely mechanical system of controlling the Communist Parties abroad. The latter, and especially those in power, present the rulers of Russia with a veritable dilemma. A strong Communist regime is not unlikely to develop the virus of Titoism, which is nothing but Stalinism transplanted to a foreign soil. Hence the ever-present need of replacing reliable men with still more reliable men, of constantly watching over the satellites and foreign Communists in general, that no man and no group of men should arise who could duplicate the characteristics of the ruling group in Russia. The price paid for the purges is not inconsiderable. They have secured for the time being that no Tito should arise in the satellites. They have in the process purged the satellite Parties of their most energetic and idealistic leaders. When the attraction and resources of Communism appeared inadequate in the Soviet Union during the last war, an appeal had to be made to Russian nationalism. But a similar recourse is unlikely to strengthen, in an emergency, the Communist regimes of the satellites.

To the West, Titoism has appeared as a doubtful and embarrassing gift. To the more naïve, Tito's Yugoslavia is the paradise regained of Communism. To the excessive optimist, it is a convenient provocation to postulate the inevitable (and painless, for the democracies) downfall and disintegration of Soviet imperialism. There are those who, as a condition of American help, would impose upon Tito the task of transforming his country into a model democracy.

If our foreign policy has to be based on something more substantial than daydreams and moralizing, then Titoism should be recognized for what it exactly is: a grave and recurrent but not fatal disease of Communism. The conditions which assured its success in Yugoslavia are not automatically reproducible in every country that has come under Communist domination. Tito's Yugoslavia is a source of actual and psychological danger for Soviet imperialism. Morally, despite the origin of their revolt and the character of their rule, the rulers of Yugoslavia deserve the credit which accrues to any group of people who prefer danger and isolation to foreign subjugation. Those are the grounds upon which the West should determine its attitude toward Tito.

BIBLIOGRAPHICAL NOTE

INDEX

Bibliographical Note

I shall mention here only some of the materials I found most useful
in writing about Communism in Eastern Europe. Two of the best in-
troductions to the subject are Andrew Gyorgy, *Governments of Danubian Europe* (New York, 1949), and Hugh Seton-Watson, *The East
European Revolution* (London, 1950). The latter, especially, deals with
social and economic as well as political institutions, and they both contain valuable bibliographies.

There is a great paucity of materials concerning the history of the
Communist Parties of the area. In the case of Yugoslavia, there is the
Historical Archive, published by the Central Committee of the Communist Party of Yugoslavia, which includes a volume on the Congresses
and Conferences of the C.P.Y. between 1919 and 1937. It is a document
of great importance for any student of the history of international Communism and should be translated into English. Otherwise, the history
of the C.P.Y. can be gleaned only from the accounts of the congresses
of the Third International and from the official version given by Tito
in his report to the Fifth Party Congress in 1948 (available in English).
Yugoslavia during World War II deserves a detailed and impartial study.
There are various accounts by British officers attached either to the
Partisans or to the Chetniks during the war. Mr. Stephen Clissold's
Whirlwind (London, 1949) stands in a class by itself. Though it is
marred by minor inaccuracies and its semi-fictionalized style, it is by
far the most informative treatment of the subject. General Fitzroy
Maclean's account in his *Eastern Approaches* (London and New York,
1950; the American title is *Escape to Adventure*) is a valuable and en-
tertaining story by the head of the British mission to Tito's headquarters.
Among diaries of the Partisans, that of Vladimir Dedijer (especially its
volumes printed before the break with the U.S.S.R.) throws the best
light on the mentality of the Yugoslav Communists during the war. In
the library of the Russian Institute at Columbia University there are two
analytical studies of the war period, both M.A. theses: Jacob B. Hoptner,
"The Foreign Policy of the National Liberation Movement of Yugo-

slavia" (1950), and Thomas Wolfe, "Role of the Armed Forces in the Soviet-Yugoslav Dispute" (1950).

The crisis of 1948 and "Titoism" are the subject of innumerable pamphlets, books, and articles published continuously in Yugoslavia, on the one hand, and in Russia and the satellites, on the other. The Yugoslavs now reprint regularly in English their more important contributions to the dispute. The Royal Institute of International Affairs published the correspondence between Moscow and Belgrade under the title *The Soviet-Yugoslav Dispute* (London, 1948). Mr. Hamilton Fish Armstrong's book, *Tito and Goliath* (New York, 1951), is an interesting and valuable study of Titoism and its implications in Yugoslavia and elsewhere. Mr. Leigh White, in his *Balkan Caesar* (New York, 1951), gives a less dispassionate treatment of the same subject. Miss Doreen Warriner's *Revolution in Eastern Europe* (London, 1950) has valuable economic data but is not free from some unfortunate political generalizations.

The only thorough way to study politics in Yugoslavia and in the rest of Eastern Europe is to supplement one's investigations by everyday reading of the Communist press and periodicals. I have been able to follow with some regularity the following newspapers: *Pravda* (Moscow), *Trybuna Ludu* (Warsaw), *Borba* (Belgrade), and *Rabotnichesko Delo* (Sofia). Even more important are the various theoretical periodicals of the Communist Parties, among which the most available have been *Komunist* (Yugoslav), *Novo Vremye* (Bulgarian), and *Nowe Drogi* (Polish). The last named is especially informative, and some of its issues used here in the text should be made available in English. The Cominform organ, *For a Lasting Peace, For a People's Democracy*, is a useful English guide to some of the organizational and propaganda problems of Eastern European Communism.

Index